Teaching for Understanding

Teaching for Understanding

Linking Research with Practice

Martha Stone Wiske, Editor

Jossey-Bass Publishers • San Francisco

Substantial discounts on bulk quantities of Jossey-Bass books are available to corporations, professional associations, and other organizations. For details and discount information, contact the special sales department at Jossey-Bass Inc., Publishers (415) 433–1740; Fax (800) 605–2665.

For sales outside the United States, please contact your local Simon & Schuster International Office.

Jossey-Bass Web address: http://www.josseybass.com

 Manufactured in the United States of America on Lyons Falls Turin Book. This paper is acid-free and 100 percent totally chlorine-free.

Library of Congress Cataloging-in-Publication Data

Teaching for understanding : linking research with practice / Martha
   Stone Wiske, editor. — 1st ed.
      p.   cm. —   (The Jossey-Bass education series)
   Includes index.
   ISBN 0-7879-1002-3 (alk. paper)
   1. Teaching.   2. Learning, Psychology of.   3. Education—Aims and
objectives.   I. Wiske, Martha Stone.   II. Series.
LB1026.T383   1997
371.102—dc21   97-17571

FIRST EDITION
HB Printing   10 9 8 7 6 5 4 3 2 1

The Jossey-Bass Education Series

Contents

Acknowledgments

The development of the Teaching for Understanding framework and the research on its use by teachers took place during a six-year collaborative project funded by a generous grant from the Spencer Foundation. Rarely are university researchers and school teachers given the opportunity to conduct sustained open-ended inquiry together free of the squelching pressure to produce immediate evidence of success. The foundation also supported a conference we held to consult with a group of scholars and educational researchers about an early version of the framework. We are grateful to the board of the Spencer Foundation and to Lawrence Cremin, who encouraged the initiation of this endeavor. We are also indebted to Patricia A. Graham, president of the Spencer Foundation, and to our program officer Rebecca Barr, who provided steady encouragement and wise guidance throughout the life of the project.

The theoretical foundations of the Teaching for Understanding project rest on decades of work conducted by the project's principal investigators: David Perkins, Howard Gardner, and Vito Perrone. Their insights and commitments shaped the intellectual direction of this effort at every turn. They began the project by convening a seminar of reflective schoolteachers and university researchers interested in collaborative inquiry toward a pedagogy of understanding. Through a series of evening conversations sustained by pizza and soda, this seminar established a form of collegial dialogue that came to be a hallmark of the project.

Teachers from Cambridge Rindge and Latin School; Buckingham, Brown and Nichols School; Newton North and Newton South High Schools; Lincoln-Sudbury High School; and English High School and Martin Luther King Middle School in Boston collaborated on the first several years of research. These teachers included

Larry Aaronson, Gayle Bartley, Wendy Bembery, Phyllis Bretholtz, Marshall Cohen, Jackie Cossentino, Joe Decelles, Sandy Dell, John DioDato, Gary Elliott, Dorothy Gonson, Dee Gould, Elizabeth Grady, Philip James, Jim Johns, Ed Joyce, Alison Kenney-Hall, Socrates Lagios, Lyn Montague, David Outerbridge, and Steve Roderick. They met regularly with university researchers to document and analyze their own practices, try experimental approaches with their classes, and extract principles from these experiences. Their thoughtful practices and contributions to collaborative inquiry rooted the Teaching for Understanding framework as firmly in classrooms as in the halls of the academy.

Of all the schoolteachers who made essential contributions to this inquiry, four are especially important. Lois Hetland volunteered to work with the Teaching for Understanding framework in its infancy and developed its power as a guide for reflective practice. Bill Kendall also wrestled with the framework in its early days and, with unusual courage, perseverance, skill, and humor, illustrated how to integrate its precepts into traditional high school mathematics courses. Eric Buchovecky first worked with the Teaching for Understanding framework as a student teacher and went on to use it both in his own classroom and in his work with other teachers. Joan Soble served as an astute critic, a talented interpreter, and a devoted supporter of Teaching for Understanding. Their sustained, probing, and wise collaboration as talented teachers, as scholars of their subject matter, and as learners about learning was essential to the rigor and power of this endeavor. All four teachers participated in writing one or more chapters of this book, and they continue to support ongoing inquiry around Teaching for Understanding.

The Teaching for Understanding project benefited from the impassioned and skilled work of a group of researchers at the Harvard Graduate School of Education. They conceptualized teachers' practices in relation to current research on teaching and learning, refined the elements of the framework through numerous rounds of revision, consulted with teachers about designing and enacting curriculum based on the framework, and analyzed the work of teachers and students to characterize and assess the results of Teaching for Understanding in classrooms. This group included Tina Blythe, Veronica Boix Mansilla, Eric Bondy, Anne

Chase, Ada Beth Cutler, Roger Dempsey, Howard Gardner, Karen Hammerness, Elizabeth Hodder, Rosario Jaramillo, Peter Kugel, Catalina Laserna, Fiona Hughes-McDonnell, Barbara Neufeld, Judy Pace, David Perkins, Vito Perrone, Alexandra Rehak, Rebecca Simmons, Chris Unger, Noel White, Daniel Gray Wilson, and Martha Stone Wiske during one or more years of the project. Joyce Conkling, Dorothy MacGillivray, and Matthew Woods contributed to the conceptual development of the project while providing essential administrative support.

Of all those who guided the evolution of Teaching for Understanding, Rebecca Simmons deserves special appreciation. As the project manager, she provided both intellectual guidance and daily coordination of a complex endeavor with multiple interwoven strands. She also worked closely on the early planning of this volume.

Many people provided assistance in the preparation of this book. Tina Blythe consulted about its contents while she prepared a companion volume, *The Teaching for Understanding Guide,* designed to give teachers and teacher developers practical guidance in using the Teaching for Understanding framework. Joe McDonald read an early draft and made sound recommendations for bringing it to publication. Lesley Iura, our editor at Jossey-Bass, provided excellent advice about shaping chapters to convey the results of this project vividly. Kristi Hayes cajoled authors gently, transformed their materials into beautifully formatted final form, and delivered the goods on time. Their advice and help undoubtedly strengthened the final product, and for that I express heartfelt appreciation on behalf of all the project members.

This book emerged through years of dialogue so that every page bears the fruit of several minds. I found the collaborative process of synthesizing the work of many thoughtful educators enormously satisfying. As editor of this volume, I feel fortunate to have worked with such a generous, astute, and dedicated group of authors and colleagues.

Cambridge, Massachusetts
September 1997

Martha Stone Wiske

The Authors

Martha Stone Wiske is a lecturer and researcher at the Harvard Graduate School of Education, where she also codirects the Educational Technology Center. She works on the process of school-university collaboration, the relationship of educational research and practice, and fostering educational improvement with the integration of new technologies in schools. She is the author of numerous articles on these subjects and coeditor of *Software Goes to School: Teaching for Understanding with New Technologies* (with D. Perkins, J. L. Schwartz, and M. M. West, 1995). Wiske is currently exploring the use of telecommunication to promote collaboration among teachers, researchers, and educational developers interested in using new technologies to support teaching for understanding.

Veronica Boix Mansilla is a researcher with Harvard Project Zero. Her work focuses on the nature of understanding within and across disciplines such as history, science, and the arts—a subject about which she has given seminars and authored and coauthored several papers. Boix Mansilla taught primary school for five years and, in 1996–97, taught part-time at the Central Park East Secondary School in New York City. A doctoral student at the Harvard Graduate School of Education, she is currently investigating students' beliefs about the nature and purpose of historical and scientific knowledge.

Eric Buchovecky collaborated with the Teaching for Understanding project while teaching physics at Belmont High School. He currently teaches at the Francis W. Parker Charter School, Fort Devins, Massachusetts.

Roger Dempsey, a former kindergarten teacher, was a researcher with Harvard Project Zero for seven years, where he studied the theory and application of multiple intelligences in young children, enhancing disciplinary understanding in teachers and students, literacy-based afterschool programs, and early childhood learning in children's museums. He is currently working with Harvard's Office of School Partnerships, promoting and developing collaborations between the Graduate School of Education and area school systems.

Howard Gardner is professor of education at the Harvard Graduate School of Education and codirector of Harvard Project Zero. Gardner is the author of several hundred articles and fourteen books, including *Multiple Intelligences* (1980), *Frames of Mind* (1983), *The Unschooled Mind* (1991), and *Leading Minds: An Anatomy of Leadership* (1995). His newest book is *Extraordinary Minds* (1997). He has taught from kindergarten through graduate school and also taught piano for ten years.

Karen Hammerness is a doctoral student at Stanford University. Her work focuses on the concept of teachers' vision, which includes an effort to expand upon the concept of vision by investigating teachers' imaginations, passions, and cognition. She is currently exploring the sources, contents, and role of vision for a range of teachers. She is also a researcher at Stanford on a project that endeavors both to design teacher communities and to investigate the process of teachers' learning of new pedagogy. Before coming to Stanford, she was a researcher for the Teaching for Understanding project at Harvard Project Zero.

Lois Hetland is a researcher and project manager at Harvard Project Zero. She taught elementary and middle school children for seventeen years and, from 1992 to 1996, was a teacher-researcher on the Teaching for Understanding project. A doctoral student in human development and psychology at the Harvard Graduate School of Education, her research focuses on the arts as cognitive domains, their relationship to deep understanding, and their role in educational reform. She consults with educators nationally and internationally on Teaching for Understanding and multiple intelligences. Hetland is coeditor and author of the chapter "Teaching for Understanding," in *The Project Zero Classroom: New Approaches to Thinking and Understanding*, a publication of Harvard Project Zero.

Rosario Jaramillo is a professor of history learning and teaching in the history department of the Universidad Javeriana in Bogota, Colombia. Jaramillo collaborated with the Teaching for Understanding project at the Harvard Graduate School of Education. As a researcher in this area, she is conducting a cross-cultural comparison of students' understanding of history. She also consults on Teaching for Understanding and on the teaching and learning of history in schools.

David Perkins is senior research associate at the Harvard Graduate School of Education and, since 1972, codirector of Harvard Project Zero. Perkins is the author of over 130 articles and several books, including *Outsmarting IQ: The Emerging Science of Learnable Intelligence* (1995), *The Intelligent Eye: Learning to Think by Looking at Art* (1994), and *Smart Schools: Better Thinking and Learning for Every Child* (1992). He is coauthor of *The Thinking Classroom: Learning and Teaching in a Culture of Thinking* (with Shari Tishman and Eileen Jay, 1995).

Vito Perrone is senior lecturer on education and director of teacher education at the Harvard Graduate School of Education. He has been a public school teacher; a university professor of history, education, and peace studies (University of North Dakota); and dean of the New School and the Center for Teaching and Learning (both at the University of North Dakota). He has served for twenty-six years as coordinator of the North Dakota Study Group on Evaluation and is actively engaged in the life of elementary and secondary schools. He has written extensively about such issues as educational equity, curriculum and progressivism in education, and testing and evaluation. His numerous publications include *101 Educational Conversations with Your Child* (1992–1993), a series of books for parents; *Expanding Student Assessment* (1992); *A Letter to Teachers: Reflections on Schooling and the Art of Teaching* (1991); and *Working Papers: Reflections on Teachers, Schools, and Communities* (1989).

Ron Ritchhart has taught elementary school and middle school mathematics for fourteen years, receiving the Presidential Award for Excellence in Science and Mathematics Teaching in 1993. He is the author of *Making Numbers Make Sense* (1994) and editor-author of *Through Mathematical Eyes: Exploring Functional Relationships in Math and Science* (1997). He is currently a researcher and doctoral student at the Harvard Graduate School of Education, where his work centers on the creation of classroom cultures and practices that support mindful, self-directed learning.

Chris Unger is currently a principal investigator at the Harvard Graduate School of Education. He is interested in the design of teaching, learning, and learning environments that promote student and teacher understanding both in and outside of schools, fostering meaningful inquiries that individuals see as relevant to them and their lives. Since the development of the Teaching for Understanding framework, he has worked with hundreds of teachers and dozens of schools in the United States and South America. He is currently working on the application of Teaching for Understanding as a framework to guide personal and organizational inquiry.

Daniel Gray Wilson is a researcher with Project Zero at the Harvard Graduate School of Education. He is currently academic coordinator of postgraduate studies at the Universidad Jorge Tadeo Lozano in Bogota, Colombia. He works with groups of teachers at various levels from kindergarten through university who are using the Teaching for Understanding framework in Colombia.

Teaching for Understanding

The Importance of Understanding

Martha Stone Wiske

Consider these images of students at work in school:

Joan Soble's English students are presenting their analysis of T. S. Eliot's poem *The Love Song of J. Alfred Prufrock* at the Cambridge Rindge and Latin High School's Arts Open House. They annotated each page of the poem with their interpretations of the literary and symbolic allusions. For the open house, they prepared posters with each page of the poem accompanied by their essays and visual images. The students discussed what they hoped visitors to their booth would understand from their presentation and tailored their efforts to support that understanding. They hope visitors will not only understand the meaning the students developed through their analysis of the poem but will also engage in making their own interpretations. The students want visitors to understand that reading symbolic poetry requires readers to reflect on their own associations.

Geometry students in Bill Kendall's class at Braintree High School are meeting in trios to think about the data they just collected in the hallway outside their classroom. They placed a mirror on the wall and moved two members of their trio around on the floor tiles until both partners could see one another in the mirror. Having collected data about angles and distances on several trials, they are now looking for patterns in their results. Bill has asked them to use what they learned about similar triangles to explain these findings.

Eric Buchovecky's physics students are concluding their unit on machines by presenting research they conducted on an everyday object of their choice. Their task is to apply the laws of mechanics that they derived from experiments in explaining the workings of their machine. One student is displaying his work about a nail clipper. His report includes diagrams as well as text to explain how this simple machine takes advantage of the laws of physics.

In the seventh grade at Shady Hill School, Lois Hetland's students are meeting in pairs to examine the life album that each student prepared about an important figure of the Colonial period in American history. The albums include artifacts and an essay in which students analyze the sources they used in their biographical research and explain their subject's place in history. As students examine their classmates' albums, they answer questions posed by the album's author to help readers check their understanding of its main points. In an oral presentation to the class, each student compares the person he or she studied to the founding fathers the class had researched as a group.

Why do we think these kinds of exercises develop as well as demonstrate students' understanding? How do teachers decide on topics around which to focus their curriculum? How do students come to understand important academic subject matter from these exercises? How do teachers learn to teach this way? What is the evidence that students learn from such performances?

In this book a group of reflective schoolteachers and researchers from the Harvard Graduate School of Education answer these questions based on a six-year collaborative research project. They describe the theoretical foundations underlying a specific Teaching for Understanding framework, the process and results of using the framework in a range of classroom settings, and the implications for teacher education and school change. The book is addressed to a broad audience including teachers, school leaders, policymakers, parents, teacher educators, and educational researchers because all these groups must synchronize their efforts in order to make teaching for understanding a reality in schools.

Nearly everyone agrees that students in schools need to develop understanding, not just memorize facts and figures. Business leaders embrace these goals because most workers must know how to learn and think in order to succeed in this era of constant change and technological development. Politicians have always claimed that citizens of a democracy must critically analyze information and ideas to make reasoned and responsible choices, not just remember what they are told. In the past decade learning theorists have demonstrated that students do not remember or understand much from didactic instruction. To understand complex ideas and modes of inquiry, students must learn by doing and actively change their minds. New curriculum standards issued by educators in a wide range of subject matters call for schoolwork to focus on conceptual development, creative thinking, problem solving, and the formulation and communication of compelling arguments. Similarly, new assessment standards decry testing students' recall of isolated bits of information with multiple-choice tests. They recommend more authentic, embedded, performance-based assessments integrated with instruction.

Despite a growing consensus regarding the desired ends of education, the means to achieve this agenda are not well specified. Most schoolteachers are still surrounded by curriculum materials, role models, standardized test mandates, teacher evaluation guidelines, daily schedules, and years of experience that reinforce traditional transmission-based instruction. Most textbooks and curriculum guidelines impel teachers to cover vast amounts of information. Few teachers have been given opportunities to reflect on the essential ideas and modes of inquiry in the subjects they teach. Many teachers who have begun to incorporate more project-based curriculum are not sure how to link "hands-on" activities with "minds-on" learning. Perhaps teachers' most difficult challenge of all is designing assessment strategies that address the new agenda in ways that are clearly feasible and fair.

General policies and broad guidelines are not specific enough to help teachers design curriculum, plan educational activities, and assess student work. Before they can respond to the ubiquitous calls to teach for understanding, teachers need answers to the following questions:

1. What topics are worth understanding?
2. What about them must students understand?
3. How can we foster understanding?
4. How can we tell what students understand?

The Purpose of this Book

From 1988 through 1995 the group of researchers at the Harvard Graduate School of Education collaborated with teachers from nearby schools on research to address these questions. This book summarizes the project's results.

The heart of both the project and the book is a four-part framework whose elements address each of the questions just posed. First, define what is worth understanding by organizing curriculum around *generative topics* that are central to the subject matter, accessible and interesting to students, and related to the teacher's passions. Second, clarify what students will understand by formulating explicit *understanding goals* that are focused on fundamental ideas and questions in the discipline, and publicize these goals for students, parents, and other members of the school community. Third, foster students' understanding of these goals by engaging learners in *performances of understanding* that require them to extend, synthesize, and apply what they know. Rich performances of understanding allow students to learn and express themselves through multiple intelligences and forms of expression; they both develop and demonstrate understanding. Fourth, measure students' understanding by conducting *ongoing assessment* of their performances. Such assessments are most educationally powerful when they occur frequently, are based on public criteria directly related to understanding goals, are conducted by students as well as teachers, and generate constructive recommendations for improving performances. Ongoing assessments inform planning and measure students' understanding.

The Teaching for Understanding (TfU) framework structures inquiry to help teachers analyze, design, enact, and assess practice focused on the development of students' understanding. It does not prescribe answers to the questions but rather provides clear, coherent, and specific guidance to help educators develop their own answers. Research on the development and use of this framework in schools has not only produced a practical tool for improving practice but also illuminated conditions that promote reflective practice.

In keeping with the collaborative process of the research, this book represents a continuing dialogue relating pedagogical theories with practice. Its authors include educational researchers and teachers from a range of schools. Their commingled voices recount the roots, development, application, and implications of the TfU framework. Although every chapter lists primary authors, invariably these writers drew upon the shared body of understanding and examples developed by a large group of collaborators over five years.

The Teaching for Understanding Project

A brief history of the project illuminates the context within which the research unfolded, thereby informing its interpretation. In 1988–89, project directors Howard Gardner, David Perkins, and Vito Perrone invited a small group of university-and school-based colleagues to plan research toward a pedagogy of understanding. Most of the university participants were associated with Project Zero, a research center at the Harvard Graduate School of Education directed by Perkins and Gardner. Project Zero researchers study human cognition in a range of domains and seek to apply their findings to the improvement of thinking, teaching, and learning in diverse educational settings. Both this planning effort and the resulting five-year research program proceeded with funding from the Spencer Foundation.

During the first year of research, the project directors assembled teachers of English, mathematics, history and social studies, and science from six secondary schools and one middle school in Massachusetts. They met with a group of researchers interested in learning, pedagogy, teacher development, and school improvement. A total of approximately twenty teachers and fourteen university-based researchers (many of whom had previously taught school) formed groups focused around particular subject matters and began by preparing cases about the teachers' best efforts to teach for understanding. Through analysis of these cases in light of current educational research, the groups gradually formulated the features of teaching for understanding into a preliminary framework. Teachers from a wide range of schools participated in a series of two-hour meetings during which they were introduced to the framework and helped to use it for designing a curriculum unit. These teachers of various subject matters generally endorsed the emerging framework and recommended further refinements.

During the third year of the project, classroom research with the preliminary framework demonstrated that coming to understand how to teach for understanding is a complex process. Based on these findings, we designed an intensive collaborative action research project with four teachers, working in four schools on different subject matters. This study, conducted in 1993–94, analyzed the process of learning to teach for understanding, the nature of classroom practice informed by this framework, and the work of students in these classes.

As this research progressed, members of the project responded to requests from school people who wished to learn about the Teaching for Understanding project. During the writing of this book, project researchers and teachers introduced our TfU framework to more than two hundred educators around the United States and in several other countries. They consulted in more than twenty schools with clusters of teachers who made a sustained commitment to revising their practice with this framework. These experiences informed the book and motivated both its development and the design of the complementary handbook *The Teaching for Understanding Guide*,[1] which is a step-by-step guide to using the TfU framework with teachers.

Contents

This book explains the foundations of the Teaching for Understanding framework and summarizes research on its use with teachers and students in schools. Each chapter is titled with a question that instigated the research and analyses it reports. This rhetorical form invites readers to join a continuing inquiry, which is the hallmark of teaching for understanding. Readers may enter this dialogue in various places depending on the questions of primary interest to them. The chapters need not be read in any particular order.

The sequence of parts corresponds roughly to the chronology of the project. Part One traces the roots of the project and the theoretical foundations of the framework. In Chapter One Vito Perrone answers the question *Why Do We Need a Pedagogy of Understanding?* His response encompasses the history of efforts to formulate a pedagogy of understanding, including the rationale for such an educational agenda, the components of related efforts, the challenges they have encountered in American schools, and the reasons for recent interest in this endeavor. David Perkins delineates the project's answer to *What Is Understanding?* in Chapter Two. He defines understanding as a performance, a capacity to think and act flexibly with what one knows, and distinguishes this conception from the more common view of understanding as a mental representation. The implications of this performance view of understanding are fundamental to the TfU framework.

The formulation of the TfU framework and its enactment in practice are the focus of Part Two. In Chapter Three, *What Is Teaching for Understanding?* Martha Stone Wiske outlines the four elements of the framework: generative topics, understanding goals, performances of understanding, and ongoing assessment. Her summary of the formulation of these elements through collaborative research with schoolteachers portrays the framework as a structure for continuing inquiry by teachers, researchers, and others who wish to support understanding in schools and elsewhere. Wiske, Karen Hammerness, and Daniel Gray Wilson answer the question *How Do Teachers Learn to Teach for Understanding?* in Chapter Four. They summarize research on the process of coming to understand the TfU framework, illustrated by vignettes of two teachers, Joan Soble and Bill Kendall. In this work, learning to teach for understanding is conceived as a series of understanding performances guided and supported by the framework itself. *How Does Teaching for Understanding Look in Practice?* is the subject of Chapter Five. Here Ron Ritchhart and Martha Stone Wiske with Eric Buchovecky and Lois Hetland summarize themes from research conducted with several teachers, illustrated with vignettes of classroom practices.

In Part Three the focus shifts to students and learning for understanding. Veronica Boix Mansilla and Howard Gardner address the question *What Are the Qualities of Understanding?* in Chapter Six by presenting a framework for assessing the dimensions and depth of students' understanding of academic subject matter. They delineate the theoretical foundations underlying this analytic framework and illustrate its practical value in analyzing students' performances and products. The next three chapters deal with different aspects of students' work in classrooms guided by the Teaching for Understanding framework. In Chapter Seven, *How Do Students Demonstrate Understanding?* Lois Hetland, Karen

Hammerness, Chris Unger, and Daniel Gray Wilson portray pictures of individual students' work from four classrooms and characterize it in terms of Boix Mansilla's framework. Chapter Eight provides a more comprehensive and quantitative answer to the question *What Do Students in Teaching for Understanding Classrooms Understand?* Here Karen Hammerness, Rosario Jaramillo, Chris Unger, and Daniel Gray Wilson summarize quantitative ratings of student work in TfU classrooms and discuss factors that may explain variations in these statistics. Members of the project also conducted research on students' perceptions about the processes of learning and teaching, which they report in Chapter Nine. In *What Do Students Think About Understanding?* Chris Unger and Daniel Gray Wilson with Rosario Jaramillo and Roger Dempsey describe students' beliefs about the nature of understanding and their perceptions of their teachers' practice. They also correlate these beliefs with the students' understanding of academic subject matter.

In Part Four we turn to the challenge of supporting wider use of Teaching for Understanding. In Chapter Ten Vito Perrone offers his response to the question *How Can We Prepare New Teachers?* He describes a year-long course in the teacher education program at the Harvard Graduate School of Education that both models the TfU framework and guides new teachers to use it in designing their own practice. *How Can Teaching for Understanding Be Extended in Schools?* is the question Martha Stone Wiske, Lois Hetland, and Eric Buchovecky address in Chapter Eleven. They summarize two different ways of supporting TfU and draw conclusions for school leaders who wish to promote this agenda.

In a concluding chapter Howard Gardner assesses the TfU project in relation to abiding educational concerns and initiatives. He perceives TfU as a way to transcend long-standing controversies between traditionalists and progressive reformers and to mobilize teachers, administrators, families, and students around education for understanding.

Audience

Because Teaching for Understanding requires the combined and coordinated efforts of a wide range of people, this book addresses a broad audience, including educational researchers with an interest in practice to reflective practitioners concerned with the conceptual foundations underlying their work. Thoughtful educators—including teachers, school administrators, curriculum directors, and professional developers—interested in TfU in middle and high schools are perhaps the primary audience. Chapters Three through Five and Seven through Nine provide detailed pictures of the process and effects of integrating the TfU framework with classroom practice. The book is also directed to educational researchers and teacher educators who study theories of pedagogy and ways of relating them with classroom practice. Chapters One, Two, Three, and Six clarify the theoretical foundations underlying this project and the process of collaborative action research through which it evolved. Chapter Ten is particularly addressed to teacher educators.

This book may also be of interest to groups who are attempting to coordinate "top-down" and "bottom-up" efforts to reform schools. For those involved in restructuring schools and developing schools as centers of inquiry, the Teaching for Understanding project illuminates the educational processes at the center of their concerns. For policymakers who argue for pedagogy focused on understanding and performance-based assessments, this book depicts how such policy initiatives may play out over time with teachers and students in school classrooms. Chapter Eleven focuses especially on the role of TfU as a framework to guide and align classroom practice, teacher development, and the process of organizational learning in schools.

Both the book and the research project it describes emerged through teachers' dialogue with researchers, relating analytic formulations with educational practice. Readers may join this ongoing inquiry at various starting points in the book, depending on their particular interests. However you begin the dialogue, we hope that reading this book will stimulate you to cultivate your own community of colleagues with whom to develop your understanding of teaching for understanding.

Foundations of Teaching for Understanding

Why Do We Need a Pedagogy of Understanding?

Vito Perrone

Teaching for understanding—the view that what students learn needs to be internalized, able to be used in many different circumstances in and out of classrooms, serving as a base for ongoing and extended learning, always alive with possibilities—has long been endorsed as a primary educational goal in the schools. Seldom, however, has such an end become the norm. Both the widespread appeal of this educational direction and the equally prevalent failure to enact it helped generate the research program reported in this volume.

A brief review of educational history establishes the enduring quest for a pedagogy of understanding and illuminates its principal features. The parallel account of barriers to teaching for understanding in American schools, however, provides a sobering reminder that this elusive goal warrants more concerted attention. Moreover, recent initiatives to reform curriculum and assessment standards underscore the breadth and intensity of current interest in this agenda. Each of these topics is discussed as a means of framing the context and the contributions of our work around teaching for understanding.

Historical Context

Renewed interest in teaching for understanding during this closing decade of the twentieth century is partly a reaction to the narrow skills-oriented curriculum that dominates schools as well as

considerable evidence that large numbers of students are not receiving an education of power and consequence—one that allows
them to be critical thinkers, problem posers, and problem solvers
who are able to work through complexity, beyond the routine, and
live productively in this rapidly changing world (in what is often
referred to as the "global economy").[1] In some respects the current
circumstances are similar to those a hundred years ago, when a
progressive education movement was beginning to gain momentum that also had as a stated goal deeper understandings of what
students studied in the schools. Although we believe that the particular Teaching for Understanding (TfU) framework on which
this book is based has many unique qualities, it clearly builds on a
long history of belief that schools need to engage students more
intensely and with understanding as the centerpiece. We further
believe that keeping this historical base before us is important.

Philosophically as well as in practice, teaching for understanding is almost as old as human history itself. Various religious traditions, for example, have been guided by prophetic teachers who
spoke in parables and metaphors, asking their followers to make
new connections within their various worlds, construct mental images that go beyond their current understandings, and imagine
themselves and their circumstances differently. Plato, one of the
Western world's great teachers, taught through elaborate alle-
gories; in China, Confucius set images off against words. Although
contemporary pursuits of understanding may not explicitly cite
such sources of inspiration, they can easily be related to these earlier educational efforts.

Educational history is also filled with master-apprentice relationships through which various arts and crafts were taught for
understanding. Apprentices learned how to approach the quality
of work of the masters by stages, gradually perfecting the various
elements of the art or craft and at some point developing their
own signatures. That important learning comes by doing something—acting on aspects of the world, actually understanding the
processes and the medium—was conventional wisdom in these
teaching and learning relationships.

Use of the word *understanding* in particular educational formulations also has a long history. The *Oxford Dictionary of the English Language* tells us that by the early medieval period the word

had a fairly modern meaning: grasping the idea, comprehending something, being aware. In 1898 the *Universal Dictionary of the English Language* defined *understand* this way: "To apprehend or comprehend fully; to know or apprehend the meaning, import, intention, motive of; to perceive by the mind; to appreciate the force or value of; to attach a meaning or interpretation to; to interpret; to explain; to be an intelligent and conscious being." Our Teaching for Understanding framework defines understanding in similar terms.

Educationally, understanding has almost always been valued, at least rhetorically. Since the beginning of schools as we know them in this country, understanding has been a stated goal. The path to understanding has not always been clear, however, and inequities in the pursuit and achievement of understanding have long existed even as they were long unattended. For many years after schools were established, for example, the educational needs of women were seen as minimal, with basic reading and writing and family arts considered more than sufficient. The goal of understanding, that deeper engagement with intellectual pursuits, was for much of the eighteenth and nineteenth centuries usually reserved for selected groups of predominantly white males.

The Common Schools

The "common school" movement, with its principal origins in the 1840s, began with hopes for a powerful education for all children. The "three R's" of reading, writing and arithmetic were clearly seen as critical, but according to the early common school evangelists—Horace Mann, Henry Barnard, and John D. Pierce—more was expected. The nurturance of democratic life was a particularly important purpose, the implication being that schools and democratic action were closely linked. Educational ideas emanating from Europe, which greatly inspired Mann and others, also supported active learning and student construction of knowledge—central ideas to any epistemology of teaching for understanding.

Friedrich Froebel's work, for example, was especially influential on America's educational reformers, particularly in relation to the earliest years of the school cycle. His garden metaphor—with its sense of unfolding, blooming, and flowering—underscored the developmental quality of learning. For Froebel, educational experiences build on each other and are therefore related. In his terms, the more significant various experiences are the larger their educational potential. Because such continuities were important, Froebel encouraged children to return often to previous experiences. He understood students would bring something different to the experiences each time, thereby enlarging them, imbuing them with new possibilities, and thus extending their understandings. Linear views of education, which became solidified in various nineteenth-century textbooks and educational expectations, would have seemed to Froebel and his followers antithetical to good education and the development of understanding.

Johann Pestalozzi and Johann Friedrich Herbart wrote about pedagogy more directly than Froebel. Responding to an educational system that was linear and fact oriented, Pestalozzi eschewed memorization, the verbalization of rules and concepts in the absence of understanding, and indeed all learning activities that could not easily be connected to the learner's life. His pedagogical points of departure were the child and the child's experiences, the concrete materials with which the child worked, and the relationships of these materials and experiences to other objects and ideas—which is essentially the basis for understanding. Student interests were considered critical and seen as important starting points for learning, especially learning that would be internalized.

Herbart viewed all learning as relational, causing him to criticize the isolated learning of disconnected topics that was beginning to shape curriculum in the schools. For him, each new stage of learning had to be integrated with previous learning, the aggregate constituting the base for further learning. His pedagogical approach sought entry points connected to previous learning, strong links to the interests of students, and consolidation around generalizations or principles to guide ongoing learning in school and in life. Herbart's ideas resemble Alfred North Whitehead's later formulation of a continuous learning cycle around romance, precision, and generalization, the latter equating to our definition of understanding.[2]

The point of this brief introduction to some of the central ideas of these European educators is to establish that many of the conceptions undergirding our TfU formulation were present in discussions of early common schools in the nineteenth century. That they existed in the language does not necessarily mean they existed in practice, but without the language the practice would likely have been less constructive than it was.

Although the common schools hardly became the enlightened educational settings Mann, Barnard, and Pierce envisioned, they were quickly incorporated into the universal fabric of American society. Schools proliferated much more quickly than Mann could ever have envisioned, especially after the Civil War, but pedagogical practices and teacher preparation lagged behind this rapid growth. As the schools increased in number and became incorporated into state systems they also became more systematized and formal. The graded structures of today's schools had become the norm by 1870. Covering the material encompassed within first-, second-, and third-grade readers became a dominant theme in the schools. Memorization took up much of a child's time. As the factory became a dominant force in the American economy by the latter nineteenth century, the factory metaphor pervaded the language of the broader culture, including schools.

Universal attendance through the elementary grades was the stated goal of the common schools, but it was difficult to achieve. Fewer than 25 percent of those who began school in the nineteenth century completed elementary school programs. Further, in spite of the best hopes of such egalitarians as Mann the common schools, especially in the East, served mostly the poor and lower middle classes (with blacks generally excluded). Those with means found other institutions for their children.

Widespread public support for secondary schools did not develop until the closing decades of the nineteenth century. Unlike the elementary schools, secondary schools in the late nineteenth century were classically academic in nature and attracted few young people from working-class or newly arrived immigrant families. Not until the 1920s did the high schools begin to attract these populations in any significant numbers. By then they had become different institutions with a broader curriculum, vocational education programs, and diverse levels of academic expectations.[3]

The nineteenth-century effort to expand educational opportunities was fraught with difficulties not unlike those currently faced by a myriad of developing countries. Fiscal support was inadequate and school facilities could not be built rapidly enough to accommodate the increasing numbers who wished to attend. Moreover, the surrounding social order was in a state of rapid transition, especially in the urban areas. Urban population, for example, increased from 9.9 million in 1870 to more than 30 million by 1900. Many major U.S. cities doubled in population in this thirty-year period, and racial, ethnic, and religious concerns related to the massive migration and immigration in the latter nineteenth century proved vexing in public schools. Much in the philosophical discourse supported a pedagogy of understanding, but putting the ideas into practice was still difficult.

The Progressive Movement

In this late nineteenth-century period of social and economic transformation, concerns about the directions of schools foreshadowed what was to become a burgeoning progressive reform movement in the early years of the twentieth century. The basic challenges focused on breaking the linear curriculum chain, the rote nature of teaching and learning, and the formalism and growing centralization of schools. Brooks Adams, a prominent historian and Boston school board member, framed the critique as well as anyone in an 1879 *Atlantic* essay. He wrote, "Knowing that you cannot teach a child everything, it is best to teach a child how to learn," and proceeded to show that most school practice had no connection to such a purpose. Such a critique was elaborated upon by a sufficient number of educators and educational critics to encourage the beginnings of an important reform movement.

Among early reformers, Francis W. Parker, referred to by John Dewey as the "father of progressive education,"[4] stands out. Accepting the superintendency of Quincy, Massachusetts, in 1873, Parker made a public commitment to bring back enthusiasm for teaching and learning. Influenced greatly by Pestalozzi's ideas, Parker quickly initiated policies to end the linear, lockstep curriculum along with the traditional graded readers and spellers. Further, Parker encouraged teacher initiative in the development of curriculum, recommended using newspapers, magazines, and field trips into the community as a basis for studying local history and geography, and introduced manipulative devices for teaching arithmetic. He wanted students to make learning their own—something internal and usable beyond school. Nothing, he believed, should be taught in isolation; the weekly spelling list was one of his most potent examples of wasted opportunities for learning. Student interest was critical. How teachers approached children and their learning, the content they stressed, the materials they used, the relationships they forged between what was studied and the world were more important to Parker than coverage of any specific curriculum.

Parker's reform efforts were large for the day, assuring that controversy would swirl around him. Some of his critics in the state department of education thought the Quincy schools were abandoning reading, writing, and mathematics and "experimenting with children." Parker responded in his 1879 annual report to the school committee with words often repeated by reformers in subsequent eras: "I am simply trying to apply well established principles of teaching. . . . The methods springing from them are found in the development of every child. They are used everywhere except in school."[5]

Our approach to Teaching for Understanding, as presented in this volume, benefits from the legacy of Froebel, Herbart, and Pestalozzi and of practitioners such as Parker. But it draws more centrally on the work of John Dewey, especially on the large vision of democratic schooling he articulated: an education of power and consequence assured for all students.

Dewey stressed the need for a "new pedagogy" that calls upon teachers to integrate the content of schooling with the activities of daily life. He understood the prevailing separation between school and life as assuring a limited education for children and young people, essentially emptying the possibilities. In addition he viewed education at its best as growth in understanding, capacity, self-discovery, control of events, and ability to define the world—in other words, as always leading somewhere. Dewey focused on the child *and* the curriculum, taking seriously both students' interests and intentions and teachers' choices about entry points to content, questions to pose, and activities to pursue. The discovery and forging of relationships were critical to his pedagogy—the known to the unknown, the new to the old, the problematic to the certain. Such relationships are, of course, critical to understanding.

In Dewey's vision the organization of subject matter was especially important.[6] He advocated organizing instruction around
themes with broad possibilities, accessible at many levels of complexity with natural connections to other content areas.[7] This is
very close to our definition of *generative topics*. Overall, what should
be taught, Dewey argued, "would justify itself because it answered
questions the student himself asked."[8]

The best of Dewey's thought, though developed well in many
small private institutions and some public schools that have sur-
vived into the present, often became diluted in the mainstream
public schools. Cremin argued that Dewey's influence on American education was profound and that the schools quite universally
adopted many of his ideas and language, such as the child as a
point of departure, greater egalitarianism, a broader view of the
subject matters, more active learning, and the introduction of
vocational education and the arts.[9] Dewey himself, however, was
unenthusiastic about most of what he saw.[10] As put into common
practice, Dewey's ideas often lacked coherence and vitality.[11] An
education of power requires, of course, more than words and
intentions.

Progressivism moved from Dewey's interest in a fusion of teaching and learning, pedagogy and curriculum, process and content,
school and life, to more focused though less integrated concerns
about method, process, and curriculum. Kilpatrick, for example,
codified Dewey's emphasis on active learning by explicating a more
formal "project method."[12] In its application, however, the project
method appeared to make content much less important than
process. It helped push some progressive educational thought toward the either-or dichotomy that Dewey expressed concern about
in *Experience and Education*.

Progressivism suffered in the 1930s from the difficulties of the
Great Depression and the overwhelming demands of World War
II that drew public attention away from the schools. By the 1950s
it had become popularly identified with a process approach to
learning that gave too little attention to subject matter. Cremin
considered progressivism to have ended with the passing of the
Progressive Education Association in 1955, but by then it had long
passed its vital years. Cremin closed his book on the subject by suggesting that perhaps "[progressivism in education] only awaited

the reformulation . . . that would ultimately derive from a larger resurgence of reform in American life and thought."[13] This may well have been prophetic.

Crosscurrents of Reform from 1960 to 1980

The 1960s proved to be years of massive social change in the United States. The civil rights movement that gained momentum in the late fifties was a fulcrum for social and political reform in the sixties. The inequities in American life became increasingly apparent and were understood to require a large-scale public response. The failure of the educational system to provide quality schooling on an equal basis to all Americans became a potent public issue. Support for pluralism, long cast aside in the wake of melting pot theory, grew with the recognition that it was necessary for the creation of a more workable social democracy.

Depersonalization, generated in part by increasing levels of technology and bureaucratization in virtually all phases of American life, produced a sometimes radical response. Awareness of the rapid depletion and defacement of natural resources stimulated an increased concern for "spaceship earth." And the war in Vietnam, which proved to be more unpopular than any previous U.S. military involvement, brought protest to a high level. This milieu generated a new wave of educational reform that echoed earlier reform efforts.

Some 1960s educational reforms were characterized in the popular press as merely romantic—related to the general questioning in American society about lifestyle and cultural change—but they certainly included serious inquiry into pedagogy around the matter of understanding. Jerome Bruner, in many respects the inheritor of Dewey's vision of possibility for children and their learning, provided the dominant intellectual influence. Bruner advocated an approach to thoughtful subject matter learning that made solid connections to the lives of learners—to their need for understanding content, not merely their ability to repeat textbook formulations.[14]

Bruner's ideas were central to much of the 1960s curriculum reform work. His well-known social studies curriculum *Man:*

A Course of Study,[15] for example, was designed explicitly to help students think about the world of human beings in the United States and in other cultures in more reflective, analytical ways. This curriculum celebrated complexity and challenged students and teachers alike to think, to go beyond what was presented. Arguing that any subject can be taught in an intellectually responsible way to learners of any age, Bruner directly challenged the popular notion that the early years of education and the early phases of study in a field of inquiry should be dominated by routine skill building.

Just as important as his pedagogical and curricular stance was Bruner's grounding of that posture in the emerging field of cognitive psychology. Bruner made the educational community aware of school learning as a process sensitive to cognitive and developmental factors. He underscored the importance to the learner of gradual mastery of several symbolic systems and modes, and experimented with different ways of representing abstract ideas to learners of different ages.

Along with *Man: A Course of Study,* several other experimental curricula of the period were committed to the notion that youngsters can not only learn about various academic disciplines but can engage them in ways significantly parallel to the work of professional practitioners, leading in the process to understanding. For example, *Science: A Process Approach*[16] and *The New Social Studies*[17] sought to introduce students directly to the kinds of inquiry processes scientists and historians exercise. Disciplinary habits of mind—problem posing, interpretation, reflection, seeking counterevidence, asking why it matters—were understood to be critical, as they are important bases for understanding.

Among the various curriculum projects of the period, the *Elementary Science Study* (ESS) is particularly illustrative of themes that correspond well to many of our views about teaching for understanding. The introduction to the guide for this curriculum states: "It is apparent that children are scientists by disposition: They ask questions and use their senses as well as their reasoning powers to explore their physical environments; they derive great satisfaction from finding what makes things tick; they like solving problems; they are challenged by new materials or by new ways of using familiar materials. It is this natural curiosity of children and their freedom from preconceptions of difficulty that ESS tries to culti-vate and direct into *deeper* channels. It is our intention to enrich *every* child's understandings. . . ."[18]

In regard to teaching strategy, the ESS guide states: "We want students not only to recognize scientific authority but also to de-velop both the confidence and the skills to question it intelligently. For this reason we feel it is necessary for the student to confront the real world and its physical materials directly, rather than through intermediaries such as textbooks. . . . We caution teachers against explaining things prematurely and against overdirecting student exploration."[19]

In this unprecedented period of curriculum reform, inquiry as a model of discourse was reaffirmed—questioning, maintaining a healthy skepticism, developing hypotheses, experimenting, exam-ining a range of confirming and disconfirming data, and articu-lating a variety of possible explanations. An open-endedness was advocated, including the active use of materials and the develop-ment of ideas based on careful observation over time. There was talk of the need to "uncover a subject" rather than "cover a sub-ject." The goal was understanding, not the amassing of isolated information.

The eventual outcome of this flurry of activity is all too well known: the initiatives foundered and faded into the "back to ba-sics" movement of the seventies and eighties.[20] Several forces con-tributed to a resurgence of less active, less complex paradigms. A fundamentalist backlash, for example, discouraged federal partic-ipation in innovative programs such as *Man: A Course of Study.*[21] Fur-ther, the university-based disciplinary scholars who led many curriculum projects of the 1960s often held unrealistic expecta-tions about teachers' comfort with the new, more complex ideas and about the schools' commitment to their particular vision of education. In fact, to carry out these various curricular reforms schools would have had to alter many of their long-standing prac-tices and structures. In addition the values of progressivism—including skepticism, questioning, challenging, openness, and seeking alternative possibilities—have long struggled for accep-tance in American society. That they did not come to dominate the schools is not surprising.[22]

Current Context

As we near the close of the twentieth century, the equity and excellence of our schools are being criticized and interest in teaching for understanding is once again on the rise. The basic skills-oriented education that has tended to dominate the last two decades seems too little. Once more school critics are calling for students to go beyond facts, to become problem solvers and creative thinkers, to see multiple possibilities in what they are studying, and to learn how to act on their knowledge.

Although the current interest in teaching for understanding will undoubtedly encounter barriers, conditions give some cause for hope that present efforts may succeed where earlier progressive movements fell short. A groundswell of public concern about the schools is certainly one critical factor; the country's educational system has lost considerable luster regarding both universality and quality. Further, widespread recognition of the need for change has fueled the popularity of multiple large-scale educational experiments. Perhaps the most visible example is the Coalition of Essential Schools led by Theodore Sizer, which emphasizes that "less is more" in regard to what is taught and learned. The coalition also endorses intellectually challenging instructional activities and assessment focused on essential questions and "habits of mind." Such efforts give the general idea of teaching for understanding a particularly friendly reception.

Teaching for understanding is now also the focus of critical attention by academic scholars in the various disciplines. This bodes well for a pedagogy of understanding, especially if attention is given to the lessons learned in the 1960s. One distinction between current disciplinary curriculum efforts and those of the 1960s is that arguments for different curricular formulations and pedagogy are not being translated into specific curricula that call upon teachers to be technical intermediaries. Renunciation of "teacher-proof" packages represents an important advance because such directions contradict the epistemological premises of teaching for understanding.[23] Changes in pedagogy that require students to be more deeply involved in their own learning—to demonstrate understanding through performance—are not likely to succeed without the greater autonomy of teachers individually and collectively.

In place of the detailed curriculum packages created in the 1960s, recent reform efforts have stressed more open-ended curriculum and assessment guidelines or frameworks. Since the National Council of Teachers of Mathematics issued its curriculum and evaluation standards in 1989, most other major discipline-based professional organizations have also begun to define guidelines for curriculum and pedagogy in their respective subject matters, drawing heavily on disciplinary scholars, educational researchers, and classroom teachers. In addition the majority of state education agencies are now developing curriculum frameworks that call for significant changes in the focus and process of education. All these initiatives give significant attention to teaching and learning for understanding.[24]

Current Curriculum Standards and Frameworks

The curriculum standards and frameworks now being developed emphasize the need for students to make sense of key concepts in the disciplines, develop intellectual dispositions and habits of mind associated with inquiry, construct their own understandings rather than merely absorb the knowledge created by others, and see connections between what they learn in school and their everyday lives. Given the focus on understanding, the new standards call for teachers to make judicious selections of curriculum content, be more clear about their purposes or goals, and make assessment rooted in performance more integral to the teaching-learning exchange. Superficial coverage of overly broad content and multiple-choice tests that feature recall of information are not viewed as virtues. More thorough inquiry is recommended around a smaller number of critical ideas, concepts, and themes that are studied in depth, returned to at different grade levels, and connected both to ideas across various fields of inquiry and to students' personal lives. Evidence of these priorities can be found in virtually every recent effort to define the nature of subject matter curriculum. Several examples follow.

Science

The National Committee on Science Education Standards and Assessment notes: "As the body of scientific knowledge has exploded, high school courses have become cluttered with so much new vocabulary, often exceeding that of foreign language courses, that terms can only be memorized rather than understood."[25] Teaching less more deeply is the overriding concern of this science education effort. Content is defined broadly within four general and equally weighted categories: science subject matter, the nature of science, the application of science, and the contexts of science. The latter three, the committee suggests, have been absent from much of science curriculum, leaving students without much understanding of science. Regarding subject matter, the committee says:

> Subject matter is *fundamental* if it:
>
> - represents central scientific ideas and organizing principles;
>
> - has rich explanatory and predictive power;
>
> - motivates the formulation of significant questions;
>
> - guides fruitful observation; and
>
> - is applicable in many situations and contexts common to everyday experience.[26]

In the area of life sciences for grades 9–12, the following subject matters are deemed fundamental understandings: the chemical nature of life processes; matter and energy in biological systems; the molecular basis of heredity; and variation, diversity, and the evolution of species. We can imagine a yearlong course developed around these four topics. Importantly, the committee offers a wide array of examples—possible entry points to each of the topics.

The second area of science content, the nature of science, includes "knowledge of the inquiry process, the ability to design and carry out an investigation, perspectives associated with critical thinking or 'habits of mind,' and other positive attitudes usually associated with learning."[27] The committee's comments about the inquiry standard, some of which follow, indicate its views about both the central goals of science education and effective teaching-learning processes (and they match much of what grows from our TfU framework).

Inquiry is the process by which scientists pose questions about the natural world and seek answers and deeper understanding, rather than knowing by authority or other processes. Approaching the study of school science in a questioning mode is, therefore, in harmony with the practice of science, as compared with presenting science by talking about it.

Inquiry in science follows no single pathway. Exploration can lead to many questions. Carefully planned experiments can proceed in a predictable fashion or yield startling data that lead to new questions and new investigations. On the other hand, the process of inquiry is not random; once a question is posed, the search for answers follows a purposeful sequence of experimentation, data collection, analysis, and the drawing of conclusions.

When students engage in inquiry, they use a wide range of tools and skills, make choices among alternatives, and determine what events are important. They use both practical, hands-on skills and thinking skills. Inquiry in the classroom can and should engage students in inquiry as it really is—a series of creative, iterative, and systematic procedures.

Inquiry in the classroom is a means of promoting and supporting students' curiosity and questioning spirit. Inquiry is a critical component of the science curriculum at all grade levels and in every domain of science.[28]

Standards regarding the other two categories—applications of science and contexts of science—emphasize rich performances, with students being expected to formulate their own directions for focused discussions, investigate the history and social context of science, and identify the uses of science. Self-evaluation is also a priority.

The committee is suggesting a major shift in the direction of science education. Recognizing the difficulties in effecting change in the 1960s science reform period, it acknowledges the need to support teachers as they rethink their teaching of science.

Mathematics

The National Council of Teachers of Mathematics (NCTM) has made understanding the uses of mathematics its central focus. Thus it has challenged the traditional separation of math into independent subject areas of algebra, geometry, trigonometry, analysis, statistics, and probability, proclaiming that students at all grade levels should understand mathematics as a fully integrated field of inquiry aimed at helping them solve problems, communicate, reason, and make connections. Such goals mean that "students should be exposed to numerous and varied interrelated experiences that encourage them to value the mathematical enterprise, to develop mathematical habits of mind, and to understand and appreciate the role of mathematics in human affairs; that they should be encouraged to explore, to guess, and even to make and correct errors so that they gain confidence in their ability to solve complex problems; that they should read, write, and discuss mathematics, and that they should conjecture, test, and build arguments about a conjecture's validity."

Though recommending particular content to be taught at each cluster of grade levels, the NCTM standards do not stipulate detailed curriculum requirements. Instead the emphasis is on integrating topics so that students make sense of mathematical ideas in relation to one another and to the everyday world. The "standards call for a shift in emphasis from a curriculum dominated by memorization of isolated facts and procedures and by proficiency with paper-and-pencil skills to one that emphasizes conceptual understanding, multiple representations and connections, mathematical modeling, and mathematical problem solving."[29]

A more integrative, functional orientation toward mathematics is also endorsed in *On the Shoulders of Giants,* the report of the Mathematical Sciences Board of the National Research Council, National Academy of Sciences: "What humans do with the language of mathematics is to describe patterns. Mathematics is an exploratory science that seeks to understand every kind of pattern—patterns that occur in nature, patterns invented by the human mind, and even patterns created by other patterns. To grow mathematically, children must be exposed to a rich variety of patterns appropriate to their own lives through which they can see variety, regularity, and interconnections."[30]

The board proceeds to outline five thematic topics concerning fundamental and universal patterns in nature and the world of ideas: dimension, quantity, uncertainty, shape, and change. Shape, for example, may seem most related to geometric conceptions but certainly is not limited to geometry. We can imagine a world of shapes, artworks as shapes, even ideas as shapes.

Humanities

The humanities fields are also far along in a similar rethinking process. In its document "Criteria for Planning and Evaluating English Language Curriculum," the National Council of Teachers of English (NCTE) makes clear its support for active learning and for tying what is studied to the world of the students. It also emphasizes the relatedness between and among students' language arts experiences, choices, and performances.

Its curriculum document is instructive. For oral and written language the NCTE guide suggests that the curriculum be "consistent with the premise that the content of language study often comes from real life, [requiring] student application of language [and] consistent with the premise that acquiring information *about* language does not necessarily improve oral or written language performance."[31] A good literature curriculum "accommodates students being allowed and encouraged to select and read all types of literature, classical through contemporary, and recognizes the importance of student involvement in literary texts." The guide recommends a media curriculum that "incorporates study of such nonliterary modes as film, newspapers, magazines, television, radio [and] provides for both study of and production of media."[32]

The NCTE statement notes that teachers are expected to be critical decision makers about curriculum and students are expected to be meaning makers. Like other professional organizations, NCTE has strongly endorsed understanding over surface knowledge; it reaffirmed this in a recent NCTE standards document.[33]

Calls for reform in social studies have come from the National Commission on Social Studies and the Bradley Commission. Both name history as the base of the social studies curriculum and stress that schools cannot continue to treat history curriculum as coverage and memorization of large numbers of dates and names. In *Charting a Course: Social Studies for the 21st Century,* the national commission urges that "teachers must select vigorously, highlight and interpret the material, challenge students to think deeply and synthesize widely."[34] Moreover, it suggests teachers begin with such premises as "students know more about the world than is readily apparent" and "different students know somewhat different things."[35] Teachers must, in other words, begin with students and their existing understandings.

The national commission outlines three major periods of history for study during a three-year sequence of courses at the secondary level, with specific topics to be addressed in each:

World and American History and Geography to 1750

Emphasis on major civilizations and their salient characteristics—economy, government, religious practices, gender roles, technological innovation, codification of law, connections to surrounding civilizations/cultures.

World and American History and Geography, 1750–1900

Emphasis on the democratic revolution, the industrial and technological revolution, and modern growth and mobility of population.

World and American History and Geography Since 1900

The democratic idea and its worldwide expression in diverse forms; the industrial-technological transformation which has altered conditions of life and landscape everywhere, even where modern industry has not established itself; and demographic shifts arising from the triumphs of modern medicine, transportation, technology and change in family relationships.[36]

The Bradley Commission asks teachers to "resist the impulse" to put everything into any single course: "The first step in teaching well . . . is to limit what you try to do."[37] Beginning with a narrative—a good story—is stressed by the Bradley Commission (as well as the national commission), which notes that "the great teacher is able to take the best, most engaging stories from each era of history and set them as stepping stones." Further, by "using the analytical techniques of the historian, teachers can draw out of [the stories] the 'vital themes and habits of mind'" desired.[38]

The foregoing directions leave teachers with considerable room to make decisions about curriculum. Thomas Holt, recent past president of the American Historical Association (AHA) and professor of history at the University of Chicago who has taken a particular interest in the teaching of history in the schools, notes in this regard:

> American history can be taught in an infinite variety of ways. It would be fallacious, therefore, to insist upon one particular selection and organization of topics and themes. . . . The vitality and effectiveness of a course depends on what both student and teacher bring to the classroom. It is their ability to adjust and respond to what they find . . . that wins teachers the status of professionals as opposed to assembly-line functionaries.

> This caveat not withstanding, it is possible to suggest some basic principles for constructing these diverse classroom experiences. . . . The basic premise of the Curriculum Task Force report [of the AHA] has been that the political demography of and cultural communication in the modern world requires an education that prepares students for a lifetime of active and effective participation in the political, social and economic life of the nation. . . .

> Whatever the particular features of an American History course, . . . [they] cannot emphasize unity to the exclusion of diversity in the American experiences, the inspirational without its problematic moments, its achievements without its failures.[39]

The goal of the various frameworks and standards for teaching history, including those developed more recently for U.S. history and world history by the National Center for History in the Schools, clearly speak of the need for "a rich network of understandings."[40]

The overall point of exploring, albeit briefly, the more recent work around curriculum in the various subject matters is to make even more clear how relevant our Teaching for Understanding agenda is at this time. There is, we believe, a real chance to alter the ways teaching and learning proceed.

Current Assessment Standards

Alongside efforts to alter the substance of curriculum and methods of pedagogy are constructive revisions in assessment policies, instruments, and practices. In addition there is a growing understanding that revising assessment policies is not merely a necessary consequence of educational change but a particularly good impetus to initiate wide-scale improvement in schooling. These performance-oriented directions are consonant with teaching for understanding. They may in fact help teachers alter their pedagogy with a greater focus on understanding. A brief review of the history of educational assessment and a somewhat fuller summary of recent assessment initiatives in the United States underscore that new forms of assessment must be part of teaching and learning for understanding.

For much of the past century in the United States, learning typically was considered to be a matter of students absorbing information from lectures, readings, and demonstrations and then being tested to see what they had learned. Tests usually were given at the end of a week, a unit, or a course, and students' performance on these usually thirty- to fifty-minute exams were thought to represent what they had learned.[41] Some schools and teachers might use essay tests or open-ended questions, but for purposes of ease and efficiency, short answer, multiple-choice, and machine-scorable items were often favored. The latter, often standardized and norm referenced, were used in most schools to judge subject matter achievement in comparison to that of students in other schools. They were also used to measure aptitude and intelligence.

To be sure, other forms of assessment have been the subjects of experimentation. Dating back to the nineteenth century, some schools mandated exhibitions of various sorts, ranging from senior orations to full-fledged scientific experiments. And in the progressive era attention was paid to student projects, often initiated by the students themselves and sometimes going beyond linguistic and mathematical demonstrations to involve more artistic forms of expressions. The products of such efforts were often exhibited or made the subject of public presentations. But even where experimental approaches to assessment were developed, the tests that most often counted remained the year-end, higher-stakes tests produced beyond the classroom doors.

In the mid-1980s a widespread effort began again in the United States and certain European countries to rethink educational assessment. This effort was generated by an increasing recognition that standardized tests, which had expanded greatly in use over the previous decade, and the weekly classroom tests, which focused mostly on information retrieval, were severely limited. New insights into learning, drawing particularly on cognitive psychology, called attention to the importance of mental representations of knowledge and challenged the belief that such representations could be adequately tapped through the occasional use of decontextualized, unsituated instruments or altered much without considerable opportunity for practice. Other important factors in the reevaluation of assessment were a heightened focus on the development of critical and creative thinking, a belief that important lessons for assessment existed in such domains as the arts, and a demonstration that it is in fact possible to achieve consensus in assessing the quality of more complex products through such means as holistic scoring and "descriptive review."[42] Finally, of considerable importance was the growing consensus that current schooling does not foster long-term commitment to learning or sophisticated mastery of disciplinary knowledge.

Over the past decade many fresh efforts at assessment have been organized. A brief survey would certainly include the Coalition of Essential Schools' emphasis on graduation through exhibitions; the New Standards Project, with its call for performance-based examinations, projects, and portfolios; experiments in various states (California, Connecticut, New York, and Vermont) with performance-based and portfolio assessments; the efforts to experiment with such forms by numerous other institutions ranging from the Educational Testing Service to the National Center for Evaluation, Standards, and Testing, the Council for Basic Education, and the Performance Assessment Collaborative in Education; and the growing lists of content and performance standards that have been developed by literally dozens of disciplinary groups throughout the land.

An account of the history of this effort must note, however, that there have been severe critics of the move toward performance-oriented forms of assessment. Predictably, some are defenders of the status quo who would lose much of their influence if the current instruments of assessment lost hegemony. But even individuals having much more sympathy for the effort to reform assessment express reservations based on cost, the ambiguities of many of these instruments and rubrics, and the necessary disruptions caused by a shift from one form of assessment to another.

In sum, then, the interest in performance-based assessment has grown steadily in recent years (though not without controversy) and is becoming part of the contemporary educational landscape. Any systematic approach to teaching for understanding must include a similarly focused strategy for helping both teachers and students monitor progress and assess evidence of understanding.

The Challenges

Even as there is growing interest in teaching for understanding along with a history in which it received support, constraints still persist. Any formulation of teaching for understanding must take account of these barriers if it is to become a practical formulation for changing teaching and learning practice in the schools.

At least four major challenges must be met: assuring an education of power to all students, not just the socially and academically elite; designing curriculum that both meets widely endorsed standards and responds to the needs of individual teachers and learners; producing clear evidence of learning so that students and educators are accountable for their work; and stimulating widespread appreciation for and endorsement of understanding as a central educational goal.

Suitability for All Students

Over the long history of public education in the United States, an education of power has been endorsed fully for only certain students. In the early years, for example, most students had only limited access to public schools; even when opportunities expanded at the close of the nineteenth century, they were limited for the majority of students. The percentage advancing to secondary schools, for example, was negligible. As access to public education increased during the past century, the forms of education provided by schools changed in ways that still kept education for understanding—what we define as a more powerful education—outside the reach of most young people.

Faced with rapidly increasing numbers of students, schools became in the twentieth century ever more bureaucratized, standardized, and segmented. As one response, separate schools or tracks within schools provided vocational training or basic education for many students thought to lack the ability or the need for more rigorous academic work. In these settings, where students were often from lower socioeconomic classes and minority populations, the focus was on practical skills or the rehearsal of "basic skills" rather than the development of critical thought. Though more expansive intellectually, even the academic tracks tended in most settings to be structured around coverage of standard textbooks and preparation for various standardized tests. Learning in such academic environments tends to require a fairly narrow band of linguistic and representational understandings, disregarding the rich range of interests and forms of expression that students might otherwise embrace. Moreover, teachers have remained the focal point, dominating most of the discourse and in the process supporting considerable passivity among students. A performance orientation, with students being "the workers" (to use a Coalition of Essential Schools' principle), has not been common.

A pedagogy of understanding must be flexible enough and attractive enough to serve all students. It must work for students at all levels of academic ability and achievement. It must engage the full range of intellectual possibilities so that students can bring all their talents to bear on their schoolwork. Moreover, it must be adaptable to all subject matters and grade levels.

Rigorousness Yet Responsiveness, Specificity Yet Flexibility

One of the major dilemmas for any curricular framework is the requirement that public schools provide all students with comparable high-quality educational opportunities while responding to local priorities and individual needs. The curriculum must engage students in work that is widely viewed as important and intellectually challenging, promote the fundamental values of a democracy, and enable students to move freely among schools without confronting totally unfamiliar intellectual expectations. Thus the curriculum in various schools must have some common standards.

Yet a pedagogy of understanding, more so perhaps than other educational goals and approaches, must also be responsive to the interests and needs of particular students and teachers in specific local contexts. If the aim of education is understanding, then students must become actively engaged in making ideas their own. The curriculum must relate to the students' concerns, interests, and experiences. Teachers cannot simply deliver a standardized message but must tailor general guidelines to suit their particular students. They must also be able to shift the focus and pace of curriculum on a daily basis to maintain the intense engagement that understanding requires.

There is another reason why a pedagogy of understanding must honor teachers as the primary decision makers about curriculum. Such a pedagogy assumes that all learners must construct their own understanding. Identifying one's own interests, developing one's own arguments, discerning the new layers of questions beneath every provisional set of answers are all concomitant with constructing one's own understanding rather than merely absorbing knowledge made by others. If teachers are expected to foster these kinds of opportunities for students, however, they must be afforded similar opportunities as professionals. This does not suggest that teachers must invent everything; their time is too limited for that. While avoiding the excessively detailed curriculum packages that leave teachers no room for invention, a curriculum framework must provide sufficient numbers of possible directions to help teachers select and refine classroom activities and materials.

A pedagogy of understanding must provide guidance for choosing what to teach and for designing a curriculum that will meet general standards of quality. At the same time it must endorse teachers as the ultimate decision makers and support their ongoing inquiry into fundamental educational questions about what to teach, how to teach, and how to know what students are learning.

Accountability

Any framework intended to guide public education must, of course, yield evidence that students are learning. Despite widespread criticism from educators, the ubiquitous presence of standardized testing attests to the ongoing interest in monitoring educational productivity. Test scores are currently taken as indicators of the achievement of individual students. And through comparisons of test results across classes, schools, districts, or states these standardized tests are also being used to evaluate teachers and institutions. Although few believe that such tests are a particularly good indicator of the work that really matters, few other types of evidence currently possess widespread support.

Other forms of assessment are needed that can provide program accountability for students, teachers, and school programs. Ideally such assessments would not only satisfy the multiple stakeholders who are concerned about school quality but also inform the students, teachers, and administrators as they work directly on developing understanding. If assessment does not support such a classroom-oriented purpose it will not be particularly useful. A major strength of the Teaching for Understanding framework is the element of *ongoing assessment* that supports student understanding. Connecting this element of the framework to a portfolio process can raise the visibility of student work, producing in the process a powerful form of accountability. Furthermore, it is also clear that demonstrations of understanding, *understanding performances* in our TfU framework, are not yet common enough in schools—not yet part of the parent and public consciousness about what students are learning. If they become more commonplace, the focus on these standardized tests that educators and students have known for so long can be expected to decline.

Broad Appeal

Throughout this chapter, perhaps the most fundamental barrier to teaching for understanding has been implied but not directly named. Many Americans are deeply suspicious about the value of academic rigor and independent thinking as universal aims to be addressed by public schools. Even among those who endorse these goals for some students, not all believe they are appropriate for all students. Many others think they are unrealistic to achieve in public schools. These doubts are reflected in the structure of schools where class periods last fifty minutes or less, where middle and secondary teachers see 120 or more students per day, where students take as many as six separate subjects a day, where lock-step coverage of a standard curriculum sequence is required. They are just as deeply yet perhaps more subtly expressed in school cultures where time and resources are dedicated to sports, administrative meetings, and many other distractions from the basic agenda of teaching and learning subject matter for understanding.

No curriculum framework can directly confront the multiple deeply rooted structures and cultural norms that interfere with teaching for understanding. Nevertheless, a pedagogy of understanding must generate, attract, and hold the widespread endorsement of rigorous academic work by students, teachers, and administrators in schools as well as by the parents, policymakers, educational researchers, and others who concern themselves with schools.

The purpose of this book and of the educational research and development on which it is based is to promote teaching for understanding that will gradually generate widening circles of endorsement. The framework we present to guide TfU is informed by lessons from the past and fueled by current opportunities.

Chapter Two

What Is Understanding?

David Perkins

What is understanding? When students attain understanding, what have they achieved? One could hardly ask a more basic question toward building a pedagogy of understanding. If the aim is a way of thinking about teaching and learning that puts understanding up front on center stage most of the time, we had better know what we are aiming at.

Knowledge, skill, and understanding are the stock in trade of education. Most teachers show a vigorous commitment to all three. Everyone wants students to emerge from schooling or other learning experiences with a good repertoire of knowledge, well-developed skills, and an understanding of the meaning, significance, and use of what they have studied. So it is worth asking what conception of knowledge, skill, and understanding underwrites what happens in classrooms among teachers and students to foster these attainments.

For knowledge and skill, a rough answer comes readily enough. Knowledge is information on tap. We feel assured a student has knowledge when the student can reproduce it when asked. The student can tell us what Magellan did, where Pakistan lies, what the Magna Carta was for, what Newton's first law of motion is. And if knowledge is information on tap, skills are routine performances on tap. We find out whether the skills are present by turning the tap. To know whether a student writes with good grammar and spelling, sample the student's writing. To check arithmetic skills, give a quiz or assign a problem set.

But understanding proves more subtle. Certainly it does not reduce to knowledge. Understanding what Magellan did or what Newton's first law means calls for more than just reproducing information. Understanding also is more than a routine well-automatized skill. The student who deftly solves physics problems or writes paragraphs with topic sentences may not understand much at all about physics, writing, or what is being written about. Though knowledge and skill can be translated as information and routine performance on tap, understanding slips by these simple standards.

So what is understanding? One answer lies at the heart of this book and this project; it is simple but rich with implications. In a phrase, understanding is the ability to think and act flexibly with what one knows. To put it another way, an understanding of a topic is a "flexible performance capability" with emphasis on the flexibility. In keeping with this, learning for understanding is like learning a flexible performance—more like learning to improvise jazz or hold a good conversation or rock climb than learning the multiplication table or the dates of the presidents or that $F = MA$. Learning facts can be a crucial backdrop to learning for understanding, but learning facts is not learning for understanding.

This performance view of understanding contrasts with another view of understanding prominent in both our everyday language and in cognitive science. We often think of an understanding as some kind of a representation or image or mental model that people have. When we achieve understanding, we say, "I've got it." Understandings are things possessed rather than performance capabilities. There is a real issue here. Which view is better, and why? The answer offered here delves both into an analysis of concepts and into ideas about constructivism from contemporary cognitive science. Readers who think the performance view is obviously sound and feel no need for a disquisition about the mechanisms of understanding could well skip to the next chapter and the teaching framework based on this idea. Readers who wonder about whether this performance view makes sense or how it can hold its own against the representational view of understanding had best read on.

A Performance Criterion for Understanding

"What is understanding?" is a tricky question. But in practical terms people are not so bewildered. We know it when we see it. Teachers and indeed most of us seem to share a good intuition about how to gauge understanding. We ask learners not just to know, but to think with what they know.

For example, one teacher who participated in this project was introducing the taxonomy of plants and animals. To probe the students' initial understanding of classification systems, she asked them to construct one. Almost everyone has a drawer full of junk at home—old pencils, can openers, nails, worn spoons. Her assignment for the students: survey the contents of a junk drawer and create a classification system for its contents. How they did this made them more aware of classification as an enterprise, told the teacher what they understood so far, and allowed her to highlight some of the purposes and challenges of designing a classification system.

Much later on in developing the same theme, the teacher assigned a more traditional but also challenging task. The students were to use a "key" of critical features to classify organisms. If they could make the taxonomy work, this would show at least a partial understanding.

Two ideas follow from these commonsense observations. First, to gauge a person's understanding at a given time, ask the person to do something that puts the understanding to work—explaining, solving a problem, building an argument, constructing a product. Second, what learners do in response not only shows their level of current understanding but very likely advances it. By working through their understanding in response to a particular challenge, they come to understand better.

The notion that people recognize understanding through performance not only makes common sense but appears throughout a range of research in human cognition. Swiss developmental psychologist Jean Piaget tested children's understanding of basic logical structures by setting tasks for them to perform—for instance, seriating a collection of sticks from smallest to largest. Investigators of students' understanding of physics pose qualitative problems that ask students to think about the physics rather than turn a well-practiced quantitative crank. For instance, when an object is dropped from an airplane will it hit the ground ahead of the plane, directly under the plane, or behind the plane, neglecting air friction? With no numbers in sight, students' answers and explanations reveal whether they understand the physical principles involved.

To make a generalization, we recognize understanding through a *flexible performance criterion*. Understanding shows its face when people can think and act flexibly around what they know. In contrast, when a learner cannot go beyond rote and routine thought and action, this signals lack of understanding.

A Performance View of Understanding

The flexible performance criterion signals the presence of understanding. But does it tell us what understanding is? The core proposal here is that yes, it does: not only do people recognize understanding through flexible performance, but it is reasonable to view understanding as a flexible performance capability. An understanding of Newton's laws or the Civil War or the subjunctive tense amounts to nothing more or less than a flexible performance capability around those topics. To understand a topic means no more or less than to be able to perform flexibly with the topic—to explain, justify, extrapolate, relate, and apply in ways that go beyond knowledge and routine skill. Understanding is a matter of being able to think and act flexibly with what you know. The flexible performance capability *is* the understanding.

All this becomes easier to articulate and elaborate with the help of a key term: *understanding performances* or, equivalently, *performances of understanding*. By definition, understanding performances are activities that go beyond the rote and the routine. An understanding performance is always something of a stretch. The teacher who asked students to sort their junk drawers was calling for an understanding performance because they had never done such a thing before and had to think about it. Had they already done it five times, asking them to construct one more variant would not be much of an understanding performance. Exactly because understanding performances ask the learner to stretch, they lead to advances in understanding as well as displays of understanding.

Performances of understanding contrast with important routine performances called for by life in general and schooling in particular. Well-practiced knowledge and habits figure fundamentally in grammatical speech, knowing the multiplication tables, manipulating algebraic equations, recalling the times and places of historical events, and so on. In no way does the emphasis on performances of understanding mean to slight the importance of basic knowledge and skill. Indeed, we would all be profoundly crippled without an undergirding of the rote and the routine. Nonetheless, understanding demands something more.

Of course, the contrast between understanding performances and routine performances is not absolute. It involves degrees. Remembering one's phone number seems little more than a well-practiced reflex, about as far from a performance of understanding as one can get. But remembering a friend's new phone number can involve recalling a few digits, guessing at another, asking yourself whether it sounds right, checking whether the first three digits match well the person's locale. This is a much more active, constructive process, a process of extrapolating from what you remember specifically to the whole number. It is, in effect, a small-scale understanding performance. Though remembering often amounts to a simple act of recall, it can demand much more.

Inevitably, what counts as a performance of understanding will vary with a person's sophistication. A physics problem that challenges high school students and so lets them demonstrate and extend their understanding might be mere routine for a graduate student. Broad developmental factors may figure as well. A task that puzzles a six-year-old with its intricate logic may appear transparent to the same child at fifteen. Finally, what kinds of performances signal understanding varies with the field and context, which place more priority on some kinds of performances than others. A writer of a short story need not necessarily strive to have the characters argue cogently with one another; what counts is the revelation of character through the argument. But an essayist had better have the argument straight.

A further complicating factor recognizes that many different kinds of performances of understanding apply to the same topic. Students may attain one handily while finding another difficult. Students who can explain in their own words the historical forces behind the Boston Tea Party may have trouble relating it to other more contemporary cases of social protest. Students who get the idea of a physics concept may have trouble with the math while others who master the math may miss the point.

All this might be read as a challenge to a performance view of understanding. It seems that the performance view leads into a maze of subtle distinctions: performances of different kinds, learners of different levels, topics with different demands. But if matters are complicated, it is not because of the performance view of understanding but because of understanding itself. Different topics and disciplines *do* pose distinctive demands; understanding *does* come in degrees; people of differing experience and development *do* display more or less insight. These complications hold regardless of the theory of understanding. If anything, it is reassuring to find that they can be expressed in performance terms, more encouragement for a performance view.

The Representational View of Understanding

The natural response to the flexible performance view of understanding is "Instead of what?" That is, with what alternative conception of understanding does the flexible performance view contrast? The answer is that what might be called a *representational view* of understanding thrives in both everyday discourse and psychological theory.

In casual speech it is commonplace to say things like these: "I see what you mean." "I see the point." "I see through you." "I see the answer." "I see the trick." Such phrases testify to a firm link in folk psychology between perception and understanding. Just as we see houses and trees, in a metaphorical sense we see what we understand. Seeing involves taking in visually, capturing some kind of an internal image of what we have seen. Following through with the metaphor, understanding-as-seeing requires achieving a mental representation that captures what is to be understood.

Psychological research often echoes this folk conception in a more sophisticated way. Understanding depends on acquiring or constructing an appropriate representation of some sort—a schema, mental model, or image. For example, Richard Mayer reviewed a series of experiments addressing diverse science and engineering concepts.[1] The findings showed that what Mayer called *conceptual models* promote understanding. Conceptual models are flow diagrams and similar representations—for instance, of a radar system. They are generally presented to students prior to a textual explanation. Learners gain by internalizing these models. Students generally benefit from conceptual models, solving problems much more flexibly than students not given conceptual models. However, they make little difference for students with good background knowledge and high aptitude for the topics, presumably because these students construct their own models.

The well-known sourcebook *Mental Models,* edited by Gentner and Stevens, includes a number of articles that argue that understanding of science concepts depends on runnable mental models.[2] These are imagistic constructions that people can run or manipulate to test questions about the behavior of a system, such as the operation of an electrical circuit imagined as the flow of a liquid through the wires.[3] Philip Johnson-Laird and Ruth Byrne offer an analysis of formal reasoning that foregrounds the role of representations in modeling situations and mediating reasoning.[4] They propose that people work from the givens of a logical argument to build "possible world" scenarios and test questions of entailment by examining and manipulating these scenarios. Noel Entwistle and Ference Marton introduced the concept of "knowledge objects," representations that students construct through intense study for exams or other purposes.[5] Students can survey these knowledge objects in a bird's-eye manner and navigate through them flexibly to answer questions and write essays. Numerous other scholars have proposed representational accounts of understanding, including Roger Schank's "explanation patterns,"[6] Stellan Ohlsson's "abstract schemas,"[7] and the "epistemic games" of Allan Collins and W. Ferguson[8] and of David Perkins.[9]

Turning to developmental research, Piaget argued that sophisticated thinking reflects the acquisition of schemas for a small set of fundamental logical operations. Some neo-Piagetians, though suggesting that development proceeds much more domain-by-domain than did Piaget, also foreground the role of schemas. For example, Robbie Case and his colleagues see development as dependent on the advance of several "central conceptual structures," including one concerning narrative and another concerning quantity.[10]

All these cases involve representations in one or another sense, but they are not all the same. In fact, it is useful to recognize two different kinds of representations. The first might be called *mental models*. These kinds of representations are mental objects that people manipulate, run, or tour in the mind's eye. Mayer's conceptual models and Entwistle and Marton's knowledge objects have this character. The second might be called *action schemas*. Sometimes representations are taken to lie in the background, not inspected consciously by any inner eye but somehow guiding our actions. So, for example, we do not have to examine any central conceptual structure for narrative with our mind's eye to encode narratives; we simply do it, governed somehow by the central conceptual structure.

How does all this relate to a performance view of understanding? The representational view explains understanding in a fundamentally different way. Understanding lies in possession of the right mental structure or representation. Performances are part of the picture, but simply in consequence of having the right representation. A flexible performance capability is a symptom. It does not constitute the understanding but simply signals possession of the appropriate representation. In contrast, the performance view says that understanding is best seen as lying in the performance capability itself, which depending on the case may or may not be supported partially by representations.

The next two sections build a careful argument for preferring a performance view of understanding over a representational view. The performance view may seem persuasive enough already, but there are technical sides to the issue that deserve attention.

But does it matter practically? The distinction between the two might appear to have as little significance as the fine points of doctrine that spawn religious splinter groups. Yes, it *does* matter in ways explored in the last two sections, which draw out what a performance view of understanding says about teaching and learning.

Why Prefer a Performance View over Mental Models?

The basic problem with a representational view is this: although representations certainly play an important role in some kinds of understanding, it is difficult to sustain the general case for understandings *being* representations in any interesting sense.

Remembering the contrast between mental models and action schemas, consider the case of mental models first. Does it make sense to say that understanding something *is* having a mental model of it? No, because we can have a mental model of something without understanding it, as gauged by the flexible performance criterion. A mental model is not enough for understanding simply because it does not do anything by itself. For performances that show understanding, a person must operate on or with the model. For instance, suppose a student tries to understand electrical circuits through the image of fluid flow. Then it is not enough for the student to imagine fluid in the wires or even in motion. The student must imagine what happens to the fluid as it passes through resistors and other circuit elements and read off the consequences from the model. In other words, the student has to manipulate and interrogate the model. To recall a phrase mentioned earlier, the model is a "runnable" mental model and nothing will be got from it without running it.

A defender of mental models as understanding might propose that, although not logically sufficient, mental models are generally practically sufficient: with the representation in mind, the person can easily show the flexible performance called for. But this is not so. Simply told to think of electricity as fluid flow, a learner might not know what to do to reason with the image. In the case of logical reasoning, people commonly fail to make appropriate inferences, displaying such classic errors as affirming the consequent and denying the antecedent instead. Johnson-Laird and Byrne interpret the errors as reflecting how the reasoners mistakenly manipulated schematic mental models.[11] Likewise, you may have a good model of your neighborhood and yet give inaccurate and misleading directions—forgetting for the moment a turn you knew was there and would never miss yourself. In general, the point is that effective manipulation of a model to yield flexible performances cannot be taken for granted. Mental models are often complex, demanding of short-term memory, tricky to track when running, or challenging to handle in other ways.

To all this, the defender might reply, "Well, of course, when I say understanding is a matter of having a mental model, I don't mean just having the model in mind but being able to work with it." But this is exactly the concession the performance view wants.

So far, the point is that mental models are not enough for understanding by themselves. But are they even necessary? Certainly not always, because people understand some things without mental models. For instance, in a practical sense we understand the grammar of our mother tongue without any explicit access to the rules that govern grammatical speech. We pass the test of flexible performance: we can encode grammatical speech, produce it, discriminate grammatical utterances from ungrammatical utterances, correct ungrammatical utterances to make them grammatical, and indeed start with grammatical utterances and rework them to make them ungrammatical in interesting ways, as poets and novelists sometimes do.

Someone might object that though we may be able to do all these flexible things, most of us do not really understand the grammar of our mother tongue because we cannot immediately identify the rules, analyze their function, make comparisons with other languages, and so on. This makes an important point. It signals that we have what might be called an *enactive understanding* of the grammar of our language but lack a reflective understanding of it. Moreover, academic contexts usually call for a reflective understanding too: the ability to talk about grammar, not just to function grammatically.

Still, enactive understanding is a kind of understanding; it passes the test of flexible performance. The understanding may be partial, but all understandings are partial—one never understands everything about anything. And it is an important kind of understanding. The student of French who can discuss French grammar but not use it flexibly is missing something. So enactive understanding is an important kind of understanding that need not involve any explicit mental model.

Thus it should not be left out of the picture. Enactive understanding with no conscious mental models at work is commonplace, not rare. There are principles of conversational turn-taking that people have assimilated but do not know as such. Yet people behave according to them in a flexible manner. Most of us understand how to have a graceful conversation without studiously contemplating the patterns of turn-taking that govern it. We flexibly handle many motor demands: we walk carefully on ice, catch ourselves when we start to slip, and dodge around a particularly slippery spot with hardly any awareness of the governing principles or mechanisms. Most of us have everyday musical ability: many people learn to carry a tune and sing or whistle ornamentations and variations with no knowledge of music notation, scales, or any of the paraphernalia of Western musical formalism. All these are possible even if we have no developed way of representing to ourselves or thinking about what we are doing.

Even when people do have explicit mental models to help them with their grammar, conversations, walking on ice, or singing, it is clear that the models do only part of the work. As we flexibly and fluently converse, navigate, or sing, we clearly do not do so by hovering over our mental models. We act effectively with only occasional reference to them.

Related observations accompany a skeptical look at the role of representations in behavior developed by Terry Winograd and Fernando Flores.[12] Building on the work of Maturana and Heidegger, they argue that in general an organism does not require mental models to get along in the world. Moreover, mental models always involve a certain point of view and emphasis; they can inform but can also mislead. What is central is effective involvement in activity, not representations.

Why Prefer a Performance View over Action Schemas?

All this argues that mental models alone are not enough to sustain the case for a representational view of understanding. A performance view wins easily. So what about reinforcing the representational view with action schemas, that other kind of representation? If mental models do not account for grammar, conversations, walking on ice, or singing, certainly action schemas could, silently underlying and guiding behavior.

What account of understanding do action schemas offer? Perhaps it makes sense to say that an understanding *is* an action schema. But this does not add much beyond saying that an understanding is a performance capability. The action schema would be whatever it takes to regulate the performance, no more and no less. This could be called a representational view of understanding, but it is a weak one.

Moreover, there may be no action schemas at all. It is easy to presume that regularities in behavior trace back to an internal representation of some sort that regulates the behavior. But this need not be so. Turning from psychology, consider physics for a moment. Newton's laws describe how nature behaves in a deep and illuminating way. But this does not mean that nature behaves the way it does because Mother Nature monitors those laws and regulates the way things happen. The laws are descriptive, not prescriptive. Likewise, just because scholars can write down rules that describe grammatical speech or conversational turn-taking or narrative structure, this does not mean that those rules sit somewhere in the mind and exercise an executive function.

But how else could large-scale patterned behavior arise? Contemporary psychology recognizes that much behavior occurs not because of any governing executive but because tiny elements interact in such a way as to bring about large-scale patterned behavior. For instance, there is no ruler of a termite nest. The queen is basically an egg factory and there are no foremen or other managers. No termite has a grand plan for the nest. Yet as each termite follows its simple programming, the nest emerges.[13]

Connectionism, a contemporary cognitive theory, advances what amounts to a view of mind as termite-nest architecture. This school of thought argues that orderly complex behavior can emerge simply from the strengths of connections distributed throughout a neural network. The individual connection strengths are, so to speak, the contributing termites. Connectionist research demonstrates that simulated neural networks can learn to recognize letters and perform other tasks of some complexity. Yet nowhere in the neural network is there any representation of anything. For instance, in a network that recognizes letters, there is no "A area" of the network that represents A, "B area" that represents B, and so on. Rather all the connection strengths collectively help to recognize all the letters. One could call the whole network an action schema for recognizing the letters. But this is not usually what is meant by a governing representation.

The issue here is not whether connectionist theory is correct. Perhaps it will win out in the end, perhaps not, perhaps something in between. But at least connectionist theory warns us that orderly behavior in the world need not stem from some representation that prescribes it. People can have flexible performance capabilities without any representations at all in any useful sense of representation.

In summary, the case for a performance view of understanding over the rival representational view goes like this. Basically, the representational view is an effort to identify something behind the flexible performance capability, some kind of representation that enables the performance. But this move simply does not work in general. If representations mean mental models, some kinds of understanding do not require mental models. For those that benefit from mental models, just having such a model in mind does not always lead to the flexible performances that mark understanding. If representations mean action schemas, they do not add much to just saying "performance capability." Moreover, connectionist research shows that flexible performance can occur without action schemas.

These limits of a representational view of understanding should not be read as dismissing the importance of mental representations in building or displaying understanding. Both research and practical experience demonstrate that mental models are often important parts of understanding something. However, often is not always and parts are not wholes. What is left is the performance view, which says that understanding amounts to a flexible performance capability around the topic in question.

A Performance View of Learning and Teaching

Reasonable though all this may seem, does it matter to the learner and the teacher? What does a performance view of understanding recommend?

Certainly there is a contrast with some commonsense views of learning for understanding that reflect the representational stance. People often refer to attaining understanding as a matter of "getting it," "catching on," or "things falling into place." Such remarks recall the idea of understanding as perception. They suggest not only that understanding involves attaining an internal representation but that it comes quickly, like a visual gestalt.

Such a mind-set demonstrably works against invested learning. Carol Dweck and her colleagues draw a contrast between what they call "entity learners" and "incremental learners."[14] Students of these kinds have starkly different views of the nature of intellectual challenge and of what to do when challenged. Entity learners believe "you either get it or you don't." They expect to understand something by "getting it," and when this proves difficult conclude that they lack the capacity to understand. Incremental learners, in contrast, treat understanding something as a matter of extended incremental effort. These contrasting belief systems correlate with different learning behaviors. Entity learners quit too early; by exercising persistence they might win through to an understanding.

The performance view of understanding favors incremental learning and fosters incremental learners. No one views acquiring a complex performance as a matter of "getting it." Performances require attention, practice, refinement. Performances characteristically involve multiple aspects that need careful and artful coordination. Indeed, this is the principal broad-stroke implication of the performance theory of understanding: developing understanding should be thought of as attaining a repertoire of complex performances. Attaining understanding is less like acquiring something and more like learning to act flexibly.

Such a stance casts teachers less in the role of informers and testers and more in the role of facilitators or coaches. Their challenge is one of choreographing performance experiences that constantly extend students' repertoires of understanding performances, and hence their understanding. Though a teacher operating in this way may well from time to time give a lecture or grade a test, these are supportive, not central, activities. The main agenda is arranging, supporting, and sequencing performances of understanding. This vision of teaching aligns well with several contemporary conceptions of pedagogy, including cognitive apprenticeship,[15] the idea of communities of inquiry,[16] and building a culture of thinking in classrooms.[17]

With the notion of performance learning at the center, some broad principles help to define the enterprise for learner and teacher alike:

1. *Learning for understanding occurs principally through reflective engagement in approachable but challenging understanding performances.*

Engagement in performances is primary: no performance can be mastered without engagement in it. Yet in many conventional educational settings students never undertake performances resonant with certain goals of instruction. For instance, it is hoped that students will see contemporary events through the lens of the history they are studying, but no classroom time gets committed to such connection making. Also, learning benefits from *reflective* engagement, including ways of getting clear and informative feedback from oneself or others and the opportunity to think about how one is performing and how one might perform better. *Approachable* performances have an obvious importance: attempted engagement in a performance one finds unapproachable is unlikely to yield learning. And *challenge* is also central: execution of an understanding performance already well in hand is not likely to extend the performance repertoire.

2. *New understanding performances are built on previous understandings and new information provided by the instructional setting.* One cannot simply engage in an understanding performance without a foundation. Sometimes learners build new understandings entirely through reflecting on and working through prior knowledge and understandings. More characteristically, however, new information obtained from verbal definitions, distinctions, narratives, models, and the like figures in the process. This affirms the importance of making information available, even in didactic ways such as lectures, providing that performances of understanding follow that allow working through the information.

3. *Learning a body of knowledge and know-how for understanding typically requires a chain of understanding performances of increasing challenge and variety.* Unless an area of knowledge and know-how is very simple, a reasonable understanding of it involves a variety of understanding performances, including ones that the learner could not reasonably attempt early in the learning process. Accordingly, the understanding needs to evolve through a series of understanding performances that increase in challenge and variety.

4. *Learning for understanding often involves a conflict with older repertoires of understanding performances and their associated ideas and images.* Often prior understandings stand in the way of building new understandings. One barrier is misconception, especially in the sciences. For instance, common sense and common experience say that heavier objects fall faster, so the Newtonian notion that all

objects fall at the same rate (air resistance aside) seems counter-intuitive and easily dismissed. Another barrier is rigidly applied algorithms, especially in mathematics. For instance, mathematics is commonly seen by teachers and students alike as a matter of adroitness with routines for addition, subtraction, multiplication, and division. Yet another is stereotypes, especially in the social sciences and humanities—for instance, racial prejudice or blind nationalism.[18]

Throughout this project the aim has been to transform the performance view of understanding and general principles such as these into a useful framework for inspiring and guiding educational practice. The next chapter introduces that framework in detail. By way of preview, the framework foregrounds four elements. *Generative topics,* rich themes and questions, provide a fertile focus for teaching for understanding. *Understanding goals* spell out the target attainments the teacher and students aim at. The goals, shared with students early on and sometimes even coconstructed with them, provide a challenge to meet and a clear sense of direction. *Understanding performances* are flexible thought-demanding performances selected and sequenced by the teacher, again sometimes with student collaboration, to both express students' understanding-so-far and push it further. Understanding performances do not just appear toward the end of the learning sequence. They appear from beginning to end in progressively more complex and challenging forms as students advance from early and basic understanding of the generative topic toward later, more sophisticated understandings. Finally, *ongoing assessment* names the important practice of offering students frequent informative assessment throughout, not so much for grading purposes as to advance their mastery of the performances that express their growing understanding.

A Kind of Constructivism

The view of learning for understanding described here plainly has a constructivist turn, challenging the idea that learning is information centered, reframing the role of the teacher as more like that of a coach, and placing the learner's efforts to build understanding squarely in the center. But virtually all contemporary approaches to teaching and learning have a constructivist cast. What makes this one distinctive?

One answer is that it should not be *too* distinctive. There is considerable insight in a range of contemporary approaches to teaching and learning, including those cited earlier. More than that, the work discussed in this book has revealed over and over again the wisdom of teachers' practice. Many practitioners who never heard of understanding performances day in and day out teach in ingenious ways that amount to a performance approach. Indeed, a heartfelt ambition of this initiative from the beginning has been not to create something utterly new but to crystallize insightful practice into a recognizable form that others might learn about and adapt to their own idioms with their own insights.

That granted, it can also be said that the constructivism implicit in a performance view of understanding has its own character. The notion of understanding advanced here leads to a view of constructivism somewhat different from that generally heard in at least two ways:

What gets constructed: representations versus performance capability. In any version of constructivism, a fundamental question is what gets constructed. The most common answer, implicit or explicit, is a representation of some sort—an action schema or mental model. The learner assembles and revises a mental representation to fit the topic.

As already outlined, the performance view of understanding challenges the centrality of representations. What the learner acquires is not just a representation but a performance capability. Learning a topic with understanding is not so much constructing a representation to fit the topic as developing a flexible performance capability around the topic. Indeed, the very metaphor of construction becomes less apt; learners could be said to construct performances, but it is more natural to say that learners develop them or work them up.

How construction proceeds: discovery versus diverse performances of understanding. Often constructivist approaches to teaching foreground a kind of discovery process. Imagine a handyman beginning to fit shelves into a corner without a plan, getting a few hints from a neighbor, trying this, trying that, and finally working it out. Another suitable metaphor looks to scientific inquiry, a scientist formulating a hypothesis, testing it, modifying or discarding it, and finally finding a hypothesis that works. In other words, discovery is the paragon performance that both attains and demonstrates understanding. What you can then go on to do—store books on the shelf, apply the theory—is a secondary spin-off enabled by the discovery.

However, the performance view gives no special priority to discovery. Rather discovery is simply one kind of understanding performance among many; it may not figure as a pivotal performance in a particular episode of learning for understanding. The handyman might become very handy not by working out his first shelf largely by himself but by following a plan and then later adapting his initial experience to diverse circumstances. A student might come to a good understanding of Newton's laws not by some kind of scaffolded discovery process but by an up-front presentation followed by a range of ever more challenging applications and extrapolations.

Why does constructivism tend to place such a high priority on discovery? Perhaps in part because of its emphasis on representations. As the understanding supposedly *is* the mental representation, attaining that representation is key. But just telling people what to think does not usually instill good mental representations; if you merely explain Newton's laws, people don't "get it." So to arrive at a good mental representation, learners have to discover it for themselves with some help. Discovery becomes the key performance of understanding.

In contrast, the performance view has no special commitment to representations. There need be no key episode of discovering the right representation. The performance view more evokes the metaphor of developing a flexible performance capability toward mastery over time. So whether one asks learners to discover core ideas for themselves or gives them direct instruction to get them over a front-end hump becomes much more a tactical question, a matter of choosing an approach to suit the students, the topic, the moment—an exercise of sensitive and seasoned judgment.

With no sweeping policy about discovery versus up-front instruction in sight, how does a performance view inform the practice of teaching? By encouraging teachers and students alike to treat learning for understanding as a kind of performance learning. Whether learning is discovery oriented or not, students will benefit from a performance viewpoint. They will gain from an early vision of the understanding goals pursued and the kinds of understanding performances that realize those goals. They will learn from reflective engagement in performances that challenge without overwhelming them. They will advance through learning experiences sensitive to the prior conceptions they bring to the occasion, indeed from attention to all the points foregrounded in the previous section and crystallized into a Teaching for Understanding framework in the following chapter.

To sum up, the performance view of understanding yields a brand of constructivism that might be called *performance constructivism* because of its emphasis on building learners' repertoire of understanding performances more than on cultivating the construction of representations. This does not mean that performance constructivism yields a prescription for practice radically different from other varieties. Any version of constructivism allows considerable latitude; the contrasts lie in the nuances of practice, not in the big picture. In any case, constructivism with this performance character has provided the guiding image for our explorations in classrooms with students over the past several years. Its ramifications and applications are explored throughout the rest of this book.

Part Two

Teaching for Understanding in the Classroom

Chapter Three

What Is Teaching for Understanding?

Martha Stone Wiske

When understanding is conceived as the ability to use one's knowledge in novel ways, as it is in Chapter Two, the implications for pedagogy may seem simple: to teach for understanding engage students in performances of understanding. But the history of efforts to teach for understanding reviewed in Chapter One reveals that the enterprise is more complex. A pedagogy of understanding needs more than an idea about the nature of understanding and its development. A guiding framework must address four key questions:

1. What topics are worth understanding?
2. What about these topics needs to be understood?
3. How can we foster understanding?
4. How can we tell what students understand?

The collaborative research project on Teaching for Understanding (TfU) developed a way of responding to these questions in a four-part framework. Its elements are *generative topics, understanding goals, performances of understanding,* and *ongoing assessment.* Each element focuses inquiry around one of the key questions: define what is worth understanding by identifying generative topics or themes and organizing curriculum around them; clarify what learners need to understand by articulating clear goals centered on key understandings; foster students' learning by engaging them in performances of understanding that require students to apply, extend, and synthesize what they know; and monitor and promote learners' progress through ongoing assessments of their performances with criteria related directly to the understanding goals.

At first glance, the framework seems simple and rather obvious. Many teachers respond, "Oh, yes, that's what I already do," after their first brief introduction to these concepts. Five years of collaborative research have demonstrated, however, that this framework is more subtle than it first appears. Its apparent accessibility derives partly from the fact that good teachers often do incorporate these elements into their practice, or at least they intend to. Yet teachers who have used the framework to structure extended inquiry about their practice have found that it stimulates them to learn more about their subject matter, their students, and their assumptions about learning even as it guides them to make profound changes in the way they plan, conduct, and assess their work with students.

This chapter introduces the TfU framework that is the focus of the remainder of the book. A brief summary of the development of each element of the framework illuminates its evolution and explicates criteria for its enactment. Describing the framework elements individually entails a risk that each element will be perceived as a more discrete concept than it is. The concomitant danger is that the application of these concepts to practice will appear as four distinct activities. In fact, each of the elements invokes aspects of the others. As the following chapters illustrate, using these elements in practice is not one of sequentially stepping through a formulaic process. The framework evolved through synthesizing analyses of teachers' good practices with theories of effective teaching and learning; its application requires a similar dialogue. Understanding this framework (in the performance sense of using the framework to analyze, design, and enact practice) is a cyclical, reflective process in which the different elements come into play repeatedly in various sequences.

Counterbalancing these reservations are the benefits of conceptualizing the overwhelming complexity of practice with a few key ideas. By simplifying and separating the confusing continuum of pedagogy into distinct concepts, we gain a manageable grip on the inchoate confusion of life in a classroom. Each framework element, with its associated criteria, focuses attention on particular aspects of practice. Collectively they create a structure for thinking about how to bring teaching practice into more complete alignment around our most important educational purposes.

Generative Topics

Determining the content of curriculum is a thorny problem. Whose favorite ideas are addressed, whose interests are served, whose passions are engaged, who makes curriculum decisions, and how do we ensure that all students are comparably prepared? The history of previous efforts to teach for understanding, as Vito Perrone describes in Chapter One, reveals some recurring features of curriculum designed to foster understanding. One is that the curriculum taught in school relates to the concerns and experiences that occupy students in their regular lives. Perrone argues that in order to make these connections between schoolwork and students' daily lives, teachers must be primary decision makers about curriculum. Teachers must select the substance and adjust the shape of curriculum to meet the needs of their particular students. Another basic criterion for curriculum designed to promote understanding is that it does not simply impart information. Rather the curriculum must involve students in continuing spirals of inquiry that draw them from one set of answers to deeper questions and that reveal connections between the topic at hand and other fundamental ideas, questions, and problems. Yet teachers must balance these needs for curriculum tailored to particular groups of students and for open-ended inquiry with a concern for some degree of standardization, equity, and legitimacy. How should teachers choose and design curriculum that meets these various requirements?

This question occupied the Teaching for Understanding project and its group of university-based researchers and teachers from middle and high schools who taught a range of subject matters—history, mathematics, science, and English. They readily acknowledged Dewey's idea of organizing curriculum around themes as a fruitful starting place.[1] But the question of which topics to select remained. A list of generative topics for different subject matters would be too cumbersome. Instead of stipulating particular topics, this collaborative group set itself the task of defining criteria to help teachers identify and evaluate generative curricular topics.

Teachers approached the task by describing and analyzing stories of success from their own experience—that is, curriculum units that engaged their students, sustained students' interest in continuing inquiry, and led them to see larger connections. The group of teachers and researchers discussed examples of effective curriculum units, prepared written cases about them, and analyzed the cases for recurring features. The concept of justice proved to be a generative topic for an English teacher whose course centered around trial scenes in literature. A biology teacher organized her course around the definition of life. A history unit on the Industrial Revolution proved to be generative as students compared conditions in the late nineteenth century with current workplaces.

As teachers examined these examples, they questioned whether generativity inhered in the topic or in the way it was taught. Certainly the generative potential can be drained from any topic if it is taught as a series of right answers in a didactic way. Nevertheless, teachers concluded that certain topics are more easily treated in generative ways. The researchers brought to the discussion their understanding of pedagogical principles, theories of cognition, and ideals based in the history of education and the results of educational research. They pressed for a synthesis of criteria that were refined through subsequent rounds of inquiry with teachers who used the concept to formulate their curriculum. Eventually the group concluded that a topic is likely to be generative when it is central to the domain or discipline, is accessible and interesting to students, excites the teacher's intellectual passions, and is easily connected to other topics both within and outside the particular domain.

Central to a domain or discipline. Curriculum built around generative topics engages students in developing understandings that provide a foundation for more sophisticated work in the domain or discipline. Such topics are typically regarded by professionals in the field as related to central concepts, enduring controversies, or important modes of inquiry in their discipline.[2]

Accessible and interesting to students. Generative topics are related to students' experiences and concerns. They may be approached through a range of entry points—from various disciplinary perspectives, through multiple learning modes or intelligences,[3] from different cultural points of view, with a variety of learning materials and resources. The generativity of a topic varies depending on the age, social and cultural contexts, personal interests, and intellectual background of students.

Interesting to the teacher. The generativity of a topic depends as much on the way it is taught as on its substantive characteristics, hence the teacher's investment in the topic is important. A teacher's passion, curiosity, and wonder serve as a model of intellectual engagement for students who are just learning how to explore unfamiliar and complex terrain with open-ended questions.

Connectable. Generative topics are readily linked to students' previous experiences (both in and out of school) and to important ideas within and across disciplines. They often have a bottomless quality, in that inquiry into the topic leads to deeper questions.

These criteria proved to be comprehensive yet manageable enough to help teachers of different subject matters identify generative topics around which to organize their curriculum. For instance, English teacher Joan Soble built one unit of her writing classes for freshman around the concept of place. The class read and wrote about place as a geographical, social, and metaphorical concept. Bill Kendall organized his yearlong geometry course around the generative topic of mathematics as the study of patterns, encompassing both visual and numerical regularities. More detailed descriptions of these units are included in Chapter Four.

Eric Buchovecky, a physics teacher, focused on the topic of simple machines, which encompassed central concepts in mechanics, everyday machines like corkscrews and garbage cans with step-on lids, and scientific processes linking systematic experimentation with theory building. Lois Hetland, a humanities teacher committed to a yearlong investigation of Colonial American history, focused one unit on biographies of Colonial figures with the question, "What picture of Colonial history do we perceive through the lens of biography?" Students began by reading about any person they wished and thinking about how that person's life illuminated the time period in which the individual lived. These students proceeded to study the Founding Fathers through group projects and then to conduct individual projects on a Colonial figure of their choice. Teachers' work on these units is analyzed in Chapter Five and their students' responses are discussed in Part Three.

Teachers and researchers found one strategy particularly helpful in uncovering and enhancing the generativity of a topic. Working individually or with a group of colleagues, a teacher develops a *concept map* with the topic in the center. Using the criteria for generative topics as a stimulus, the teacher draws a link from this central topic to related ideas, such as the teacher's own passions, issues that interest students, rich educational resources, and important ideas in the subject matter. As ideas are generated the teacher adds them to the map, making links to related nodes. Such a map helps reveal generative connections. It may also draw attention to particularly rich concepts by revealing those with multiple links.

Understanding Goals

Understanding goals state explicitly what students are expected to come to understand. Whereas generative topics or themes outline the subject matter that students will investigate, goals define more specifically the ideas, processes, relationships, or questions that students will understand better through their inquiry. Through their reading and writing about place, Joan Sobel's students came to understand the role of metaphor in literature and the value of metaphor in expressing their own ideas effectively. Through their investigations of machines Eric Buchovecky's students understood the principles of mechanics so that they could apply them to explain the workings of everyday objects like nail clippers.

Unlike the other three elements of the TfU framework—generative topics, performances of understanding, and ongoing assessment—the concept of understanding goals was not part of the earliest formulations of the framework. The value of this element emerged only as teachers and researchers began trying to design materials and activities for teaching generative topics to their students and to define criteria for assessing students' performances. Sometimes the teacher-researcher teams stalled as they tried to move directly from generative topics to curriculum designs. Some of the activities they considered would clearly appeal to students, but they seemed rather frivolous or remote from the core ideas of the generative topic. Designing worthwhile performances became easier once teachers were able to articulate specifically what they wanted students to understand about the designated topic or theme. The need for clear goals also became apparent when teachers attempted to assess student performances. Defining assessment criteria depended upon the articulation of understanding goals.

Just as the value of explicit understanding goals emerged slowly in the Teaching for Understanding project, it is frequently the most elusive element for teachers as they work with this framework. The meaning of understanding goals and their role in relation to the other elements evolved considerably during the course of the project. A similar evolution is often apparent as teachers struggle to articulate their goals and use them to focus their practice. Several factors appear to make this element of the framework particularly difficult, yet important.

Teachers' goals are always complex and often inchoate, as teachers embrace multiple and often intertwined purposes. Teaching for understanding is often only one of several agendas that they value and pursue. Attempting to define understanding goals requires teachers to distinguish these particular end goals from intermediate academic goals (such as practicing basic skills) and from other kinds of agendas (such as learning to cooperate or learning to keep orderly notes). These other agendas may be important, but attending to them does not necessarily lead directly to developing students' understanding.

Managing complex agendas is demanding both socially and politically as teachers are expected to serve multiple purposes. Even simplistically, the two agendas of teaching students and teaching subject matter can seem to be competing imperatives. Furthermore, teachers must appease multiple constituencies, including students, parents, administrators, politicians, business people, and taxpayers, not to mention their own personal values. Failing to explicate a specific list of goals from this complicated set of demands is understandable, perhaps even advantageous, for teachers caught in the cross fire of multiple mandates.[4]

Another reason that many teachers encounter difficulty in defining understanding goals for their students is that they have a vague or limited conception of the subject matter they are supposed to teach. Many teachers' ideas about their subject are defined by the curriculum materials, frequently textbooks, that they are accustomed to using. Few of these materials are organized around understanding goals, however. They are frequently too broad and shallow, focused around facts, formulaic operations, and superficial and excessively large sets of information rather than the "big ideas" that understanding goals should address.[5]

Goals derived from such materials tend to focus on remembering information or correctly following stipulated procedures. Furthermore, traditional curricular materials are often designed to be taught in a specific sequence, thereby reinforcing the expectation that students must learn in this sequence in order to avoid confusion or misunderstanding. Teachers whose familiarity with their subject is shaped primarily by textbooks are unlikely to imagine goals that might require superseding or altering the sequence of the topics in their traditional materials.

Unless teachers have opportunities to develop their own understanding of the richly webbed core concepts and modes of inquiry in the fields they teach, they are not likely to perceive their goals in such terms.[6] Few schools make such opportunities a priority for their in-service teacher development activities.

Some teachers confuse understanding goals with overly narrow behavioral objectives. Veteran teachers who remember these empty formalisms from their training and teacher evaluation conferences sometimes resist defining explicit understanding goals because they seem too oppressive and constraining. Especially when goals are derived by teachers directly from traditional curriculum mandates or materials, they often sound like the sort of narrow objectives that are unlikely to stimulate the development of rich understanding.

Finally, teachers have difficulty articulating understanding goals because their most fundamental aspirations for their students are deeply rooted in assumptions and values that usually remain tacit. Surfacing such tacit knowledge is intellectually difficult and often personally revealing. To articulate goals one must put into words ideas that may be inchoate and private partly because they are so heartfelt.

Despite these difficulties (perhaps because of them), understanding goals have proved to be an essential element of the Teaching for Understanding framework. To leap past the narrow and restrictive associations that teachers may first bring to this concept, it is often helpful to focus on the large purposes that teachers hope to address. "What do you most want your students to understand by the end of their term or their year in your class?" is a question that often draws teachers' fundamental goals to the fore. Answers often point to long-term, overarching understanding goals, such as "Students will understand how to express themselves clearly, both orally and in writing."

Because these overarching goals tend to be the ones that teachers and students revisit over the course of a year or a term, they have been called *throughlines* by some members of the Teaching for Understanding project. The word comes from Stanislavski's method acting school[7] and signifies a fundamental theme in a play on which an actor can focus the portrayal of his or her character.

Lois Hetland used the term for the overarching questions that focused her class throughout its yearlong study of Colonial America. She was able to formulate these questions after a year of work with the TfU framework, during which time she thought and talked frequently with her research partner about what she most wanted students to understand. Near the beginning of her second year of work with the framework, Hetland posted her throughlines on the wall of her classroom. The list included such questions as "How do we find out the truth about things that happened long ago and/or far away?" "How can you connect your personal interests/passions/ideals to your schoolwork?" "How do we discover central themes?" She introduced these questions to students, parents, colleagues, and the administrators in her school by saying, "These are the questions we're going to get smarter about during this year."

Concept maps, as described earlier, may not only enrich teachers' conceptions of the territory of generative topics but also help teachers reveal tacit goals. As teachers prepare such maps they may uncover their assumptions about the links between main ideas within and across subject matters. Nodes in such maps that are linked to many other ideas are often worth singling out as the focus of understanding goals.

Another strategy that has helped teachers articulate their tacit goals is a set of sentence stems that begin with phrases such as "Students will appreciate . . ." or "Students will understand. . . ."

Completing such sentence stems helps teachers distinguish understanding goals from understanding performances, a subtle distinction that is not easy to make at first. We have found that goals phrased as "Students will understand how to [for example] express themselves vividly" tend to be richer than those with the form "Students will understand that they can express themselves vividly." The former usually leads readily to the definition of powerful understanding performances. The latter often points toward inert factual information or articulates a remote rather than intense relationship between the student and the subject matter.

As teachers consider their long-range goals in relation to particular curriculum units or assignments, they can often articulate a more specific set of understandings. These are in effect subgoals. Students approach the overarching goals by developing understanding of these preliminary ideas and processes in particular units or assignments. For example, an overarching goal for a high school Spanish teacher was "Students will understand Spanish as a language of everyday communication." He planned a unit in which students would develop and perform skits in Spanish that portrayed characters wrestling with a social problem. At first his understanding goals for the unit focused on students' collaboration processes, problem-solving skills, and proper grammar. After reflecting further on his overarching goal, he realized that his central purpose was neither the development of social skills nor the perfection of formal grammar, but students' understanding of Spanish as a working language. He phrased one of the understanding goals for this unit this way: "Students will understand how to express themselves effectively in Spanish about a realistic problem." With this goal in mind he designed the unit to include performance of the skits followed by a question-and-answer period with other members of the class in Spanish.

Teachers and researchers clarified and elaborated the concept of understanding goals as they used it with the other elements of the TfU framework to clarify and guide classroom practice. Eventually the project determined that understanding goals are most useful when they are explicitly defined and publicly posted, when they are arrayed in a nested structure with subgoals leading to overarching goals, and when they are focused on key concepts and modes of inquiry in the relevant subject matter.

Explicit and public. Understanding goals are most powerful if they are explicit and public. Teachers must often do significant intellectual work in order to unearth their tacit goals and disentangle their understanding goals from their other agendas. The value of this effort is enhanced if teachers then articulate their primary understanding goals to their students and other key actors in the school context—parents, administrators, colleagues. Publicly posted understanding goals help everyone know where the class is going, mark progress, and focus attention on the main agenda. Many teachers find that students and other members of the school community participate in refining understanding goals once they become the subject of public conversation.

Nested. A nested set of understanding goals helps clarify the connections between any particular exercise and the larger purposes of the course. Overarching goals that focus an entire course or year of work are related to unit-level goals defined for a particular curriculum unit that might take a week or more to complete. For instance, if an overarching goal for the year is to understand mathematics as the study of patterns, the goal for a unit may be to analyze regularities in the relationships among elements of similar triangles. Similarly, the goals for a specific assignment or lesson are directly linked to more comprehensive understanding goals. Thus the goal for a particular lesson might be to understand how to compare ratios as a way of analyzing patterns in similar triangles.

Central to the subject matter. Understanding goals focus on those ideas, modes of inquiry, and forms of communication that are essential if students are to understand the subject matter at hand. These may be concepts that are richly webbed to other ideas or that must be clearly understood in order to develop more sophisticated understandings. What is important is that understanding goals draw teachers and students toward the center of significant work rather than toward the peripheral areas of their agenda.

In the last year of the Teaching for Understanding research, project members devised a framework for explicating aspects of understanding goals more completely.[8] Members of the project defined four dimensions articulating the scope of understanding across all subject matters: knowledge, methods, purposes, and forms of expression. They also specified levels for gauging the depth of understanding. The understanding framework that integrates these dimensions and levels is explained in Chapter Six. Preliminary work with this framework leads us to believe that it might help teachers develop, critique, and refine goals that address the full range and depth of the understanding they hope students will develop.

Performances of Understanding

Performances of understanding are perhaps the most fundamental element of the Teaching for Understanding framework. The conception of understanding as a performance rather than a mental state underlies the entire collaborative research project on which the framework is based.[9] The performance view emphasizes understanding as the ability and inclination to use what one knows by operating in the world.

It follows that understanding is developed, as well as demonstrated, by performing one's understanding. This assumption is reflected in many learning situations, such as learning to play a musical instrument, learning a sport, learning a craft, and learning various arts. Indeed, most learning outside of school proceeds by engaging learners in increasingly complex performances. Within schools, however, students often spend their time on tasks that are only remotely related to the performances their teachers hope they will ultimately master. The obvious value of performances, for educational advancement as well as assessment, makes them central to teaching for understanding.

In an early phase of the TfU project the collaborative research teams attempted to specify scenarios that teachers could enact to foster their students' understanding. Teachers had many different strategies for such fostering, however, and the notion of scenarios seemed too specific to accommodate teachers' need for flexibility. Despite considerable variation in these teachers' approaches, a common feature of their classrooms was that students spent much of their time engaged in performances of understanding. Thus this element of the framework focuses attention on what students rather than teachers do. Indeed, teachers who work with the framework often note that one source of its educational value is the way it causes them to analyze what their students are doing and learning.

As teams of teachers and researchers attempted to define and design performances that would develop and demonstrate students' understanding of important goals, they had to distinguish performances of understanding from other kinds of activities. They recalled the project's definition of understanding as "going beyond the information given"[10] to extend, synthesize, apply, or otherwise use what one knows in creative, novel ways. Performances that fulfill this definition include explaining, interpreting, analyzing, relating, comparing, and making analogies. As the research teams examined the generative topics and understanding goals they had identified, they incorporated verbs like these in answering the question, "What might students do to develop and demonstrate their understanding?"

Answering this question reminds teachers that students can undertake a much more varied range of activities as part of their schoolwork than is encompassed by typical assignments. If students use the full spectrum of intelligences,[11] not just the verbal and mathematical ones that schools typically emphasize, they may perform their understandings in a myriad of creative ways.

For example, students in Eric Buchovecky's physics class kept journals in which they reflected on the forms of inquiry they used to investigate an everyday machine of their choosing. They employed words, drawings, and demonstrations to explain the workings of their chosen machine using the concepts of mechanics. Students in Joan Soble's English class created visual "maps" of their life journeys to develop their understanding of metaphorical places, which they then incorporated into an autobiographical essay. Bill Kendall's geometry students took mirrors to the corridor outside their classroom, created triangles where they could see their classmates' reflections, and counted floor tiles to analyze similarities in these triangles. These performances focus on understanding in ways that many traditional school activities do not. Instead of rehearsing or recreating knowledge produced by others, performances of understanding engage students in creating their own understandings. Broadening the vision of learning performances without losing the focus on understanding is an important feature of this element of the TfU framework.

As teachers on the research teams incorporated understanding performances into their classrooms, they recognized different types of performances. Like understanding goals, performances tended to be conceived as nested clusters or linked chains. Often teachers began designing a curriculum unit by identifying culminating performances—that is, final projects or products that students might produce at the end of the unit to demonstrate their mastery of understanding goals. Teachers realized that students must engage in preliminary performances or subperformances in order to develop understanding of ideas and processes they can synthesize in the culminating performance or product.

Eventually, research teams working with teachers of different subject matters recognized a common progression of categories of performances designed to foster understanding. Across the progression, teachers maintained a dual focus on students' interests and the target understanding goals so that the chains of performances were both generative and challenging. Three progressive categories are common:

Messing about. Named after David Hawkins's memorable phrase,[12] *messing-about* performances acknowledge his respect for initial inquiry not yet structured by discipline-based methods and concepts. They usually come at the beginning of a unit and serve to draw students into the domain of a generative topic. They are typically open-ended and approachable on multiple levels so students can engage them no matter what the students' prior level of understanding. These activities help students see connections between the generative topic and their own interests and previous experiences. Messing about may also provide both the teacher and the students with information about what students already know and what they are interested in learning. It may be designed to engage students in performing their initial understandings and confronting some of the phenomena or puzzles that the generative topic presents.

Guided inquiry. Guided inquiry performances engage students in using the ideas or modes of inquiry that the teacher sees as central to understanding the identified goals. During the early stages of a unit or a course of study the performances may be relatively simple or elementary. In fact, teachers may focus on such basic skills as close observation, accurate recording of data, use of rich vocabulary, or synthesis of notes from multiple sources around a specified question. Developing such skills may entail performances of understanding so long as they are undertaken to help students achieve an understanding goal—understanding how to analyze empirical data to refine theories, for example, or understanding how to express oneself vividly by using a varied vocabulary.

As students develop understanding of preliminary goals through early performances, they can engage in more complex forms of inquiry. The guidance that teachers provide during later phases of work helps students learn how to apply disciplinary concepts and methods, to integrate their growing body of knowledge, and to perform increasingly complex and sophisticated understandings.

Culminating performances. Culminating performances may be similar to the projects and exhibitions that many teachers assign as final products to complete a curriculum unit. Their distinguishing feature in the TfU framework is that they clearly demonstrate students' mastery of the designated understanding goals. Such performances typically invite students to work more independently than they did on preliminary performances and to synthesize the understandings they have developed throughout a curriculum unit or series of units.

Performances of understanding as an element of the Teaching for Understanding framework should be distinguished from two other kinds of common classroom activities. Activities are performances of understanding only if they clearly develop and demonstrate students' understanding of important understanding goals. Many hands-on activities do not engage students in performances of understanding because they are not focused on important goals or because they do not require students to stretch their minds. Another common educational activity that people may wrongly equate with TfU is project-based curriculum. Teachers need not design complex projects in order to teach for understanding.

The framework can be readily applied to relatively traditional classroom lessons and activities so long as they are designed to engage students in performing their understandings. For example, teachers may assign students a short story to read and ask them to identify elements of the story that make it strong. Such an assignment may develop and demonstrate students' understanding of plot, character development, and setting without requiring a major departure from the traditional curriculum.

To summarize, effective performances of understanding do each of the following:

Relate directly to understanding goals. Performances of understanding engage students in work that clearly advances specified understanding goals. This criterion protects against designing projects that may look spectacular without really addressing the core curriculum.

Develop and apply understanding through practice. Performances of understanding are designed in iterative sequences so that students build from their initial skills and knowledge toward the target understandings. Students may draft, critique, and revise a performance one or more times.

Engage multiple learning styles and forms of expression. Performances of understanding are designed so that students learn through multiple senses and kinds of intelligence. They also permit students to use various media and forms of expression.

Promote reflective engagement in challenging, approachable tasks. As David Perkins explains in Chapter Two, a performance of understanding requires a student to think, not simply recall or repeat routine knowledge or skills. Performances of understanding must be approachable by all students yet challenging enough to stretch their minds.

Demonstrate understanding. Performances of understanding are not simply private experiences but rather yield products or activities that can be noticed by others. As such they provide evidence for fellow students, teachers, parents, and others to see what a student understands. In this way, performances become a means of monitoring, publicizing, and learning from students' understanding.

Ongoing Assessment

The fourth element of the Teaching for Understanding framework is ongoing assessment of performances in relation to understanding goals. Like the idea of performances of understanding, this concept is easily grasped in relation to learning sports or the arts.[13]

In athletic and artistic contexts, learners witness model performances by both experts and other learners. They can analyze and critique these sample performances in relation to criteria to understand what an accomplished performance entails. Learners emulate these models by practicing their own performances and receiving constructive critiques of them. Learning advances from assessing one's own and others' performances in relation to clear criteria. In this way assessment both enhances and evaluates learning.

Ultimately, if instruction is effective the assessment of one's own performance becomes almost automatic; one is continually comparing one's present performance with where one was earlier and where one wants to be. In athletics or the arts, the use of a decontextualized standardized test disconnected from daily work, or a final examination given only at the end of a period of learning, would make no sense. Indeed, when "high stakes" public performances take place in these fields they in most cases simply confirm what the learner already knows from hours of practice and observation.

Given the reasonableness and longevity of such assessment procedures, one wonders why it seems exotic to suggest translating lessons from the fields of art and athletics to the context of teaching subject matter in school, particularly middle and high school. Granted, exhibitions were a common practice in the nineteenth century and various versions of performance and portfolio assessments are increasingly popular today.[14] Yet these approaches are still rare in schools; furthermore, they are seldom designed systematically to encourage the development and demonstration of explicit understanding goals.

As a constitutive part of the performance approach to understanding, the early formulations of the Teaching for Understanding framework called for a definition and delineation of the performances or exhibitions of understanding that students are expected to accomplish. For instance, students in English classes ought to know about the kinds of essays they are to write or the kinds of talks they are to give, including criteria and rubrics for evaluation. Students in history classes ought to know about the kinds of historical analyses they are expected to write or the kinds of syntheses they will be required to make of data that they collect or review. Students in science classes ought to know about the uses to which they will be putting theories and concepts and about the kinds of experiments that they are supposed to design and analyze. And so forth. Clearly defined performances, along with examples of less and more successful efforts on the parts of students, are regarded as a necessary ground of departure for a serious effort in ongoing assessment.

The collaborative research teams that first used the TfU framework in classrooms attempted to define criteria based on the designated understanding goals with which to assess every significant performance of understanding. The expectation was that prespecified criteria would be presented to students at the time they received an assignment. Then both students and teacher could use criteria not only to monitor draft performances but also to plan next steps in the teaching and learning process.

As teachers began to work with the concept of ongoing assessment, they refined ideas about how and when assessment rubrics might best be designed. Teachers did not always find it possible or pedagogically advantageous to stipulate assessment criteria at the very beginning of a unit. Particularly when their students were engaged in performances new to the teacher as well as the students, teachers were hard put to produce a complete set of assessment criteria in advance. Teachers often became more conscious of their own tacit criteria as they examined students' early draft performances and recognized features of both strong and weak examples. Furthermore, teachers found that their students learned from analyzing model performances and participating in the process of defining assessment criteria.

Some teachers perceived that very specific criteria during the early stages of developing performances of understanding (for example, during messing-about performances) tended to constrain students. They preferred to develop criteria with students and then publicize assessment guidelines part way through the period of *guided inquiry* when students were developing early drafts of their performances. Teachers varied in the timing and the process by which they developed criteria. In all cases, however, they developed clear criteria directly related to understanding goals, discussed them with students, and publicly posted assessment criteria early in the process of practicing performances of understanding.

In addition to exemplar performances and assessment rubrics, another key component of ongoing assessment is that students and the teacher *share* ongoing responsibility for analyzing how students are progressing toward high-level performances. Teachers discovered that ongoing assessment was most useful when everyone in the class participated in the process. Students learned from analyzing the work of their peers. They saw multiple ways of approaching the assignment and came to understand the meaning of criteria as they used them to provide feedback to peers. By the same token, students benefited from discussions and critiques of their own work with suggestions for improvement. Students collected and preserved examples of their performances to monitor areas of growth as well as areas where obstacles remained. Sometimes such collections are called *process-folios*.

As teachers developed multiple forms of ongoing assessment, the TfU research teams perceived some common categories of assessment activities in relation to the types of understanding performances. Ongoing assessment of messing-about performances is usually informal and conducted primarily by the teacher rather than students. Teachers may assess such performances informally to discern what their students already understand and where they need support, but these assessments are rarely recorded formally in relation to explicit criteria.

During the guided inquiry phase of instruction, ongoing assessment tends to become more formal and to involve students. Early guided inquiry performances may include critiquing sample performances such as models supplied by the teacher or early drafts of work done by members of the class. Discussion of these models develops and demonstrates students' understanding while contributing to the definition of criteria for assessing students' own performances. As clear criteria are formulated, teachers may use them to structure peer assessments of student work, either in pairs or in small groups. Students develop understanding of the meaning of the assessment criteria from assessing peers' work. They may also learn how to improve their work from their peer's feedback before the criteria are used to evaluate individual student performances.

By the time students begin drafting their culminating performances they are familiar with the criteria that will be used to evaluate their final products. But even at this stage of instruction the concept of ongoing assessment serves formative as well as more summative purposes. Students may conduct peer or self-assessments of early drafts to inform subsequent revisions. Teachers may require students to submit a self-assessment form along with their final product. These formats of ongoing assessment remind students to monitor their work and provide the teacher with more insight into the students' thinking than the product alone may offer.

As the members of the research project analyzed features of effective ongoing assessment during the collaborative research process, they summarized criteria for this element of the framework. Ongoing assessments are based on public criteria related to understanding goals, take place frequently, are conducted by students as well as teachers, and inform planning while they gauge students' progress:

Relevant, explicit, and public criteria. The criteria for assessments are directly tied to understanding goals. They are articulated early in the process of drafting performances of understanding, although they may evolve over the course of the performance, especially if it is unfamiliar to the teacher. Criteria are made public to the students, who are given opportunities to apply and understand them before they are used to evaluate the students' performances.

Frequent assessments. Assessments occur frequently, from the beginning of a curriculum sequence until the end. Specific assessment activities are conducted in conjunction with every significant performance of understanding.

Multiple sources. Students benefit not only from their teachers' assessments of their work but also from conducting assessments of their own and peers' performances.

Gauge progress and inform planning. Assessments look forward to next steps and backward to monitor and evaluate progress. Students learn not only about how well they have carried out a performance but also about how they might improve performances. Ongoing assessment of students' performances informs teachers about how to respond both to individual students and to the whole class in designing subsequent educational activities.

Ongoing assessment is often named as the most challenging element of the Teaching for Understanding framework. Part of its difficulty arises because teachers must understand the other elements of the framework in order to approach this one. They must specify clear understanding goals and design specific performances of understanding in order to define appropriate criteria for assessing performances. Furthermore, public posting of assessment criteria disrupts the culture of secrecy that attends most forms of testing in schools.[15] Involving learners in assessment of their own and classmates' work invites students to take more responsibility for their own learning. Indeed, it requires teachers to relinquish their role as the sole arbiter of excellence and to negotiate intellectual authority with their students. These shifts run counter to the norms in many classrooms and may require both students and teachers to take on new roles and relationships.[16]

Interaction of the TfU Elements

Although each element of the Teaching for Understanding framework can be used as a focus for analyzing particular aspects of educational practice, the power of this framework derives from the coherent integration of all four elements. Teachers who use the framework to intensify their efforts to teach for understanding may start by thinking about any one of the elements. Some teachers prefer to begin by talking about their overarching goals. Others find it more natural to start by examining a topic that has seemed generative in the past and reconsidering it in relation to the framework's criteria for generative topics. Still others analyze a favorite curriculum activity to see how it might be conceptualized or revised to become a performance of understanding. Some teachers start by trying to design more explicit and shared assessments of work that their class is already doing.

Wherever teachers initiate the inquiry, each element of the TfU framework leads into thinking about the others. As teachers use the framework to design and enact curriculum, refinement of one element generates changes in the others. For example, as teachers analyze a successful curriculum activity in terms of an understanding performance, they may ask, "What made this so rich? What understandings did students perform?" Answers to these questions may clarify understanding goals that had not previously been explicit. Attempting to define criteria for assessing performances also leads teachers to reexamine their understanding goals; as these become more explicit and clear, teachers often realize that even their favorite performances could be redesigned so that students spend more effort performing important understandings. In reviewing criteria for generative topics, teachers often see ways of adding or modifying performances to enhance connections between students' interests and the key ideas in their discipline. In short, each element of the framework invokes the others.

As teachers shift attention from one element of the framework to another, attempting to maximize the extent to which they meet the criteria for each element, they gradually sharpen the focus of their curriculum design on understanding. This process of progressively refining practice to center on understanding continues as teachers move from planning to enacting their curriculum designs. New generative aspects of a topic may be revealed as students exercise their ingenuity in developing performances that address their personal interests and express their particular talents. New entry points, links to other subjects, additional layers of questions become apparent as students perform their understandings. Sometimes students' performances display understanding of ideas or modes of thinking that the teacher values but had not consciously defined and espoused. Articulating the qualities of good performances often helps both teachers and their students clarify understanding goals.

Ongoing assessment of student performances reveals the quality of the curriculum design as well as the extent of students' understanding. As teachers engage in ongoing assessment, they notice how students are responding to the assignment. Sometimes it becomes obvious that the assignment requires students to spend a great deal of time on activities that are either trivial or largely unrelated to the understanding goals. The assignment may have to be altered to increase the proportion of time that students are engaged in performances of understanding. By the same token, ongoing assessment of students' early drafts may reveal that some or all of the class need help developing preliminary understandings in order to succeed on the final project.

Overall, the process of using the framework is not one of finally getting it right, once and for all. Whether analysis of practice with the framework reveals problems or progress, it stimulates teachers to make interacting adjustments in various aspects of their curriculum and pedagogy. Like understanding itself, using the Teaching for Understanding framework to improve plans and practice is a continuing inquiry.

The Nature and Role of the Framework

The Teaching for Understanding framework is founded on a definition of understanding as creative performance. Thus understanding always entails personal invention; it can never be simply transmitted from a generator to a recipient but must be constructed from the learner's own experience and intellectual work.

During the course of the TfU project, the participants—both teachers and researchers—came to realize that learning to teach for understanding is itself a process of developing understanding. The early formulations of the project spoke of developing teaching scenarios to exemplify a pedagogy of understanding. As the collaborative research teams attempted to specify the scenario concept, they realized that the participating teachers varied too much for their approaches to be fruitfully characterized in this way. The focus of the research project shifted from documenting standard teaching moves to characterizing what learners did to develop their understanding and how teachers supported them. As the concept of scenarios gave way to the idea of a teaching for understanding framework, the purpose of the research shifted from documenting how teachers implement effective scenarios to the process of understanding (in the performance sense) the framework.

As the focus of research shifted from implementing to understanding teaching for understanding, the roles of the research participants also changed. When research focused on implementation, the role of the teacher was to enact the desired pedagogy and the role of the researcher was to foster and document this enactment. This generated adversity when teachers felt pressured to enact an alien design and researchers felt they must urge teachers to test their product.

When members of the project reconceived the endeavor of learning to teach for understanding as an example of developing understanding, the roles of both teachers and researchers shifted in subtle ways. They became partners in an open-ended inquiry in which all participants shared responsibility for developing their understanding. The researchers wanted to understand how to conceptualize, characterize, and assess the TfU framework; the teachers wanted to understand how they could improve teaching and learning in their own classrooms by using this framework. These twin endeavors—refining the theory and the practice of teaching for understanding—were mutually informative.

The shift from implementing a fixed framework to understanding an evolving framework permitted and required the development of trust and reciprocity in the relationships among research participants. Pairs of teacher and researcher partners developed close relationships, characterized by mutual respect and joint commitment to a shared endeavor.

This history is recounted here in order to illuminate not only the process of developing the Teaching for Understanding framework espoused in this book, but also its nature and the form of its utility. The TfU framework that emerged from this collaborative research is not a set of predetermined scenarios or a recipe for successful practice. It can not be transmitted and implemented in a direct, linear way. Just as the educators who developed this framework had to create intellectually stimulating and personally engaging dialogue and relationships to foster their own understanding of these ideas, so will others who wish to understand TfU. They will have to conduct open-ended inquiry to construct their own understanding of this framework in relation to their personal practice and context.

The Teaching for Understanding framework provides a structure and a language to organize inquiry. Dialogue with the framework can bring tacit goals and unconscious pedagogical expertise into clearly articulated forms that can be assessed, ratified, or revised. As a structure for inquiry, the TfU framework supports teachers as continuing learners. Instead of pointing out their shortcomings or directing them to follow any particular strategy or curriculum design, it endorses their professional authority and autonomy. The role of this framework is not to dictate a mindless enactment of someone else's prescription but to stimulate and help educational colleagues to be mindful in articulating their own prescriptions.

Conceived in this way, the TfU framework suggests a way of steering a course between two dangers that have plagued attempts to improve education in the past. One danger is attempting to produce a "foolproof" curriculum that does not leave sufficient room for teachers to exercise their professional prerogatives and responsibilities. The other is honoring teachers' individuality to the extent that insufficient guidance and support is provided to stimulate significant improvement. The TfU framework is intended to be used with teachers in ways that mirror the experiences they are asked to give students—that is, defining clear goals, supporting performances that pursue those goals, and providing criteria for assessing and improving the elements of teaching for understanding, all the while leaving room for teachers to express their own talents and pursue their own passions. In this view both the framework and curriculum are conceived not as products to be implemented but as structures to guide a process of negotiating meanings.[17]

The gist of this account is that the TfU framework serves not only to orchestrate teaching subject matter to students in classrooms but to provide a structure for guiding professional development. Further research with groups of teachers in various school settings suggests that the framework can also structure more broad-based initiatives aimed at developing schools as learning organizations.[18] No matter what the context, the learners, or the substance of the goals may be, if the focus of the effort is the development of understanding then the TfU framework is a useful way of structuring dialogue and designs for learning. Furthermore, when the same framework is used for various kinds of learning initiatives within a context, participants gain when students, teachers, and organizations are learning in complementary ways.[19]

The Teaching for Understanding framework guides teachers to revisit age-old questions about what and how to teach. It encourages them to continue learning about their subject matter as they develop more powerful generative topics and to articulate more penetrating understanding goals. It helps them listen to their students to learn how they are making sense of the curriculum and to adjust in order to respond to the students' interests, strengths, and weaknesses. It invites them to keep refining assignments so that they serve to maximize students' engagement in performances of understanding. It guides them in clarifying the development, communication, and application of assessment criteria so that students advance their understanding as rapidly and fully as possible.

Chapter Four

How Do Teachers Learn to Teach for Understanding?

Martha Stone Wiske
Karen Hammerness
Daniel Gray Wilson

If using the Teaching for Understanding (TfU) framework is a process of inquiry rather than the implementation of a tool, how does this work with teachers? How do teachers of different subject matters, in varied settings, make sense of the framework? How do they interpret it in relation to their particular students, curriculum priorities, resources, teaching approaches and circumstances? How does their understanding evolve? What helps and hinders their progress? What common patterns can be discerned across cases? These questions were the focus of research during the fourth year of the project in order to demonstrate how this framework might prove useful on a broad scale.

Work with teachers during the early years of the project revealed that learning to teach for understanding is itself a process of developing understanding. From this perspective the TfU framework itself offers a structure for guiding the process. Action research combines support for change with analysis of the change process. In this project, action research on learning to teach for understanding became a mirror image of the TfU process that teachers enacted in their classrooms. For both the research and teachers' practice the TfU framework structured the definition of goals, support for performances of understanding, and regular opportunities to assess and improve those performances. With the framework as the conceptual structure for this research, we defined four types or levels of understanding TfU, each associated with particular performances of understanding.

- *Comprehension.* Identify the four key elements of the framework exemplified in written, oral, or video descriptions of practice; analyze practice with reference to the four elements and their criteria.
- *Design.* Design curriculum units that exemplify all four elements of the TfU framework; plan units around generative topics with explicit understanding goals, activities that engage students in performances of understanding, and materials and strategies for conducting ongoing assessment.
- *Enactment.* Teach a curriculum unit that enacts the four key elements and uses them to focus student learning on specified understanding goals.
- *Integration.* Design and teach a sequence of curriculum units over several months or more in ways that exemplify the TfU framework and *ramp* students up to increasingly sophisticated performances and to understanding of at least one overarching goal.

The TfU framework asserted that teachers' understanding could be developed as well as demonstrated by engaging and supporting them in these kinds of performances. Although the sequence may imply a certain progression in the types of performances, we did not expect to orchestrate them in any lockstep order.[1] Performances of any type may enhance understanding of a different type in a mutually reinforcing, recursive way, rather than in a strictly linear sequence. The integration level of understanding TfU is a culminating performance, however, that depends upon and synthesizes the other three types of understanding.

Prior research had shown that learning to teach for understanding takes time, along with sustained commitment and support. Accordingly, we elected to work intensively for a year with a small set of teachers who had already demonstrated a serious interest in using and reflecting on the Teaching for Understanding framework. We looked for teachers who taught different subject matters to a range of students in varied kinds of schools so that their experiences might suggest lessons for a broad array of teachers and settings. The four teachers were Joan Soble, an experienced teacher of English at a comprehensive urban high school; Bill Kendall, a veteran mathematics teacher in a high school serving students from predominantly middle- and working-class families; Lois Hetland, who taught an integrated humanities strand in the seventh grade of a progressive private school and had already worked intensively with the Teaching for Understanding framework for a year; and Eric Buchovecky, a second-year science teacher in a suburban high school who had been introduced to the TfU framework in his teacher education program at the Harvard Graduate School of Education.

During the 1993–94 academic year each of these teachers worked closely with a researcher from the Teaching for Understanding project. The teacher-researcher partners met together for a three-day workshop in August to discuss examples of curriculum based on the TfU framework. Each teacher also began planning a unit to teach in the fall. During the following year the researchers met the teachers each week in their classrooms to observe, consult, and document progress. Researchers prepared field notes about these meetings, teachers kept reflective journals about their experiences, and the research team met weekly to compare and analyze these data on understanding TfU. Three times during the year, the research-teacher partners met together for a full day to exchange ideas and strategies about teaching for understanding and about learning to teach with the TfU framework. Teachers and researchers jointly defined the agenda of these meetings to focus on key challenges and successes in understanding the framework.

Throughout the year, both teachers and researchers engaged in many cycles of talking, writing, planning, trying things in the classroom, and reflecting on that experience. Through talking and writing about practice with the language of the framework, they developed comprehension of TfU. Through trying to articulate generative topics and understanding goals and drafting plans for student performances, they developed and demonstrated understanding at the design level. As teachers tried their designs in the classroom, they came to comprehend the meaning of the framework elements and to understand how to enact them in practice. Gradually, teachers found that these cycles of thinking, planning, doing, and reflecting deepened their commitment to TfU as well as their understanding so that the framework became integrated into their usual practice.

Each researcher-teacher pair prepared two reports about the year of research. One report documented the process of learning to teach for understanding. This chapter draws primarily on those reports and includes vignettes taken from the reports on Joan Soble's and Bill Kendall's experiences learning to teach for understanding. A second report about each teacher portrayed classroom practices exemplifying the elements of the framework. Chapter Five is based on those reports and contains comparable vignettes of Lois Hetland's and Eric Buchovecky's classroom practice. These vignettes provide an integrated picture of the TfU process in particular cases and contexts, but each was constructed to illustrate patterns of experience common to many teachers. The themes discussed in both chapters reflect findings drawn from all four teachers and others who have worked with the TfU framework.

From Romancing the Parts to Embracing the Whole of TfU

Joan Soble is an English teacher at Cambridge Rindge and Latin High School, where she has taught for the past seven of her fifteen years of teaching. Joan heard about TfU from several colleagues who participated in the early years of the project. Her first direct contact came when she joined a panel of teachers asked to review and critique the TfU handbook. She responded enthusiastically to the TfU framework and was thoughtful in using it to outline a unit for her writing class (called Writing Workshop).

Joan's school is subdivided into houses, each with its own focus, faculty, and students. Her house, the Pilot School, encourages a democratic community where students are expected to take responsibility for their learning and teachers are especially careful to foster and respect students' initiatives. Because of the Pilot School's geographical as well as philosophical proximity to the Harvard Graduate School of Education, its faculty often collaborates on educational research. Teachers here are encouraged to reflect on theory in relation to practice more than in many schools.

Joan taught four English courses per semester. She planned to use TfU to improve Writing Workshop, an introductory writing course designed primarily for ninth-grade students at risk for failure. These students are "perpetually overwhelmed," Joan noted. "This is a group of kids who are relieved when they make it through school. It's a good day when they don't get into trouble." For several of them English was a second language; some feared they would grow up to be homeless or the victims of violence. All regarded writing as a great challenge. "These are kids who tell you they 'really can't do this.' They worry that they can't fill a page. My job is to help them transform their expectations of themselves."

Getting Started

Joan hoped TfU would help her develop a more powerful, connected, and compelling curriculum for the class. "I have always felt that I gave interesting writing assignments," she said. "But I began to see a pattern: as soon as the kids finished the assignment, the momentum was over. We would have to build it up all over again, and sometimes that didn't happen." The course seemed dull and disconnected. Joan hoped TfU would help her focus curriculum on important understandings about writing, sustain students' attention to revision, and develop their understanding of a topic by delving into it more deeply as the course progressed.

Yet Joan wondered if TfU would work with her students: "So many activities that the other TfU teachers do seem to require that students show understanding through language, and they focus on higher-level thinking. What about students who can't express themselves that well in language yet? What about students who need to develop some basic skills as well as work on higher-level thinking? Will TfU really work for my kids?"

Joan's research partner, Karen Hammerness, had taught English herself. They began during the three-day August workshop to develop Joan's plans for the introductory unit of Writing Workshop. Joan thought one of the most helpful exercises was listing their understanding goals in the center of a big sheet of newsprint, around which they summarized a set of understanding performances to address those goals. The visual depiction of central goals related to a sequence of instructional activities was clear and coherent.

Talking and writing about her goals with Karen and exchanging reflections on this experience with other teacher-researcher partners helped Joan begin to comprehend understanding goals.

During the following year Joan and Karen met weekly for several hours to discuss how the course was unfolding, review students' progress, develop curriculum plans, and discuss Joan's developing thoughts about the framework. Karen visited Joan's class weekly and took notes or videotaped. It was particularly important to Joan that Karen understand the context of her classroom, the nature of her students, and the severity of the challenges they faced. "You have to know my kids," she said. This knowledge gave Karen both insight and credibility in advising Joan about how to apply TfU in her classroom. "I was glad that while Karen was my research partner she was also a sympathetic and highly observant educator. Sometimes we could talk about what worked and what didn't work in the classroom, even if it wasn't directly related to TfU."

Comprehending the Generative Topic

Reviewing her first year of work with TfU, Joan perceived that she had "great romances" with individual elements of the framework. "For each piece of the framework, there was a protracted period when I was trying to figure out its limitations and potentials, thinking it was the most important part, and then ultimately deciding it worked best in conjunction with the other elements."

Joan's first positive connection was with the concept of the generative topic. It addressed her problem of engaging reluctant students and sustaining their attention. Joan had always discussed central issues as part of her teaching but had not previously planned as systematically to organize a sequence of assignments around one idea.

"Writing about place" was the generative topic she chose, in part because it served as a common focus for the teachers of history, math, and science with whom she was designing an interdisciplinary course. Joan also thought this topic would interest her students because they could start by writing about places that were familiar. Many of them had moved from other countries and were concerned about establishing themselves in a new place. And, she observed, "I know my students like to write about themselves."

From their personal and concrete starting place, Joan planned to move students to thinking and writing about more abstract places: their place in society and in the future, and place as a metaphor for a state of mind. Joan thought this topic would engage students' emotions and hold their interest, allowing her to build their confidence and skills in writing more than a few sentences.

Struggling to Define Understanding Goals

Although Joan easily selected a generative topic, she had difficulty articulating the understanding goals. She worried that predefined goals would interfere with the richness of generating curriculum by exploring the exciting ideas and questions that emerged during class. Her initial goals were complicated and overly broad. During the August work session, Joan wrote this goal: "Students will understand how to think critically about a wide range of sources, such as books, movies, personal experiences . . ." Some early goals described behaviors without articulating the substance of the understandings she hoped students would develop. In October, Joan wrote: "Students will understand that you can compare pieces of writing and make decisions about which pieces you want to keep working on and/or place in your portfolio."

Articulating clear understanding goals was hard for many reasons. Joan was not accustomed to thinking about goals for students in relation to the discipline of writing. Although she was implicitly aware of central concepts in reading and writing English, Joan did not usually plan curriculum with explicit reference to the structure of her discipline. Joan was not sure how ambitious her goals for these students should be. Perhaps her initial goals should be at a mechanical level and become more abstract. She puzzled over translating her own goals into language that would make sense to her students while still conveying the complexity and richness of disciplinary understanding. Karen helped by asking questions and suggesting revisions that sharpened and deepened the focus of Joan's goals. Through cycles of designing draft goals, talking about them with Karen, and reflecting on them in relation to key concepts in language arts, Joan developed her comprehension of understanding goals.

Designing Understanding Performances

Joan felt "confident and comfortable" designing engaging performances. For example, she wanted students to create a *Place Mat,* a
visual collage, as preparation for writing about their favorite place.
After students made their collages, Joan asked them to reflect on
how they selected and placed their images to convey the desired
impression: "Is making this collage anything like writing a paper?"
Students did notice similarities in selecting and relating items to
emphasize important ideas. Although Joan had previously included
some artistic activities to motivate students, when she reviewed this
activity in relation to her understanding goals she saw more clearly
the need to link such performances to understanding the writing
process. The art pieces helped students stir their memories and
formulate ideas. As students moved between their art work and
their writing, Joan saw that the Place Mats helped students articulate their ideas and make choices about placement, style, and tone
in both pieces.

Yet Joan wondered if TfU required that she dream up more
"unconventional performances" rather than revise her traditional
assignments. She also worried about basic skills. If TfU focused on
larger disciplinary understandings, how would she teach students
the phases of the writing process, develop vocabulary, and improve
sentence structure? "Skill building will probably have to be separate from my 'understanding curriculum,'" Joan mused in October. "Grammar doesn't seem to have a deeper meaning that could
connect to understanding."

Linking skill development to understanding performances was
a topic at a meeting with the other teacher-researcher pairs that
fall. Teachers shared strategies and philosophies concerning this
challenge. By exchanging examples of their designs for understanding performances and critiquing them with colleagues who
shared their TfU language, teachers developed comprehension of
TfU and enhanced their capacity to design curriculum with this
framework. They concluded that skills should be developed in the
context of draft performances of understanding. Following this
thinking, in conversations with Karen, Joan clarified her fundamental goal: students will understand how to express themselves
in writing. At the end of October she wrote in her journal, "As I

think of it, [vocabulary development] is so related (finally!) to the mission of the course: it encourages revision . . . and suggests that vocabulary acquisition is a means to enhance self-expression."

Enacting Ongoing Assessment

Joan developed another early romance with the ongoing assessment element of TfU. It was alluring, she noted, because it was "least articulated" in her practice: "I have not always been as good at systematically asking [students] what they understand." At first Joan thought ongoing assessment meant evaluating students' understanding of her overarching goals for the class. She asked students, "What have you learned about place today? How have your ideas about effective writing changed?" But the repetition began to exasperate her students.

The mid-October meeting with the other teachers and researchers helped Joan address this problem. Other teachers described strategies for conducting both formal and informal assessments focused on understanding goals. They exchanged forms and criteria their students used to guide peer conferences about their work and questions teachers asked as they walked around the class listening to students' conversations. A TfU staff member emphasized that ongoing assessment is frequent, occurs from the beginning of a unit, and provides recommendations about next steps as well as feedback on products and performances. These comments reminded Joan that assessments help students take more responsibility for their learning. As she noted, "I think my kids are still talking about learning for my benefit and not their own."

Overall, Joan said, these conversations helped her "see the whole concept of ongoing assessment more broadly." She designed assessment structures that informed students as well as herself. For example, a peer editing sheet had sentence stems for students to complete, such as, "I was really surprised when . . ." "Why did you say . . . after you said . . . ?" "My favorite sentence was . . ." Joan's students also kept writing portfolios. They defined goals for improving their writing, using a "goal-setting" form (see Exhibit 4.1). At the end of each unit students selected examples of writing for their portfolios with associated journal entries and

Exhibit 4.1. Joan's Goal-Setting Form.

GOAL-SETTING FORM   **WRITING WORKSHOP**

Name _____   Date _____

SKILLS AND ACTIVITIES OF WRITING WORKSHOP

In the blanks that follow, put the number that describes your skill level:

> 1 = I already do this excellently
>
> 2 = I'm okay at this, but I'd like to improve
>
> 3 = HELP! I really need work on this

Vocabulary

___ learn new vocabulary words

___ use new vocabulary words correctly in sentences

___ use new vocabulary words correctly when I'm writing stories, essays, and freewrites

Sentence Structure

___ write complete sentences (no fragments or run-ons)

___ write different kinds of sentences

Writing Content

___ write good physical descriptions

___ write pieces that describe well how I feel

___ write pieces that appeal to all of the senses

___ write pieces that contain vivid, well-chosen words

___ write pieces that show imagination

Writing Process Elements

___ write pieces with definite beginnings, middles, and ends

___ begin new paragraphs when I should

___ write long enough pieces

___ always write enough to explain exactly what I mean

___ write things that say exactly what I want to say

___ write good first drafts

Exhibit 4.1. Joan's Goal-Setting Form *(continued)*.

___ write good revisions

___ write good final papers with good revisions and editions

___ make up good titles

___ make helpful comments about other people's writing

___ explain why one piece of writing is better than another

___ follow the multistep writing process

Mechanics

___ use apostrophes correctly

___ spell long words correctly

___ spell words that sound alike correctly

___ use capital letters when they're needed

___ use commas correctly

Other

___ do my homework on time

___ enjoy writing

___ use writing as a way to express myself

Now that you've gone through this list of possible areas of expertise, improvement, and disaster, choose some areas on which you want to work.

Which **two areas** that you designated with a "2" do you wish to focus your energy on for the next 4–6 weeks?

1._____   2._____

Which **two areas** that you designated with a "3" do you wish to focus your energy on for the next 4–6 weeks?

1._____   2._____

peer editing sheets. Students wrote a cover sheet for each portfolio submission, describing how the piece illustrated progress on their selected goals.

Rethinking Understanding Goals

For the first several months of her work with TfU Joan had qualms about the "revolution" it seemed to require. She had been attracted to TfU to validate her practice but found that this pedagogy required substantial rethinking of her craft. Designing and managing performances of understanding and ongoing assessments with a difficult group of students was very demanding. It absorbed most of her weekly meetings with Karen. Joan also had to plan and teach three other courses and work with a total of ninety students each week. Finding the intellectual time to reflect on her goals was a big obstacle.

Initially Joan was not sure that her students really needed to know her goals for the course, but gradually she saw the value of stating explicit understanding goals. One day a student asked to go to the bathroom, adding, "It's a place!" Joan realized that students "tune into the teacher's repetitions. . . . I thought that if I mentioned the goals early and often, kids would begin to listen and look for them in the coursework." During the second unit of Writing Workshop, Joan began listing goals at the top of student assignment sheets. She related goals for specific performances to her unit goals. By the third unit in late November, Joan felt she had become better at designing goals through practice, dialogue with Karen, and time for reflection. See Exhibit 4.2 for a summary of Joan's goals in the three units.

Karen reminded Joan that public assessment criteria clearly related to understanding goals were important. She suggested that Joan involve students in defining criteria for good writing. Joan thought her students would be comfortable starting with the question, "What makes a piece of writing complete?" Pairs of students read two different essays (each focused on a place) and discussed criteria for completeness. Through further class discussions Joan pooled students' ideas into a list of criteria for the beginning, middle, and end of a piece of writing. She posted this list on the classroom wall and used it as the basis for peer conferences and

Exhibit 4.2. Writing Workshop Unit Goals.

Unit One: Writing About Places (September–October)

Understanding Goals: Students will understand . . .

  1. . . .that their ideas and feelings can be expressed in writing

  2. . . .that writing is a multiple-step process

  3. . . .that "place" plays significant roles in all of our lives

  4. . . .that they can compare pieces of writing and make decisions about which pieces they want to keep working on or place in their portfolio

Central Understanding Performances: "Place Mats" of students' favorite places, essays describing those places, one-page description of Cambridge, students create criteria for good writing

Unit Two: A Scientific, Objective View of Place (November)

Understanding Goals: Students will understand . . .

  1. . . .that in certain disciplines and professions, any writing about place conveys reality through both description and measurement

  2. . . .that the goals of different writers—geographers, navigators, cartographers, geologists, naturalists, oceanographers—affect the balance of description and measurement in their writing

  3. . . .that "scientific" writing about place can lead naturally to writing about human nature

  4. . . .that creating a complete piece of writing can also involve steps such as collecting data and making measurements

Central Understanding Performances: Essay on how technology changed students' views of the world, map of "world at age seven" and essay about perspective of the world at age seven, creation of criteria for a "complete" piece of writing, creation of writing portfolio

Unit Three: Metaphorical Places (mid-December–end of January)

Understanding goals: Students will understand . . .

  1. . . .the factors that affect your place and others' place in society

  2. . . .that these factors can be written about in such a way as to make your audience understand where and how you see yourself as fitting into society

  3. . . .that one's place in society can affect one's power and freedom

  4. . . .that the act of writing about one's understanding of one's place in society is empowering

  5. . . .that place can be used metaphorically in your writing

Central Understanding Performances: Essay on place in society, creation of "Life Road Maps," essay describing life road toward goals, creation of criteria for effective beginning, middle, and end writing, creation of writing portfolio self-editing. These strategies sustained students' interest because they enjoyed reading one another's work, and caused them to focus on the goals captured in the criteria.

Later in the year Joan noted that one of the difficulties of articulating goals is that it takes time and thought to unearth tacit goals buried in the back of a teacher's mind. Joan called this "back-burner thinking" and explained that as her course progresses she rethinks her goals and sometimes refines, revises, or rewords them more precisely. Only after the workshop course had ended did Joan recognize that she had not explicitly expressed her most important overarching goal, although it was implicit in every performance and unit she developed. She had not directly stated to students the goal of understanding writing as a form of self-expression, although she had discussed it repeatedly and written about it in her journal. Joan noted that setting goals requires rethinking as a course progresses, probing collaborative discussion and reflection with colleagues about disciplinary concepts and methods, and continual examination of student performances in relation to clear criteria.

Integrating the Whole TfU Framework

After working with TfU for several months Joan began to feel more comfortable with it. Her course was running smoothly, designing curriculum was easier, and her students were producing some careful, powerful, and moving writing. The framework began to shift from an external object to an internal part of Joan's mindfulness about her teaching. In the early months she sometimes described Karen's role as "the guardian of the framework," but by December Joan described the TfU framework as "my teaching conscience." In January she told Karen, "The framework doesn't intimidate me anymore." Through repeated enactments of framework elements in her practice, Joan was beginning to integrate TfU into her overall teaching approach.

Joan continued to use the TfU framework in a literature course about short stories that she taught in the spring term. This course enrolled 70 percent of the ninth-grade students listed as "at risk" for failure. Absenteeism was consistently high, students rarely did homework, and they pressured Joan to lower her expectations. Nevertheless Joan worked conscientiously to integrate all four elements of the TfU framework into her curriculum plans, activities, and materials. Although Joan was often discouraged by the students' lack of participation during the term, she thought their final products demonstrated more understanding than she had expected.

In addition to using TfU ideas in her own practice, Joan also introduced the TfU framework to her colleagues. In May, Joan and a colleague offered a short course to fellow faculty as part of her school's in-house staff development program. The focus of this minicourse was performance assessments, a priority in the school district, but Joan also used the occasion to introduce the four elements of the TfU framework.

Helps and Hindrances

Joan thought TfU helped her promote and track students' understanding and adjust curriculum to their needs. "Teaching for Understanding relentlessly makes the child more central than the pedagogy," she noted. "It creates a mindfulness around a constellation of TfU concerns which work together to foster students' understanding. Understanding and good teaching aren't the results of good luck or miracles; they're the result of careful attention to four important areas [spotlighted] by this framework."

Joan claimed that Karen's assistance was a significant help in developing her understanding of TfU. Karen listened sympathetically to the full range of Joan's concerns, provided specific constructive suggestions as she coached Joan's performances of understanding TfU, and supported Joan's reflection on her discipline and her practice.

Joan's situation was challenging in several respects; her students were among the more reluctant and historically unsuccessful freshmen in her school, and she had no time built into the school day to think about TfU. Her school was supportive, however, in its endorsement of performance assessments. At times this initiative blurred the vocabulary and the specific elements of the TfU framework,[2] but overall it created an atmosphere conducive to rethinking curriculum and pedagogy with the TfU framework.

Joan herself is a contemplative professional committed to continuing her own education. In 1994–95 she arranged a partial sabbatical that she devoted to deepening her understanding of her discipline and to leading a yearlong study group for six teachers interested in more work with TfU. (Joan's strategies for supporting her colleagues' use of TfU are described in Chapter Eleven.) Continued experience with TfU in her own classroom informed Joan's consultation with her colleagues. By the same token, Joan found that helping other teachers use TfU to redesign their courses advanced her own understanding of the framework.

Relating Teaching for Understanding to the Textbook

Bill Kendall had taught mathematics for twenty years at Braintree High School (BHS) when the Teaching for Understanding project caught his attention. BHS is a large comprehensive secondary school serving students from mostly middle- and working-class parents. Bill was dissatisfied with the way he taught geometry, especially to lower-level classes. Traditional methods of giving lectures and assigning homework from the textbook bored him and his students. He wanted to include more hands-on experiences and cooperative learning, as the National Council of Teachers of Mathematics standards[3] recommended, but he worried that students did not really learn from these activities. "I've never been happy with the way it worked in the class," he said. "It all degenerates into white noise for the kids . . . they go through the motions, but they retain very little."

First Encountering TfU

Bill first worked with the TfU project during its third year, when he participated in teaching experiments designed to analyze the impact of TfU pedagogy on student learning. The TfU research team asked several accomplished teachers to teach one of their standard curriculum units using their usual best methods. Then TfU researchers redesigned the unit with the teachers to incorporate the principles of TfU and the teachers taught it a second time to a comparable group of students. As a full-time teacher, Bill had little time to redesign curriculum. So his research partner invented many of the performances for the TfU-based unit. Under pressure to complete the research in a limited time, Bill agreed to teach the project-based units the researcher designed.

The experience of teaching lessons that he had not designed, and that did not resemble his usual practice, was mixed for Bill. His students really enjoyed the two-to-three-week TfU units, in which small groups of students conducted projects that related geometry concepts and mathematical reasoning to realistic problems such as designing a parking lot to accommodate the maximum number of cars in a given area. Although students found the first project somewhat confusing, they were more capable of working effectively in groups on the second project. Because students urged him, Bill designed a project on his own at the end of the year and was pleased that it worked reasonably well.

Bill's reaction to TfU was not all positive, however. His frustrations and doubts were apparent the following August during the three-day work session with the other teachers invited to collaborate on TfU research. Unlike the teaching experiments of the previous year, which attempted to measure the impact of TfU on student performance, the goal of the present research was to understand the process of connecting the TfU framework with teachers' thinking and practice. The summer work session was intended to help teachers develop plans for the coming year, but Bill had trouble getting started. He questioned the definitions of TfU terms and worried over defining generative topics that related to his textbook.

Comprehending TfU in Connection with Bill's Priorities

When the school year began, the TfU project brought in a new researcher as Bill's partner. Daniel Wilson was a former mathematics teacher and a part-time graduate student. In his early meetings with Bill, Daniel realized that Bill did not "own" the TfU work. Although Bill had defined some understanding goals with his research partner during the summer work session, he "couldn't really remember" why they were important. Daniel concluded that his first task must be to understand Bill's priorities as a teacher and his hopes and fears about TfU.

Through several conversations, Daniel clarified both Bill's goals and the roots of his frustration. "I really want to see what will happen if I try using the Teaching for Understanding framework for the whole year with my regular textbook," Bill acknowledged. Bill valued the projects he had tried during the previous year because they involved students in using geometry to study real-world problems. He worried, however, that they took him and his students too far from the textbook-based curriculum he felt obligated to cover. "It was hard to come up with a project that covered all the math within a unit," Bill recalled, so that as the class came to the end of the project "you had to patch stuff in. Or you had to make connections that weren't really there . . . so we were stretching. It wasn't working; the connections were weak."

Although Bill wanted his course to remain closely linked to his textbook, he preferred to include some hands-on experiences that made geometry meaningful for his students. And he wanted to develop better approaches to assessment. He thought his usual text-based tests neither helped students learn nor provided a very good measure of their understanding.

Bill's major problem with TfU focused on generative topics, which he equated with curriculum projects. Besides his worry about the discontinuity between projects and his textbook, Bill wondered if mathematics was a generative subject. He observed, "Mathematics is generative only within its own field. It's there to generate more math and that doesn't help if you've got someone who doesn't understand math or doesn't want to understand math. . . . My training in mathematics is strong, but it didn't prepare me to define generative topics with meaningful applications of the math. . . . I wasn't taught that way and I don't think many math teachers are. Taking higher- and higher-level math courses isn't enough."

Designing Overarching Understanding Goals

Bill's attitude toward the TfU framework brightened noticeably in October after he and Daniel met with David Perkins, one of the TfU project directors, with whom Bill had collaborated in the past. Through discussing the central ideas of geometry within the field of mathematics, Bill reconsidered his own understanding of the subject. They wrestled with the knotty problem of defining a generative topic around which to design curriculum without disrupting the usual structure and sequence of Bill's textbook-based curriculum. The problem was resolved when they shifted the focus to ask about Bill's overarching understanding goals. The question became, "What do you most want your students to understand or appreciate about geometry when they leave your course?" With David's assistance, Bill defined his overarching topic this way: "Geometry is the study of lawfully connected patterns in the world." This captured central concepts in mathematics and addressed Bill's desire to help students apply geometry to everyday life. Bill wrote this overarching generative topic on a large poster and hung it prominently in his classroom. He announced to students that this was the main idea for their whole course.

With this topic in mind, Bill and Daniel revisited the task of designing understanding goals. Through several hours of discussion, they ultimately produced the following:

Students will understand how to

- Recognize lawfully connected patterns in the world
- Define lawfully connected patterns in the world
- Employ lawfully connected patterns in the world
- Reason logically by means of

    Decomposition
    Rearrangement
    Connecting concepts coherently

- Apply and employ math tools

Bill posted these goals on the wall of the classroom, thinking they would make his teaching agenda more explicit for his students. An unanticipated benefit was that he used the list to focus his teaching. He noted, "Those posters are as helpful to me as they are to the students. While I am teaching, those [goals] should be up-front things that I should be keeping in mind: How does geometry connect to the real world? How can I keep referring to logical arguments? What tools are we using?"

Designing Curriculum with the TfU Triangle

Freed from a preoccupation with generative topics that made him feel anxious about abandoning his textbook and doubtful about his own understanding of mathematics, Bill gained comfort with the TfU framework. He noted, "We factored out generativity for

the moment. We dwelled on goals, performances, and assessments
. . . and they seemed to form a pretty nice triangle." In planning a
unit based on a chapter in his textbook, Bill would ask himself,
"What are my goals for the unit? How can I integrate them with my
overarching goals? What understanding performance will encompass these goals? How can I assess the performance?" As he addressed these questions Bill used the TfU triangle—or "trinity," as
he called it—to relate understanding goals, performances, and assessments. From this relationship, generative action arose. This way
of thinking about interconnections among the framework elements was very different from the prior year's work with TfU that
Bill perceived as linear and rigid.

Using the trinity, Bill selected exercises from his textbook that
addressed his goals and modified them to fulfill TfU criteria. The
textbook activities did not usually connect geometry to real-world
problems that were interesting and meaningful for students, engage students in active performances of understanding, or incorporate opportunities for ongoing assessment. So Bill supplemented
the textbook exercises with activities of his own design that did
meet these TfU criteria. For example, during an early unit focused
on developing understanding of basic terms Bill asked students to
produce and label a poster with photographs of objects that illustrated each of forty key geometry terms. In addition, students wrote
a "guidebook" containing a definition in their own words and an
example of each term.

Through these two performances, students applied geometric
ideas to regular life and demonstrated their understanding of Bill's
curriculum. Bill understood students' progress well enough to
forego the test he usually gave at the end of this unit. As he graded
students' posters and guidebooks, Bill realized he should have assessed them earlier and given students some feedback before they
turned in the final products. For the next unit, he devised similar
assignments but collected them after students had completed the
first half. Bill learned how students were progressing and gave additional guidance to those who needed to make improvements.

Enacting Ongoing Assessment with Students

Assessing student performances midway in the unit was useful but
time-consuming for Bill, who taught five different classes every day.

He decided he needed to "decentralize assessment" among the students. Distributing assessment would alleviate pressure on his time, allow students to see several approaches to the assignment, and engage students in giving and getting feedback on their works-in-progress.

Bill learned some useful tips for engaging students in assessment at meetings with other TfU teacher-researcher pairs. Joan Soble mentioned that her English students were much more willing to provide pointed critiques and suggestions to fellow students when their remarks contributed to revision rather than to the final evaluation of the product. Students were reluctant to assign grades to their peers but happy to try to help them improve their writing. Joan also showed assessment sheets she had designed that guided students with questions to answer about their peers' work. Seeing other teachers' examples and describing his own experiences helped Bill understand how to enact ongoing assessment in his own classroom.

In consultation with Daniel, Bill devised ways to engage his students in peer assessments. These worked well when students understood the assignment well enough to provide helpful suggestions for improvement, but this was not always the case. For example, Bill found that students could not look at a peer's proof and figure out where it went wrong unless they understood the structure of proofs pretty well. In confronting this challenge, Bill hit upon the concept of self-revealing problems. In his unit on regular polygons, he gave an assignment that required students to use interior angle formulas to produce a tessellation. (He found this idea in a book while searching for ways to make this unit more generative and applicable to the real world.) On this assignment students could observe whether their pattern repeated precisely. This visual information provided a basis for checking their mathematical calculations.

Developing ways for students to assess their own and their peers' work and integrating ongoing assessment into curriculum seemed very powerful to Bill. He began to regard assessment as "part of the learning process—feedback advances learning."

As the year progressed Bill involved students in collaborative inquiry around more complex problems. He learned how to ramp students up to challenging performances of understanding. In the spring Bill devised a complex final project for the unit on similar triangles. Working in trios, students used mirrors in the hall outside their classroom to investigate the mathematical relationships among distances and angles in the cases where two students could see each other's reflection in the mirror.

Bill and Daniel talked at length about what students would need to understand in order to apply similarity concepts to this problem. They identified three subgoals: understand how to use algebra to calculate ratios, how to deduce mathematical patterns from data and make conjectures, and how to collaborate on inquiry in groups. They designed *subperformances* to help students develop understanding of these concepts and skills.

Bill began the unit on similar triangles in his usual way of reviewing in class the methods for setting up and solving ratio problems using algebra. Students completed the homework from the textbook without difficulty, so Bill assumed they would easily solve the first subperformance assignment, as shown in Figure 4.1.

Bill distributed graph paper and rulers and then walked around the room listening as students worked on this problem in trios during class. He was astonished to learn that most students were confused about how to proceed. "I was absolutely shocked to

Figure 4.1. Bill's Staircase Assignment.

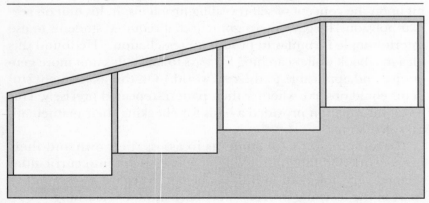

Page 499 in your textbook shows a side view of a set of stairs with a railing. Each step is actually, in real life, 7" high. Draw a sketch of this staircase and railing with all of the lengths and angle measurements marked (side view only will do).

see that some students thought they should add the values . . . that if the stair is a half inch in the picture and seven inches in reality then [they should] take every measurement and add 6.5 inches to get the answer! . . . If I hadn't done this type of assessment—gone around to each group and checked to see if everyone was understanding—then I would have assumed that they understood how to apply ratios."

Although the results were disturbing, Bill was glad he had uncovered these weaknesses in his students' understanding. Faced with this evidence, Bill rethought his unit plan. He decided to assign an additional exercise that required students to make a scaled drawing of a floor plan of a room in their own home. With this additional practice students were able to approach the mirror project more effectively.

Helps and Hindrances

Bill found working with the TfU framework during the fourth year very helpful in clarifying his goals, designing generative curriculum, and using assessments to advance student understanding. His teacher preparation courses and the process of teacher evaluation in his school had tended to emphasize lesson plans rather than the long view of his agenda. "There isn't any of this long-haul talk: are your units cohesive; is your year planned well," Bill noted, adding that he found that the TfU framework gave him a "heuristic for planning units" that was "relative easy to use once you get into it."

Working with this framework also helped Bill accomplish his desire to supplement the usual diet of lectures and homework and to involve students in more active inquiry without abandoning his textbook. "Six years ago I thought my job was to come in and clearly explain it," he said. "But it wasn't working, students were not getting it. I knew I had to get away from the constant lectures." The standards issued by the National Council of Teachers of Mathematics (NCTM) also urged Bill to use more hands-on inquiry and collaborative groups, but did not tell him how. "The TfU framework makes [the standards] manageable to the regular hard-pressed teacher who has a hundred students and five classes a day."

One reason Bill found the TfU framework more manageable during the fourth year was that he and Daniel used TfU in the context of a textbook-based geometry course. For Bill, the prospect of organizing his whole course around a series of complex curriculum projects was too difficult. In his view, TfU can be effective even if you do not "do projects, throw away your textbook, or become a revolutionary."

Before Bill could understand TfU as a tool to design curriculum, he had to interpret the elements of the framework in terms of his priorities for his own practice. To make the Teaching for Understanding framework generative for Bill, Daniel had to understand Bill's goals for his students, his preferences and concerns about his own teaching, and the limits on the risks he was prepared to take. This diagnostic work revealed the need to focus first on Bill's overarching goals. Defining them in generative terms benefited from consultation with an academic who mapped curriculum in terms of central disciplinary concepts in mathematics. Conversations with his university-based colleagues helped Bill formulate understanding goals as a touchstone on which to base his curriculum plans. "The Overarching Generative Topic has been one of the most useful things that I keep in mind when I plan a unit," he observed.

Several aspects of Bill's school setting hampered the incorporation of TfU into his practice. He reported that most administrators, teachers, students, and parents in his school have fairly traditional expectations about teaching: "Parents expect me to cover the curriculum [which] they see as the textbook. I can't change that." The school reflects the same priorities: "If you were to walk the school you would see that by and large kids are sitting at their desks and teachers are lecturing." These norms cause students to "think they need to sit there and the teacher will pour knowledge into their heads. . . . They think that on tests and homework, particularly in math, they regurgitate what the teacher did." Bill sees each of his classes for forty-five minutes daily, but his students spend the rest of the day with teachers who have little or no knowledge of TfU. He wondered, "Is just one class with one teacher for one year enough to change [students'] view of the whole school and what's going on? I don't think so. Maybe it's enough to plant the seed."

A few of Bill's colleagues expressed interest in his work with TfU. He shared some of his assignments with other geometry teachers who asked to see them. But there are few opportunities built into the school schedule for teachers to talk about teaching. Bill said that conversations with colleagues were more likely to be about "administrative trivia" than about the "nuts and bolts of what's really going on."

Under these circumstances any teaching for understanding is an uphill battle. It requires time and careful thought beyond the investment needed to teach from the textbook. At times Bill was enthusiastic about the value of the TfU framework as a practical heuristic for planning and conducting lessons, units, and courses that focus on understanding, but at other points he wondered whether he could manage to use the framework without the support provided by the research project. "I really feel that most of the stuff I have developed is because I am putting in extra time and I have [Daniel] for help. I am just still wondering if you really cut me loose, could I still do it? Would I still do it?"

A year later, however, Bill's connection with the TfU framework was still strong. "Ongoing, meaningful assessment is at the core of my teaching. It is difficult to do. I constantly question my own children about what their teachers are actually grading them on and they are usually mystified. . . . Understanding goals and performances (although I don't necessarily call them that) are important in deciding what to include in and what to exclude from my course. Unfortunately, for political reasons (parents, the College Board, the state mathematical frameworks) they are not my only consideration in planning lessons."

Bill has moved more and more to projects built around generative topics. He and a colleague took five hours to redesign a project after Bill realized that it "missed the understanding goal" of decomposing real-world shapes into regular figures found in the textbook. "It took me a few years to see this, but it is evidence of how the TfU framework has deeply penetrated my thinking."

On a broader scale Bill reported that "the culture of my school has changed, partially due to my work in the TfU project. Longer periods and more penetrating work by the students are moving into BHS. I am treated as an example of how such things can work."

Developing Understanding of TfU

These stories about two teachers' experiences illustrate themes echoed in the intensive research with two other teachers (see Chapter Five) and in consultations with dozens of other teachers about TfU. They demonstrate that learning to teach for understanding is fruitfully conceived and supported as a process of developing understanding. The TfU framework provides a useful structure for a sustained dialogue with teachers about bringing their practice into alignment with the elements of the framework to sharpen their focus on enhancing students' understanding. From this perspective, themes in the development of teachers' understanding of TfU can be clustered around the elements of the framework.

Making TfU Generative

Making TfU generative for teachers meant linking their passions to this fundamental effort to improve practice. It depended on finding an entry point to the TfU framework that addressed the teacher's interests and concerns. Bill was eager to incorporate more active performances into his lessons without abandoning his textbook. Joan was attracted to the idea of a generative topic to make her curriculum more coherent and engaging for students. Other teachers were drawn to the idea of ongoing assessment embedded in curriculum or to the value of clearly defining understanding goals. To make TfU a generative topic, teachers must be allowed to discuss and enact the ideas of the framework in ways that help them address their own concerns and passions about their practice.

Sustaining what Lois Hetland called "the fragile thread of generativity" was a sensitive process. It required a balance between building on teachers' strengths and interests and pressing toward central TfU goals that were not easy or apparently interesting to teachers. Like all good teachers, Karen and Daniel had to demonstrate their own passion for this endeavor, provide encouragement and help, and cultivate an honest and reciprocal relationship with their teacher partners. This built their credibility to probe and challenge teachers, to unearth tacit thoughts, and to question ideas or practices that were inconsistent with TfU.

Understanding the Goals of TfU

Performance-based understanding of TfU was the clear understanding goal in this research. For teachers, this goal meant using the four elements of the framework to analyze, design, and enact curriculum. Wherever teachers entered this endeavor, the researchers posed questions that guided teachers to apply the elements and criteria of the framework to their practice: What do you want students to understand? How is that goal connected to central ideas and methods in your subject? How can it be connected to students' interests and your own passions? What performances will develop these understandings? How will you and students know that they understand?

There was no one best sequence for confronting these questions. Teachers proceeded in various ways depending on their strengths and concerns. As teachers conversed about goals, performances, and assessment, TfU consultants gradually formulated teachers' ideas with the language of the TfU framework. Because teachers often found the TfU terms initially awkward and confusing, too much emphasis on the words themselves was counterproductive in the beginning. Ultimately, however, teachers came to comprehend and use the language of the TfU framework elements and criteria.

Performing Understanding of the TfU Framework

Project staff supported teachers' understanding of TfU by helping them refine performances at all four levels: comprehension, design, application, and integration. As they would with any process of understanding, teachers already had ideas, dispositions, and habits that shaped their interpretations of TfU. Building understanding of TfU required moving from wherever teachers started, sometimes explicitly confronting misconceptions, building on existing repertoires, and adjusting goals to accommodate barriers.

Teachers often interpreted TfU elements initially in terms that were already familiar and appealing to them. For example, they noticed the generative topic criterion of addressing students' interests and saw this as a way to meet the abiding challenge of engaging students, related to "student-centered," "interdisciplinary," and "authentic" curriculum. Teachers often overlooked the criterion concerning centrality to the field. As Bill discovered, mapping the curriculum in terms of key concepts in the discipline is difficult if one is accustomed to structuring courses around chapters in a textbook. At times Joan worried that motivating reluctant students conflicted with focusing on understanding goals. A major challenge in teachers' learning to teach for understanding is developing understanding of their subject in ways that reveal generative topics.[4]

The concept of understanding goals was difficult for many teachers to comprehend. Some teachers interpreted them as behavioral objectives, perhaps because TfU emphasizes understanding as performance. Like Joan, teachers resisted defining goals if they interpreted them as isolated, narrow outcome statements that unravel the richly woven fabric of their multilayered interdisciplinary curriculum. Articulating goals was difficult when teachers' agendas were deeply embedded in a tacit amalgam of values and goals concerning subject matter content, modes of inquiry, and students' individual and communal habits of mind. Extricating specific understanding goals from these inchoate ideas required many hours of thinking and talking.

As Joan discovered, defining clear goals may seem easier and more valuable as teachers confront the task of articulating explicit assessment criteria. Specifying the qualities of an understanding performance may bring tacit goals to the fore in terms that make sense to students. Teachers often find that they can induce their goals by assessing student performances and articulating the qualities of strong work more easily than they can deduce their goals by reflecting on abstract ideas.[5]

The concept of understanding performances was relatively easy for most teachers to understand at the level of comprehension and even curriculum design. Bill associated it with the "real-world experiences" called for by the NCTM standards and Joan interpreted it as "hands-on inquiry" in the Place Mat project. Teachers often equated understanding performances with project-based curriculum and designed multiweek projects including complex investigations with elaborate equipment, collaborative group learning, and students' keeping reflective journals.

Enacting complex projects in the classroom was demanding, however, especially if teachers and their students were accustomed to traditional text-based lessons, teacher lectures, and short-answer assignments requiring recall of information. Both Joan and Bill had to reinterpret the notion of understanding performances to encompass activities that more nearly resembled their accustomed classroom routines. They designed sequences of performances that gradually ramped up students' knowledge, skills, and dispositions until students could attempt more sophisticated understanding performances.

Teachers also had to resist simplistic goals and performances, such as decomposing understanding goals into isolated skills or facts. Joan worried that developing vocabulary and practicing correct grammar were not understanding goals even though her students needed to learn them. Eventually she concluded that skills and facts must be learned in the context of developing understanding. Joan then connected vocabulary enrichment to her central goal of understanding how to express oneself vividly through writing. Yet the subtleties of this idea were not easy to apply in practice. Teachers did not always see or remind their students of the relation between subperformances and the larger understanding agenda.

Ongoing assessment, like understanding performances, was an appealing idea for most teachers that proved challenging to enact. They commonly interpreted it as synonymous with portfolio or performance assessment. These assessment approaches also emphasize performances and products that are part of regular curriculum, not a separate assessment activity like traditional tests and quizzes. Ongoing assessment in TfU is distinctive, however, because it is conducted throughout a curriculum unit. Bill discovered that conducting assessments early and often, even if relatively informally, provided valuable information to both him and his students.

Ongoing assessment in TfU is also distinctive in its emphasis on clear criteria related to understanding goals, a feature that challenged most teachers. Sometimes teachers clarified their criteria only as they examined early drafts of student work and recognized features of strong versus weak examples. Teachers also found that students demonstrated and developed their understanding through participating in the definition of assessment criteria. Publicizing clear criteria at the beginning of a performance, as early versions of the framework urged, was not always possible or desirable. Indeed, this is one area in which teachers' critiques caused the project to modify the TfU framework. We learned that criteria might be developed and publicized partway through a unit while students still have plenty of time to work toward meeting the criteria in the culminating performance.

Integrating ongoing assessment into the classroom was especially difficult; for Bill, for example, grading draft performances was inordinately time-consuming. Involving students in assessment alleviated the time pressure on teachers and gave students opportunities to see and critique examples of understanding performances. As Bill discovered, however, students could not assess performances if they did not understand criteria well enough to apply them or were reluctant to assume the intellectual responsibility for critiquing their own or fellow students' work. Ongoing assessment shifted the balance of power and authority in the classroom, as it became not a tool of the teacher's control but a process whereby teachers and their students jointly learned to use explicit criteria to evaluate and improve performances of understanding. Integrating the ongoing assessment component of TfU often required significant changes in the usual norms, values, and expectations in a classroom and a school.

Refining TfU Through Ongoing Assessment

Teachers worked past many of these misinterpretations and difficulties by assessing examples of practice with the criteria for each element of the TfU framework. Consultation with TfU specialists and with other teachers involved in TfU was an indispensable format for assessing and refining TfU performances. Teachers benefited from analyzing and critiquing examples of TfU curriculum plans and materials, from applying TfU approaches to design and enactment of curriculum in their own classrooms, and from sharing strategies with other teachers. Reflecting on their own experiences with TfU helped teachers surface confusion, manage anxiety, and recognize progress. Gradually teachers understood and valued TfU well enough to assess themselves in relation to the framework. All these forms of assessment by themselves, peers, and specialists contributed to the development of teachers' understanding of TfU.

Helps and Hindrances

Intensive research with four teachers, as well as less systematic analysis of other teachers' experiences, demonstrated that understanding of TfU advances through cycles of conversing about the framework, designing curriculum, enacting these designs in classroom practice, and rethinking TfU. With sufficient support teachers gradually broaden these cycles of performances toward integrating TfU throughout their curriculum.

The concept of four levels or types of understanding (comprehension, design, enactment, and integration) proved useful in designing performances to promote TfU and in analyzing what helps and hinders those performances. Performances of all four types appeared to reinforce one another. Teachers developed comprehension of TfU as they talked about their practice with consultants who interpreted the teachers' descriptions and ideas in terms of the framework. With only a general understanding of the TfU elements, teachers began to use these ideas to design curriculum. As they did so, they benefited from the assistance of TfU consultants who, through questions and suggestions, helped them critique emerging curriculum designs with TfU criteria.

Performances of TfU at the comprehension and design levels were strongly influenced by the characteristics of the teacher and the kinds of help received. Teachers needed to understand the structure of their subject matter to identify generative topics and to define understanding goals central to their discipline. They needed to understand their students to formulate generative curriculum and goals in ways that attended to students' interests and concerns. A rich repertoire of curriculum materials and activities helped teachers design performances that addressed understanding goals and involved a range of learning modes and formats.[6]

To support teachers' understanding of TfU at these levels, the project consultants attempted to build on teachers' strengths and bolster them where necessary. For example, Daniel engaged Bill in conversations with a disciplinary specialist about his subject matter. Karen talked with Joan about how to redefine her goals in terms that addressed her central agenda. Bill consulted a range of curriculum materials to design activities to supplement the lessons in his textbook with assignments that would engage students in performances of understanding.

Understanding TfU at the levels of enactment and integration entailed a notable shift from the realm of ideas and plans on paper into the real world of schools. They required a different repertoire of performances from teachers. Teachers' performances of understanding at these levels were influenced by a host of additional factors, including some beyond the direct control of teachers and TfU specialists.

To enact TfU designs in the classroom, teachers needed to understand how to present ideas, answer questions, and guide performances so that students successfully engaged in performing their understandings. This required what Lee Shulman calls "pedagogical content knowledge,"[7] an understanding of how students think about the subject matter to be understood, including the ways they tend to misunderstand and forget it. Bill planned specific activities to ramp up his students' understanding of several subgoals. He listened to students and examined their performances closely enough to learn that he had misjudged his students' current understandings. He revised his plans to start farther back on the ramp and engage students in working toward the culminating performance of understanding. Clearly, an essential factor in applying TfU in the classroom is a teacher's capacity and inclination to listen carefully to students and to adjust curriculum in response to students. The challenge is to maintain this responsiveness to students without losing sight of understanding goals. Both Joan and Bill found that students sometimes resisted the rigor of TfU and had to be encouraged to try challenging performances.

TfU consultants faced a similar challenge in preserving the fragile thread of generativity as teachers attempted to enact TfU in the classroom. Karen had to observe Joan's classroom and appreciate the needs of her students in order to consult with Joan effectively and credibly about enacting TfU in her particular situation. Daniel had to understand Bill's personal priorities as well as the constraints of his classroom situation in order to know when to push TfU and when to back off.

Understanding TfU at the integration level was shaped by an even broader range of influences, including the school organization and community surrounding teachers' classrooms.[8] Joan's school encouraged students to take responsibility for their own learning. This aspect of the school culture endorsed the basic principles of TfU in a way that was less apparent in Bill's school; in his case an emphasis on textbook coverage and more traditional instruction caused students to regard learning as a process of absorption. Bill had to confront these expectations, norms, and requirements incrementally in order to integrate TfU into his course.

Long-term integration of TfU seems to depend on teachers' developing at least a cluster of like-minded colleagues who can help to develop school structures and cultures that are conducive to it. In the research project collegial support developed as teachers from different schools met to exchange strategies, materials, and moral support. In Chapter Eleven similar teacher study groups appear to support the integration of TfU in several schools.

Implications

Intensive research with four teachers helped answer questions about the process of learning to teach for understanding—its evolution, variations, and similarities across cases. It supported and recorded the experience of teacher pioneers who charted the unknown territory of relating the TfU framework to practice. Based on the map they helped to create, other teachers and supporters have been able to find their own ways through the TfU territory without such intensive collaboration. (See Chapter Eleven.) Here, we identify the landmarks mapped by this research and briefly discuss their implications.

Learning TfU Takes Time and Personal Support

Teaching for Understanding is a continuing, idiosyncratic, and personal inquiry, not an implementation of a standardized pedagogical model.[9] The TfU framework provides a language and structure for guiding this inquiry. Teachers can use the framework to become more conscious of their goals and more systematic and coherent in focusing both themselves and their students on the achievement of these goals. But this is not a one-time endeavor. Trying to teach for understanding stimulates teachers to become continuing learners about their subject matter, about their students, about curriculum that centers on priorities, and about ways of altering schools to emphasize the development of students' understanding. When taken seriously, the inquiry entails a profoundly personal reconception of practice, shaped by teachers' prior knowledge, skills, beliefs, and contexts.

This process was helped by developing and sustaining a professional community of learners based on reciprocity, honesty, and respect. They jointly constructed understanding of TfU through dialogue with intellectual, emotional, and logistical support for participants. In this research the role of social interaction among like-minded colleagues appeared crucial. As the TfU framework is described more fully and supplemented by various artifacts of its enactment, perhaps teachers will be able to develop understanding of TfU from these materials without so much human assistance. It seems likely, however, that the process of professional inquiry through which teachers connect TfU principles with their practice will always benefit from dialogue with colleagues engaged in similar inquiry.

The Whole of TfU Is More Than the Sum of Its Parts

As teachers' understanding of TfU evolves, they perceive it as increasingly integrated and profound. At first, its framework appears to be a relatively clean and simple model with four elements and their attendant criteria. Teachers tend to focus first on one element and then another. Through continued work with the framework, teachers see that each element interacts with the others. Eric Buchovecky said that as he focused on one element, he heard the others banging behind him "like cans tied to the car of newlyweds." Teachers who used the framework extensively found that it shifted from being an external guide to an internal lens for viewing their practice. Joan called TfU her "teaching conscience."

The discrepancy between the apparent simplicity and the actual scope of the TfU framework has both positive and negative implications. Because it looks relatively simple and highlights basic elements of practice, many teachers regard it initially as relatively straightforward and similar to what they already do. This is beneficial if it draws them into reflective inquiry about TfU but not if it makes them think there is nothing new or difficult about it. As teachers develop understanding of TfU they appreciate its comprehensive scope and its subtly profound implications for altering the focus, roles, and norms in their classrooms. For many this dawning realization is rejuvenating, but it can also generate anxiety or despair when teachers perceive that their circumstances will not support the profound changes they wish to pursue.

The Integration of TfU Requires School Change

Teaching for Understanding, in its fullest enactments, challenges the norms of many American schools. It emphasizes understanding of generative subject matter rather than memorization. Basic skills are a means toward understanding and self-esteem is a result of understanding, rather than ends in themselves. Teaching for Understanding requires both teachers and students to engage in continuing active inquiry. Participants in TfU classrooms are parties to an ongoing dialogue about understanding goals and assessment of performances. Such negotiations require teachers and students to take risks, to question, and to exercise intellectual authority. These responsibilities are not the norm in many schools and may be particularly alien to teachers of mathematics and the "hard" sciences.

TfU can be undertaken in relatively traditional school settings where textbooks and direct instruction are the norm. As Bill's case illustrates, TfU can help teachers redesign or supplement textbook assignments as necessary to emphasize performances of understanding. Teacher-led presentations can support TfU if they focus on understanding goals and are interspersed with opportunities for students to perform their understandings. Integrating TfU does not necessitate complete replacement of traditional forms of instruction.

Nevertheless, in its emphasis on public goals and performances of understanding TfU usually brings teachers and students up against business as usual in their schools. Supporting TfU is therefore not simply a matter of professional development for individual teachers. To integrate TfU into a school community usually requires teachers, administrators, students, and parents to rethink goals, curriculum, assessment, norms, and structures.[10] If this implication sounds unduly awesome, see Chapter Eleven for accounts of integrating TfU in school systems.

Chapter Five

How Does Teaching for Understanding Look in Practice?

Ron Ritchhart
Martha Stone Wiske
with Eric Buchovecky
Lois Hetland

How does Teaching for Understanding (TfU) look in practice? How do teachers exemplify the abstract elements and criteria of the TfU framework in their own curriculum and pedagogy? What moves do teachers make when they teach for understanding? Answering these questions was one purpose of a yearlong intensive collaborative research conducted with four teachers. The teachers varied in the subjects they taught, the kinds of schools where they worked, and the amount of teaching experience they claimed, but they were alike in their commitment to understand TfU.

Chapter Four included vignettes of two of these teachers, with a focus on the process of their learning to teach for understanding. This chapter draws extensively on the work of the other two teachers and shifts focus to examine how their practice exemplifies the elements of the TfU framework. The detailed depictions of two teachers' efforts to interpret, design, and enact teaching for understanding are based partly on reflective journals and reports that these teachers wrote about their own experience. The chapter is also based on a yearlong collaborative research process that included weekly observations and interviews with the teachers along with periodic reflective conversations among all four teachers and their research partners. Intensive research with these teachers, as well as observations of many other teachers who have used TfU in a wide variety of schools, framed the description of practice in the vignettes and analysis of its features.

Any picture of the TfU framework in practice is incomplete for at least two reasons. First, working with the framework is like participating in a reflective dialogue about principles and practice. It is a process of planning, enacting, and assessing practice in relation to the abstract concepts of the framework and reinterpreting one's understanding of it in light of this experience. Any attempt to capture a picture of TfU practice artificially freezes this ongoing dialogue and illustrates only a part of the process. Second, teachers are always trying to accomplish multiple purposes simultaneously, only some of which they formulate explicitly. Eric Buchovecky and Lois Hetland, the teachers in these vignettes, had many other matters on their minds even as they were thoughtfully preoccupied with TfU in their classrooms. Our research illuminates only one strand of their complex practice.

Because of these challenges, the vignettes provide inevitably limited representations of findings about the TfU framework in action. Yet they are an attempt to honor the unique, multifaceted, situated reality of teachers' practice while highlighting the elements of the Teaching for Understanding framework.

Features of Teaching for Understanding

Although teachers' work with the elements of the TfU framework is dialogic and recursive, it is helpful to analyze their moves in three broad categories related to the types of understanding described in Chapter Four: the backdrop, behind the scenes, and the action.

The Backdrop: Artful Comprehension in Context

How do teachers comprehend and use the framework to meet the particular opportunities and constraints of their teaching situation? Teaching is a dynamic act of interpretation shaped by the unique requirements and qualities of the subject area, designated curriculum, school culture, and particular students. The artistry of Teaching for Understanding lies in interpreting the framework elements and adapting them to meet the demands of a particular context while expressing the teacher's unique commitments, passions, and personality. Thus teachers incorporate their own interests and priorities into their practice of TfU, giving each classroom a distinctive feel.

Behind the Scenes: Design Moves

How do teachers prepare to teach a unit using the framework? How do the elements of the framework shape their designs of curriculum materials and activities? Teacher planning works dynamically among the elements of the framework; there is no set starting point or sequence. Articulating goals helps to define the essence of a generative topic. Analyzing performances may reveal goals that a teacher had not previously articulated. Defining ongoing assessment criteria is often particularly difficult during the process of curriculum design and may stimulate a refinement of understanding goals. Through this dynamic interplay teachers weave back and forth among the TfU elements and criteria, tightening the connections among goals, performances, and assessments in curriculum designs.

The Action: Application and Integration

How do teachers sequence instruction when using the framework? What kinds of moves do they make to enact TfU in the classroom? Although teachers' approaches vary, they often orchestrate a series of performances, within a single unit and across a sequence of curriculum units, that evolve in a characteristic pattern of three stages: messing about, guided inquiry, and culminating performance.

Teachers often initiate students' engagement with the generative topic through an initial open-ended exploration, discussion, or brainstorming session. This *messing about* (see Chapter Three) helps students perceive connections between the topic and their own interests and knowledge. Teachers build on students' initial explorations by assigning problems or projects that direct students toward central issues, questions, and understandings. Through *guided inquiry,* teachers focus students' attention and support their performances through structured assignments and ongoing assessments that are often conducted in small groups. Students learn from one another's examples and comments when they work together. As students develop knowledge and skills, their work becomes increasingly complex, open-ended, and self-directed. Teachers often conclude a curriculum unit with a *culminating performance* that each student develops more independently; it usually requires synthesis and extension of understandings that students have developed through the early phases of a unit.[1]

Within and across units, performances evolve from simple to complex, from structured to more open-ended, and from collaborative to independent. Similarly, ongoing assessments, which include student-generated as well as teacher-generated assessments and recommendations, evolve from informal to formal evaluations and from a focus on group work to individual students' performances. Throughout such a sequence of performances, ongoing assessment focuses both teaching and learning on understanding goals.

Every teacher's performance of TfU is a unique expression of his or her own characteristics and responses to particular students and circumstances. Yet these patterns emerge in the following vignettes as the teachers interpret the framework in relation to their own situations, use it to design curriculum, and apply it through continual adjustments in their classrooms.

A High School Physics Class

As a novice teacher, Eric Buchovecky approached the TfU framework with both enthusiasm and reservations. He became acquainted with the principles of TfU as a preservice teacher but feared that the framework was too prescriptive and inflexible. His colleagues dismissed the framework's applicability to science, causing Eric to question it. "Science is different," he commented initially. "Science demands that students all arrive at the same accepted conclusions [and is] associated with the mastery of factual knowledge and rigorous methodology."

Nonetheless Eric appreciated the framework's emphasis on students' active engagement in the construction of understanding. Having entered teaching "with the hope of instilling in students a fascination with the physical world while equipping them with the thinking tools necessary to explore its mechanisms more fully," he wanted to "get students to think like scientists." He believed that TfU could be a useful vehicle for achieving his goals: "My driving passion was the desire to prove that it could be done in science."

Eric's school, Belmont High School, focused on preparing its population of approximately 750 students for college within a strictly tracked curriculum using a pedagogy he described as "strongly rooted in a traditional transmission model." Though feeling largely successful with his honor students, Eric sought ways to pull in the students in his regular classes. "Coursework for these students is typically biased toward memorization and recall," he said. "The mastery that they develop often does not help them make sense of the world beyond the classroom, and they find little correlation between school and their lives. I actively engaged students in performances of understanding around topics that they find generative, hoping [they] would develop meaningful understandings that extend beyond the classroom."

The Backdrop: Clarifying Priorities

It is easy for new teachers to become swamped in the details and management issues of teaching and lose sight of both their discipline and their dreams as teachers. Eric's initial comprehension of the TfU framework depended upon his interpretation of its elements in relation to his own priorities. His TfU researcher partner, Chris Unger, encouraged Eric to begin by taking stock and allowing himself time to (in Eric's words) "refine and clarify what I would most like my students to be able to accomplish, then organize my teaching practice in a way that focuses directly on the attainment of these goals."

Eric began by reviewing problematic aspects of his previous teaching: "The Physics 1 students had difficulty generalizing patterns and concepts from specific classroom experiences. While I was trying to engage students in a multistep reasoning process that drew on the information and strategies developed through classroom experiences, they were searching their memories and their notebooks for 'the answer' that they assumed must be planted there." Eric understood that his students were accustomed to learning factual knowledge and had little experience in scientific thinking. "I recognized the need for explicit instruction about the process of scientific thinking. My students were not 'getting it' because although I was modeling the kind of thinking I wanted them to do, I was not giving them direct access to the larger scheme that was guiding my thinking."

Uncovering that larger scheme ultimately required Eric to construct a model of scientific thinking that he could articulate to his students and use as a guide in planning. Eric noted that his model (Figure 5.1) built on "the recursive nature of scientific inquiry" that flows between intuitive inferences based on initial observations and the construction of theories to explain and predict. Students enter the inquiry process with both experiences and tacit theories or models that they build on in a cycle of continuous refinement based on new information and increasing intuition. "Understanding this process and being able to apply it in a wide range of situations is the overarching goal I ultimately set for my students."

Behind the Scenes: Designing and Preparing

This overarching goal guided Eric's design and implementation of a monthlong unit investigating the physical principles of machines, "framing it," he said, "within my larger agenda as a science teacher."

Figure 5.1. Eric's Model of Scientific Thinking.

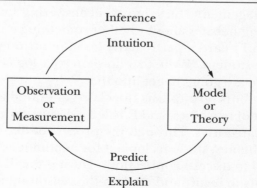

Situated at the end of a semester-long study of Newtonian mechanics, this machine unit focused on the concepts of force and energy conservation. Eric chose machines as his generative topic because it offered rich links to central ideas of physics and was highly accessible to students: "Machines are ubiquitous in our culture and all students have a wide range of personal experience with machines. In addition, the complexity and breadth of the topic allow students to generate a wide array of new questions as they develop deeper levels of understanding."

The Action: Teaching the Unit

Eric's curriculum plan displayed the progression of performances described earlier: messing about, then guided inquiry leading to a culminating performance. Throughout this sequence he incorporated many opportunities for students to demonstrate and assess their growing development of the knowledge and skills they needed to understand his overarching goals.

Messing About

Eric frequently began his units with a "brainstorming session" designed to activate students' background knowledge and introduce the unit in an accessible manner. "I gave the students ten minutes to come up with a list of twenty commonplace machines and a list of five essential characteristics of machines." During this time students worked in small groups, keeping track of their lists in a log book. Eric assessed his students' understanding informally as he moved around the room listening to their conversations and providing encouragement: "I tried to avoid answering students' questions or settling debates about whether something was a machine or not. When I heard a particularly good question or insight, I would tell the student, 'Write that down in your log book. That's a good idea! We are going to get into that.'"

From students' group lists the class generated an extensive composite list of machines, and Eric led a discussion about sorting the list into categories. Through the process of developing categorization schemes, students looked for generalities within their lists and tried to discern connections. During the discussion Eric asked students to justify and explain the reasoning behind their proposed categories. He then translated students' ideas "into language that emphasized disciplinary concepts, bridging from the informal to the disciplinary domain." After validating the utility of differing classification schemes, he proposed a system of classification differentiating mechanical from nonmechanical devices and engaged the class in identifying the various criteria that define a machine. Through debate and refinement of one another's ideas, students developed a working list of "machine criteria."

This activity enhanced the generativity of the machine unit by situating it in the real world, eliciting students' current understanding of the topic, and planting the seeds for further inquiry. Eric summarized the activity for students and placed it within the context of the entire unit:

> The bottom line is that many different criteria characterize machines. As you study machines in more detail, you'll find that some of the criteria you have come up with are more useful than others, and you'll develop new criteria. Today, as you tried to find ways to characterize machines, you began to consider some of the central questions that you will be investigating over the next month. What is the purpose of a machine? What does a machine actually do? Are there general ways to describe what all machines do? How do machines do what they do? Are there certain things common to the way all machines work? As you work on the different projects, you should keep coming back to these questions.

Eric followed up the presentation of these guiding questions with a handout that provided an overview of the entire machine unit and listed the understanding goals for the unit:

- Understand how to apply the principle of conservation of energy to solve quantitative problems in which energy is transferred.
- Understand how the principle of conservation of energy applies to and can be used to analyze simple machines.
- Understand the meaning of "ideal mechanical advantage," "actual mechanical advantage," and "efficiency" in relation to machines, and understand the differences among them. Understand how to determine each of these quantitatively for a given machine.

- Understand how to determine the forces and distances involved in the working of simple machines.
- Understand how the principles of conservation of energy, mechanical advantage, and efficiency apply to more complicated machines. Recognize and analyze simple machines in the everyday world around you.

Although some goals did not make sense to students initially, they set the stage for the future study.

Guided Inquiry

Nesting his understanding goals within his overarching goal of having students think as scientists, Eric immersed his students in a two-week investigation of a simple adjustable lever apparatus (see Exhibit 5.1 for the sequence of the entire levers investigation). Working in groups of three or four, students developed and tested theories of how forces and distances relate by adjusting the length of the lever arm and using a spring scale and metal weights to measure the forces on either end. Students recorded their ideas, questions, theories, and data in a log book and produced a final report that presented their theory with supporting evidence and a new application. Eric distributed a handout that outlined the specific report requirements.

In launching students' investigation of the lever apparatus, Eric shared with students his model for scientific theory building: "Good theories don't just pop up fully formed; they grow and change as you interpret new experiences. Play around, try different things, make guesses about what will happen. Keeping track of your ideas and observations and measurements will help you see patterns and draw better inferences. Use your inferences and intuitions to make changes to your theory of how levers work. You then have to test the theory by using it to make a prediction and then seeing if the prediction matches what you actually measure. So start playing around and see what you come up with."

As students began to explore the apparatus and gather data, Eric assessed their progress and questioned them to help them organize their thinking and articulate their ideas. In the process of explaining their actions and difficulties students often solved their own problems. At times Eric asked leading questions or suggested

Exhibit 5.1. Levers Unit: Scope and Sequence.

Day 1	Day 2	Day 3	Day 4	Day 5
Unit Launch Brainstorming Session on Machines	Messing About with the Lever Apparatus in Groups	Guided Exploration: Data Collection & Theory Building	Theory Building & Organizing Data for Reports	Writing of First Drafts for Reports
Day 6	Day 7	Day 8	Day 9	
Writing Drafts	Peer Review of First Drafts of Reports	Prepare Final Drafts	Polish Final Drafts	

specific experiments to move their thinking along. He noted a gradual decline in productivity and increasing frustration as students' work progressed: "I noticed that work in the groups had focused on making large numbers of measurements with little forethought or analysis. After two days, students in several groups asked, 'We've done all of the measurements, now what are we supposed to do?' When I asked how the measurements related to a theory, they were baffled. I realized that I needed to intervene at this point to clarify the theory building process and to demonstrate its application here."

To help them connect their data collection to the formulation of a theory, Eric asked students to make a prediction. "I hung a ten-Newton weight from one end of the lever and placed my hand on the other end. The fulcrum was positioned twice as far from the weight as from my hand. I then asked, 'Will I need to push with more or less than ten Newtons of force to lift the weight?'" After soliciting students' predictions, Eric used a spring scale to measure the force at greater than ten Newtons.

Eric: Why did you predict that I would have to push with more than ten Newtons?

Lelia: Because you have less leverage than the weight does.

Eric: What do you mean I have less leverage?

Lelia: Your side is shorter.

Eric: Now you have a theory! You predict that a greater force will have to be applied to the shorter side of the lever. You need to test it in more detail and refine it. Remember, you develop theories through a process that involves making predictions based on the current theory, making measurements to test those predictions, and modifying the original theory as needed. The more times you repeat this cycle the better your theory will get.

Students had the beginning of a theory relating the length of the lever's two sides to the amount of force needed to lift a weight but had difficulty articulating how this relationship functioned. Eric set up a new lever with a ten-Newton weight on the arm that was half as long as the arm on which the force was being exerted.

Again Eric posed the question, "Will I have to push with more or less than ten Newtons of force?" Many students called out that less force would be needed. Eric urged students to guess how much less force. Rob predicted that only five Newtons of force would be needed.

Eric: Rob, how did you come up with that prediction?

Rob: Well, it looked like the side you pushed on was about twice as long as the side with the weight. If it's twice as long, I guessed that the force would be half as much.

Eric: So your theory is that the ratio of the forces is related to the ratio of the two lengths. It seems to have worked in this case, but it needs to be tested. What we just did here gives you a whole new approach for doing experiments.

Eric thus engaged students in making predictions that drew on the intuitive understanding of levers developed by messing about. He then helped students shape their predictions into a testable theory, setting the stage for their further investigation. Students continued to record their thinking and observations in their log books, which Eric read and responded to every other day. This process of group dialogue, written reflection, and feedback from the teacher helped to shape students' understanding by highlighting their areas of comprehension and difficulty.

In a later reflection paper Eric considered the form his teaching had taken in this unit and recognized certain practices that characterized his teaching:

Students spend the majority of their time working within their groups while I monitor their progress and provide suggestions. However, when I feel that a significant number of students or groups have reached an impasse, I initiate a class discussion. Sometimes insights arise during these facilitated discussions that can move the class past the current barrier. In other cases, I need to make a more active intervention to move students into the next level of inquiry, drawing out student ideas then reframing those ideas within the disciplinary language and the larger disciplinary process. Students leave the class discussion with a richer formulation of their own ideas in relation to the disciplinary goals as well as new strategies, vocabulary, and knowledge that they can apply in their next phase of independent investigation.

Culminating Performance

As students' work progressed and their understanding of levers developed, the focus of their work gradually shifted. They moved from experimentation and theory building toward synthesis and development of a culminating performance, consisting of a written presentation of their theory with supporting evidence and application. Working from a list of self-assessment questions, students generated a draft report for peer review. As students evaluated the draft reports from other groups, they came to recognize the need for the inclusion of supporting evidence and clarity in their own reports. Responding to the peer review in their log books, students justified accepting or rejecting the critical feedback they received. Through this process students internalized the explicit criteria Eric later used to grade student work and applied it in their own formative self-assessment.

Eric repeated this cycle of theory building and testing in the class's next investigation of pulleys (see Exhibit 5.2 for the machine unit sequence). Gradually his students developed their skills in "thinking like scientists" within the context of understanding basic mechanics. Soon they were ready for a culminating project in which individuals rather than groups investigated a self-selected machine.

To explain the culminating project, Eric led the class through an analysis of a bicycle, thus providing a clear model of both the process of thinking and the product expected of students. Students applied their understanding by selecting a machine of moderate complexity, describing what it did, and explaining how it worked by noting the elements of simple machines in the mechanism. Eric gave students a list of explicit assessment criteria for the report, along with a written example that elucidated the workings of a corkscrew and demonstrated how diagrams could be helpful. Using an abbreviated and less structured form of peer review, students again engaged in a cycle of drafting, assessing, and revising their work before submitting the final report. (Chapter Seven presents work that two of Eric's students produced for their reports.)

Exhibit 5.2. Machine Unit: Scope and Sequence.

Day 1	Day 2	Day 3	Day 4	Day 5
Introductory Activity: Making Connections	Levers Investigation	Levers Investigation Continued	Levers Investigation Continued	Levers Investigation Continued
Day 6	Day 7	Day 8	Day 9	Day 10
Levers Investigation Continued	Levers Investigation Continued	Levers Investigation Continued	Levers Investigation Continued	Pulley Investigation
Day 11	Day 12	Day 13	Day 14	Day 15
Pulley Investigation Continued	Pulley Investigation Continued	Pulley Investigation Continued	Pulley Investigation Continued	Whole Class Bicycle Investigation Begin Work on Individual Projects
Day 16	Day 17	Day 18	Day 19	Day 20
Whole Class Bicycle Investigation (Project Work)	Small Group & Individual Project Work	Small Group & Individual Project Work	Culminating Individual Project	In-Class Unit Test

Summary

Using the generative topic of "machines" to capture students' attention, Eric designed understanding performances that built upon students' intuitions and hunches. Throughout the unit students' work focused on Eric's goals of developing students' understanding of both disciplined reasoning about scientific theory building and knowledge about mechanical physics. Initially, students were more comfortable measuring and collecting data connected with the lever apparatus than they were in building theories. Through questioning, Eric showed them that they did indeed have their own theories about how the lever worked that guided their prediction of outcomes. Working in groups and employing peer review, students learned to articulate their theories clearly and to refine them through a sequence of understanding performances.

Eric recognized that understanding performances take time and must develop progressively to help students transfer their understanding to novel contexts.[2] He supported their work by providing structure and information in the lever investigation, then repeating the theory-building process with somewhat less guidance in the pulley investigation, until students had enough understanding and confidence to conduct their own culminating investigations more independently. Throughout the unit Eric continually adjusted both the pace and scope of the performances to develop the habits of mind he sought to foster while meeting the needs of his students. Through ongoing assessment of classroom progress and students' log book reflections, Eric learned how to redirect both the class and individual students toward the understanding goals for the unit.

A Middle School History Class

As an experienced teacher of the humanities, Lois Hetland had long held a strong performance view of understanding. The TfU framework was compatible with her teaching style; she had organized her teaching around themes similar to generative topics for years and had extensive experience designing curriculum projects. Initially Lois saw the TfU research as an opportunity to focus on ongoing assessment, an area less cultivated in her practice. She had concerns about the framework's emphasis on setting goals, however, fearing that they would stifle her creativity as a teacher: "I felt that because of the inherent richness of the inquiry approach, goals for understanding were too complex and individualized to bother with. Each student got a great deal, and each one got a different great deal." Nevertheless, Lois was willing to explore how the framework mapped onto and enhanced her teaching.

Lois's school offered a supportive environment for innovation, promoting teacher collaboration, organizing the curriculum around *central subjects* that encouraged interdisciplinary curricula, and scheduling blocks of teaching time that varied from forty minutes to two hours. Her students were accustomed to interdisciplinary, project-based work and were generally well prepared, motivated, and supported.

Lois had a strong inquiry-based approach to teaching, involving students' construction of meaning and demonstrations of understanding through interdisciplinary projects. "I include a heavy dose of arts in my units, do a study of world geography, and coordinate projects with teachers in other departments as time and interest dictate," she said. "However, history and English are my mandated responsibilities."

Specifically, her class of independent school seventh-graders focused on the central subject of Colonial America, exploring it through various cultural perspectives. Lois felt historical scholarship entailed the responsibility "to consider multiple viewpoints and tie them together into reasonable conclusions about what happened and what can be learned from the period." She had "come to see this idea [of viewpoints and perspectives] as the one I most wanted my students to take away with them."

The Backdrop: Clarifying Priorities

In the third year of the TfU project Lois worked with her research partner, Stone Wiske, with a focus on understanding how Lois interpreted the nascent TfU framework. During her first year with TfU Lois worked extensively with ongoing assessment while organizing her teaching around generative topics and understanding performances. However, she found herself often cycling back to the idea of understanding goals, which she had initially resisted. In a year-end reflection Lois clarified the place of goals in her teaching: "Goals serve as road signs, reminding us that in addition to glorying in the journey, we have a specific destination. We want to get there, to know how far we have come, and to know how much farther we must go." After a full year of work with TfU, Lois's comprehension of the framework was still evolving.

Having seen the power of goals to focus and guide her own work, Lois wanted to make their power available to students. In the fall of her second year of work with the TfU project, she expressed the desire "to clarify my goals and post them for my students," thus making the road signs clear to all. Working initially from an implicit understanding of her purposes, Lois eventually derived the concept of *throughlines* as an expression of her overarching goals. She phrased the throughlines in the form of questions to make them accessible to students and to mobilize inquiry throughout the year. "I wrote them on construction paper and put them up in the front of the room. I was only partially satisfied—some seemed right, others felt too obtuse, and for some I was unsure. I knew my students would help me figure out how to improve them" (see Exhibit 5.3).

When students returned from their math class to find the posted throughlines, they responded immediately: "What are those?" "I don't get it. How can you multiply intelligence?"

Interest in the throughlines ranged from curiosity to a simple willingness to go along. One student commented, "Those are a great idea, Mrs. H. When I'm spacing out in class, those are just the kinds of things I think about."

Lois explained how the class would use the throughlines throughout the year: "Everything we do can connect to them, so look for the connections. As you do, we'll discover what the questions mean and get a deeper understanding of how to answer them."

Behind the Scenes: Designing and Preparing

After clarifying her goals with the publication of the throughlines, Lois looked for ways to use them to mobilize students' inquiry about Colonial America and make the subject as generative as possible.

Exhibit 5.3. Lois's Throughlines.

Throughlines for CS 93–94

Look for examples and related questions and concepts everywhere: in history, literature, other classes, your lives.

1. A. How does land shape human culture?
   B. How do people think about the land?
   C. How do people change the land?

2. A. How do we find out *the truth* about things that happened long ago and/or far away?
   B. How do we see through the bias in sources?

3. A. Why did Europeans colonize when other cultures didn't?
   B. What were the attitudes of different nations toward colonization?

4. A. What keeps peoples of different cultures from living and working successfully together?
   B. What helps overcome these difficulties?

5. How do we look at a culture?

6. How do we discover central themes?

7. How can you use multiple intelligences to approach your work?

8. How can you connect your personal interests, passions, and ideals to your schoolwork?

9. How do elements of a story connect to make bigger meanings?

10. What are the strengths and limitations of different genres of writing?

11. How are people today affected by and/or connected to decisions and/or events from the Colonial period? (Or what can we learn and how can we benefit from the study of history? Why does it matter?)

12. How does reflecting on your work and your thinking help you understand?

She addressed the criteria of accessibility, interest, richness, and connections in formulating her generative topics by considering four practical issues: What source materials are available to provide access? How will students connect ideas to their own lives? How can the study of Colonial America be linked to various disciplines? How can the topic be seen from more than one cultural viewpoint to increase its richness?

From these considerations Lois, her teaching colleague, and her apprentice teacher designed teaching units around six generative topics: the world in 1492, European antecedents, American antecedents, the original thirteen colonies, Colonial biography, and the American Revolution. Her biography unit illustrates how Lois's overarching goals, as expressed in her throughlines, motivated and guided her planning and instruction.

Lois stated the generative topic for the biography unit in the form of a question: "What can biographies tell us about Colonial history?" This topic offered students the opportunity to identify with historical figures by addressing themes important in the humanities and of interest to adolescents, such as authority, independence, fairness, social pressure, fear, and courage. Lois enhanced the generativity of the unit by allowing students to choose the Colonial figures whose biographies they studied. Resources were readily available, and the topic invited exploration through literature, promoting interdisciplinary connections. Finally, individual biographies offered unique viewpoints and perspectives on the period. By encouraging them to examine diverse biographies, Lois guided students toward understanding the complexity of the period as seen from differing cultural vantage points.

The generative topic of Colonial biographies addressed several of Lois's overarching goals, including one that encouraged an examination of history from a variety of viewpoints: "How do we find out the truth about things that happened long ago and/or far away?" Lois also formulated specific understanding goals for the unit, related to her yearlong throughlines. Lois saw these goals as flexible and evolving over the course of the unit. In a written reflection she made her view clear: "By striving to set goals, I had something explicit to compare to my plans and student performances. As goals shift, they tug on performances and assessments, causing them to shift as well. Although the goals shift, they must be set forth early, for they mark our path through the richness of the generative topic."

Lois established the following understanding goals for the unit:

I want students to understand how individuals shaped and were shaped by the culture and period in which they lived. I want them to consider what factors contribute to enhancing or limiting someone's influence and to connect some of the actions of Colonial individuals to the present shape of our nation and to their own lives and choices. I want them to understand the difference between being "influential" and being "good" or "righteous." I want them to understand that historical figures were as complex as any people alive today, full of the ambiguities and contradictions of human character with which we are all familiar.

Lois planned her unit to be "an active inquiry that grew in complexity and accountability as students engaged in their own research." Her students were accustomed to viewing history from differing viewpoints through their work in earlier units. These units developed students' skills in acquiring knowledge from various sources, analyzing and categorizing this information, and interpreting and presenting what they had learned in a variety of forms. Building on these preliminary understandings, Lois stretched her students during the Colonial biographies unit by designing work that required more independent and complex performances of understanding.

The Action: Teaching the Unit

Lois's curriculum design, like Eric's, includes a progression of performances from relatively unstructured exploration to structured investigations through which students develop the knowledge and skills to complete a more open-ended, independent, and synthetic culminating performance. This progression appears across the sequence of Lois's units and within the biography unit featured in this vignette.

Messing About

Lois introduced the generative topic of biography by asking her class, "What can biographies tell us about a period of history?" To capture students' interest and commitment to the endeavor, she asked them to choose a biography that reflected their own interests. Students' selections ranged from George Harrison to Benjamin Banneker. In discussions and brainstorming sessions that followed, Lois urged students to use instances from the specific lives they had read about to make informed guesses about the period in which the person lived.

Lois: Can you remember something your person did that was special to when he or she lived? Something you might not expect someone to do today?

Jim: Well, George Harrison painted his house psychedelic colors. Not too many people would do that now.

Lois: Why do you think he did that? Does that tell you anything about that time?

Jim: Well, people were trying to expand their minds and were interested in experimenting and trying new things. Like he also learned to play the sitar. People were curious about Eastern things—music and religion and stuff.

As the discussions progressed, Lois helped students link the specifics about the persons they had studied to more general themes, leading them to speculate about how single lives reflected universals of human behavior, characteristics of one time and place, and unique personal traits. The discussion helped students recognize that individuals are not completely free agents but are affected by the assumptions of their cultures. On the basis of students' discussion, Lois led the class in generating a list of questions that would guide understanding of both the person and the historical period in which he or she lived. Students came up with a variety of useful guiding questions:

- Why is this person remembered? Why are these people important?
- How did people become who they were?

- Did the people have to overcome any special obstacles or did they have advantages over other people?

Lois eventually formulated the students' list into a set of fourteen "questions to consider," which represented the unit-level understanding goals that guided further explorations of biography as a window onto the Colonial period (see Exhibit 5.4). Lois shared with students the role the questions would play in their work: "These questions will guide your research. In all your work, it should be obvious that you thought about them. After you read any source, go through this list and try to use the information from the source to form a tentative answer to the questions. Write about this in your Process Journal." The process journals served as a means for record keeping, self-reflection, and ongoing assessment.

Guided Inquiry

This initial open-ended inquiry set the stage for the subsequent group study of Colonial figures, focusing the general idea of biography as a vehicle for studying any historical period toward the specifics of the Colonial era. Lois's main understanding goal at this juncture was about influence: "I want my students to consider what factors contributed to enhancing or limiting someone's influence and to connect some of the actions of Colonial individuals to the present shape of our nation and to their own lives and choices, to understand the difference between being 'influential' and being 'good' or 'righteous.'"

Lois led an initial discussion centered on what being influential meant, and then opened the floor up for nominations of "Colonial people who were powerfully influential in giving our country the shape we see today." Informed by discussions at home, their previous research on the colonies, and general reference readings, students had no problem posing nominations: Paul Revere, George Washington, Betsy Ross, King George III, Thomas Paine, Ben Franklin. The fun, and students' understanding of influence, emerged when Lois asked the class to narrow the list to four individuals. Each nomination would have to be supported with convincing arguments. In lively debate students attempted to supply evidence that would convince their classmates. Eventually they winnowed the list to the requisite four.

Exhibit 5.4. Questions to Consider.

QUESTIONS TO CONSIDER

These questions will guide your research. In all your work (album, essay, annotated bibliography, presentation, study guide), it should be obvious that you thought about them.

The throughline numbers after each question suggest which of the yearlong questions each biography question might help you think about. After you read any source, go through this list and try to use the information from the source to form a tentative answer to the questions. Write about this in your process journal.

1. What attracts you to this person? (Throughline 8.)

2. A. What does this person's life show about the history and culture of the Colonial era of American history? (Throughlines 1, 2, 5.)

   B. What trends in Colonial history can we see through this person's life? (Throughlines 1, 2, 5, 6, 11.)

3. What does your person's life reveal about our present culture or your own life and values as an American? (Throughlines 1, 5, 6, 11.)

4. What does your person's life reveal about universal human nature? (Throughlines 4, 6, 11.)

5. Why is this person remembered in history? What did he or she do? (Throughlines 2, 3, 4, 6, 7, 8, 11.)

6. How did history select this person from the many people who lived at the time as someone worth remembering? (Throughlines 2, 4, 6.)

7. What advantages and disadvantages did your person have over others who lived at the time? (Throughlines 4, 11.)

8. What point of view, attitudes, and values did your person have? Be able to explain his or her biases. (Throughlines 1, 2, 3, 4, 6, 8.)

9. A. How did your person develop into the person he or she became? (Throughlines 6, 8.)

   B. Who, what, when, where, why, and how did your person live in his or her early and later life? (Throughlines 2, 5.)

   C. What important events shaped your person's attitudes and values? (Throughlines 2, 6.)

10. A. How does the individual's point of view compare or contrast to the attitudes and values of others in that time and place? Especially, compare him or her to the Founding Fathers we studied: Sam Adams, Ben Franklin, Thomas Jefferson, and George Washington. (Throughlines 1, 2, 3, 4, 6, 7, 8, 11.)

    B. How does the individual's point of view compare or contrast to your attitudes and values or those of other people who are alive today? (Throughlines 8, 11.)

Students formed collaborative groups to research each of these Founding Fathers. Lois distributed a performance guide, directing students to study multiple sources and perspectives to better reveal each of their subject's characteristics and contributions. Students identified sources of bias in their material and debated the role of viewpoint. Each group created an evolving visual display on bulletin boards and shared their developing findings through informal presentations to the class. Lois regularly asked the class to pause and synthesize the information they had gathered thus far in their process journals, directing students' attention from the individual they were studying to the period: "Based on the individual you're studying, what are you discovering about Colonial history?"

Following the alternating rounds of research and group presentations to the class, Lois asked students to "select specific facts from the presentations and guess what the period might have been like based on that information."

Di: Well, George Washington and Thomas Jefferson owned huge plantations, so the economy of the South might have been more farming. But if you look at Sam Adams or Ben Franklin, it seems like the North had more industry.

Max: Maybe that's really why the North and South fought in the Civil War?

Engaging in these understanding performances allowed students to develop a better understanding of the details of the period and of concepts such as viewpoint, influence, and the effects of culture while building up a repertoire of analytic skills and forms of expression. These performances both modeled and provided practice for students in the processes needed for the final phase of the unit.

Culminating Performance

The culminating assignment called for each student to select a Colonial personality and design a project to teach the rest of the class about that person's life. With criteria developed collaboratively with her class during the more informal group research project already described, Lois carefully detailed her expectations for this phase of students' work on an assessment sheet (see Exhibit 5.5).

Exhibit 5.5. Individual Biography Project Assessment Sheet.

INDIVIDUAL BIOGRAPHY PROJECT ASSESSMENT SHEET
Due April 4, 1994

Name: _____

Rate yourself from 1–10 (ten high) in each category and write a sentence explaining your rating.

	Student	Teacher

1. **Life Album** shows in-depth research of person, logical organization, demonstrates how individual lives help us understand history. Finished form, easy to learn from, aesthetic, creative design, makes interesting connections, uses questions to consider and throughlines, accurate list or explanation of life events, compares and contrasts individual's life and point of view to Founding Fathers' and student's own, includes visual and written materials, accurate information. Has all parts (see A, B, C).
Explanation:

A. **Study Guide for Life Album** identifies main points about person's life and the person's place in his or her culture and in history; lets students who read your album show whether they understand these.
Explanation:

B. **Annotated Bibliography** lists at least five sources (more is better) of the following types: primary document, reference, grade-level book, children's book, periodical. Bibliographic entry follows correct form. Entries are listed alphabetically by author's last name or encyclopedia article title. Annotation give strengths and weaknesses of source and compares it to other sources used.
Explanation:

C. **One-Page Essay** summarizes whether sources gave a complete and accurate portrait of the person's life, cites examples, uses essay form (introduction with opinions, body, conclusion), is neat, is mechanically accurate (spelling, capitalization, punctuation, sentence and paragraph structure).
Explanation:

2. **Oral Presentation** is easy to understand and learn from, obviously prepared, clearly projected, eye contact, states how individual's life connects to history, compares and contrasts individual's point of view to Founding Fathers' and student's own, evaluates various sources, describes process, and states main ideas of album.
Explanation:

3. **Process Folder** has notes in categories, handouts, drafts with peer and teacher comments, and this assessment sheet filled out by you. Most importantly, *Process Journal:* regular entries for three weeks, states evolving questions and conclusions, includes draft annotated bibliography, focuses on topic but describes actions too; might include sketches, plans.
Explanation:

4. **Deadlines:** turned in on April 4 or before, all parts included. *There will be no extensions for any reason whatsoever on this project.*
Explanation:

TOTAL:
COMMENTS:

The project required students to choose a Colonial figure and study how that person had been shaped by the cultural climate, how his or her life provides a window into that climate, and what effect he or she had on the world. Specifically, this culminating understanding performance required students to create text and illustrations about the selected figure in a *life album* with annotated bibliography, study guide, and oral presentation. To ensure that students continued to evaluate sources for bias and seek completeness of information on their topic, Lois required them to use at least five sources. Students were also asked to reflect on their product in a one-page summary essay of their research process supported by a *process folder* that included drafts, notes, handouts, and their process journal of ongoing reflections.

The questions to consider proved an effective tool for students as they worked. Because the questions emerged from the previously completed analysis of biography, students were clear about their meanings. From discussing these issues in relation to other figures, students knew that these were complicated questions on which people might disagree. Consequently, they did not expect to go to an encyclopedia or any one source and find answers. The questions to consider focused students' notes about what they had read on synthesis rather than the mechanistic accumulation of facts. Lois had labeled each Question to Consider with the throughlines it addressed so that students could make connections to the issues the class had dealt with throughout the year. For example, "What trends in Colonial history can we see through this person's life?" connected to throughline number two, "How do we find out the truth about things that happened long ago and/or far away?" and number six, "How do we discover central themes?"

Lois had made her goals clear on both her assignment and questions to consider sheets. In addition, the assessment sheet she provided combined standards the class had developed during the year by examining models of good work with the criteria derived from the earlier process of biographical analysis. All students worked to the same high standards. "These criteria remain the same, no matter the level of competence of the student," noted Lois. "They relate to the content of the curriculum." However, she provided differential levels of support as ongoing assessment revealed the strengths and needs of different students. Some students simply needed comments. Others needed multiple teacher-student conferences and specific suggestions for improving form and content.

The selection of a person to study, the variety of sources at their disposal, and their personal lines of inquiry shaped students' work. Kimba chose Mercy Otis Warren, Elizabeth chose Abigail Adams, and Derek chose Phillis Wheatley because each was interested in the roles of women during the period. Derek also said he selected Wheatley because she was a slave and a poet, both areas of particular interest to him.[3] Carmen's project on Paul Revere eventually took her to the Boston Museum of Fine Arts to learn about silversmithing, see Revere's silver products, and analyze the portrait of him by Copley. She also visited Revere's house in Boston's North End, interviewed a historical actor portraying him, and read about him in several works of fiction in addition to the primary and secondary sources required. Rick's research developed interests important to his family, who ran their own business and were active in politics; he chose John Hancock and focused on economics and its relation to political stance in the Revolutionary War. He looked at old maps to see where Hancock's wharf was located, causing him to wonder which parts of modern Boston were under water in Hancock's day and how Boston's business community related to Hancock's influence. Thus students' research led to connections with art, history, geography, economics, literature, and their personal concerns and interests.

As the projects developed, Lois assessed drafts, allowing her to evaluate and support students' abilities to formulate research plans and organize their projects. Students also met in groups to discuss their plans and receive critiques from peers, using the questions to consider and the assessment sheet as performance guides. At this point some students needed more guidance than others to shape and direct their work, but the review process benefited all the students by sharpening their focus early and allowing them to approach the task with greater independence. The process journals that Lois reviewed weekly provided another means for ongoing assessment. The journals allowed students to pose questions as they worked, to which Lois later responded. These questions not only elicited Lois's guidance but left a trail of students' thinking for her to follow in later assessment of the final product.

Ongoing assessment allowed Lois to tailor her attention to individual students while also providing information for adjusting her own instructional plans in response to more general needs of the class. Lois felt that part of the power of ongoing assessment lay in its ability to confer responsibility for the quality of students' work upon the students themselves. "In previous years, I have seen my students' responses to my assessments, and I didn't like it much. I spent hours writing comments. I think they paid attention, but I never got a sense that they used my suggestions to inform the next phase of their work. I suspect that they saw assessment as the end of the line." By providing clear expectations that students would reflect regularly and specifying how to do so, Lois sought to help students internalize the external criteria that the class had established.

The presentation of individual projects to the class, both through oral presentations and through reading each other's life albums, offered another opportunity for peer assessment. This process of sharing work was a dynamic portion of the instructional process; students read each album and responded to it on the accompanying study guides that the album's author had designed. The process came together through class discussions and reflections about the view of the Colonial period that emerged not only through the individual study of biography but in the group study. Every student had expertise on one figure from the period and exposure to the people studied by classmates. They all developed a general understanding of the historical period and gained different perspectives on it through biography.

Summary

This project developed students' understanding of the influence of figures from Colonial history and the viewpoints these individuals provide on the period. It directly related to Lois's understanding goals for both the unit and the year, and it incorporated performances by both groups and individual students. It fostered students' ownership by requiring them to choose their subject of study, depth by providing sufficient time to do research and explore ideas, and thoughtful interpretation by asking students to situate the individuals studied in the culture of the past while connecting them to current issues. The consistent presence of on-going and self-assessment helped students to internalize standards while shaping their current work and allowed Lois to respond to the needs of both individual students' and the class. The three phases of instruction carefully supported students' understanding and performances as they studied the generative topic of learning about history through research on individual biographies.

Analyzing TfU in Teachers' Practice

Teachers comprehend the Teaching for Understanding framework by interpreting it in relation to their own passions, the requirements of their curriculum and context, and the particular strengths and weaknesses of their own students. To understand the framework as a tool for designing curriculum, teachers must make sense of each framework element and relate these elements in a coherent way so that performances and assessments clearly advance the development of targeted understanding goals. To apply TfU elements and principles in the classroom, teachers must understand how to adapt their curriculum designs, considering students' evolving understandings and adjusting assignments to support and challenge both individual students and the class as a whole. Applying the Teaching for Understanding framework is an interactive process of considering the context, designing curriculum, and adjusting practice in response to students. The following analysis disentangles this fusion of moves to explore more fully the dimensions of teachers' dialogue relating the TfU framework to their practice.

The Backdrop: Artful Comprehension in Context

TfU encourages teachers to build on their passions, a powerful attraction for teachers that distinguishes TfU from standard curricular reform efforts.

Teachers' Passions

One teacher in the project expressed his enthusiasm for it by saying, "I use TfU to communicate who I am and what my priorities are, what I think schooling should be about." An administrator interested in school reform stated, "I want to make sure teachers know why they are teaching. TfU addresses this and cuts across all subject matters."

Lois's design of the throughlines was a powerful interpretation of the TfU framework's idea of understanding goals to express her priorities as a teacher.[4] She valued developing a spirit of inquiry in her students. Her teaching style routinely called on students to blend creativity, reflection, and knowledge from diverse perspectives to develop and demonstrate understanding. Rather than allowing herself to feel constrained by the framework, Lois used it as a springboard for her own ends. The throughlines reflected Lois's interdisciplinary focus, her desire to develop students' multiple intelligences, and her affective goals related to students' development as learners and citizens as well as her curricular goals. Lois used the throughlines to mobilize students' inquiry and connect the entire year's curriculum.

Eric had a passion for scientific inquiry and a fascination with the physical world that he wanted to share with his students. He wanted students to "think like scientists and create their own theories" rather than memorize information. He wanted students to look at the world differently and pose their own lines of inquiry. Much of the artistry in Eric's interpretation of TfU lies in his efforts to create a classroom climate that differed substantially from what his students expected.

Classroom Cultures

Teaching for Understanding is not simple or prescriptive. Teachers must incorporate into the process the unique situation of their schools, the climate of their classrooms, the dispositions and preparedness of their students, the demands of the curriculum, and their own understanding and expertise. Eric found that the mindset of his students made it a challenge to meet his overarching goal of getting students to think like scientists. He had to construct and support experiences that encouraged students' more active engagement in developing understanding. He found that for students to develop understanding, they also had to reconceptualize what it meant to do science. In addition his short class periods made it difficult for his students to conduct investigations.[5]

In his end-of-year reflections Eric commented on his success in creating an effective classroom climate: "Students entering my classes encounter a very different classroom culture. One that includes new types of performances, new standards for demonstrating and assessing understanding, and new roles for both the teacher and students. Learning to navigate this new terrain requires a significant effort." For Eric and many of his students, the TfU framework changed their perspectives on what it means to teach and learn science. One student provided a fitting contrapuntal response to Eric's early reticence about the appropriateness of the TfU framework to science by stating, "I think this kind of teaching is appropriate in science, but I can't see how it could work in social studies or English."

In contrast Lois had a more conducive situation and more teaching experience and expertise. This is reflected in her more thorough integration of TfU into the sequence of a yearlong cohesive progression, an additional form of artistry. When teachers move to this integration level, the TfU units occurring early in the year may have quite a different focus from later units. Early in the year curriculum units emphasize developing processes, skills, and habits of mind within the field of study. In later units students draw on this foundation and progress more rapidly into explorations of content.

In creating TfU classrooms, teachers work to share authority with students and to create a community of learners.[6] This is a gradual process that builds on trust and mutual respect nurtured over time. Eric incorporated students' ideas and interests and engaged them actively in the process of setting standards. Lois gave her students a great deal of choice and responsibility in selecting project topics and designing their inquiries. She also encouraged her students to take an active role in refining the throughlines. Throughout, teachers work toward becoming more explicit with their students about their overarching course goals. In doing so teachers chart the domain of study and become more open to alternative paths to reach those goals.

Behind the Scenes: Design Moves

Both Eric and Lois were well versed in their disciplines and felt passionate about them. Yet they worked initially from implicit goals, understandings, and beliefs that they struggled throughout the year to articulate explicitly.

Rethinking the Discipline

For Eric, part of the process of connecting his existing curriculum to more generative topics involved articulating what it means to engage authentically in doing science. Discussions with his research partner helped Eric formulate this idea. In the machine unit Eric linked these increasingly articulated concepts, methods, and modes of thinking in the discipline to subject matter content and made them the focus of motivated, purposeful inquiry in framing the generative topic. Lois did not fully articulate her overarching goals until her second year of working with TfU, after much reflection and consultation about the disciplines of English and history. Lois and Eric's experiences suggest that other teachers, especially those with less expertise in their disciplines, will have to struggle to move beyond narrow textbook conceptions of their subject matters.[7]

Some teachers found it effective to rely on collaboration with colleagues or the organization of the textbook to facilitate the task of reconceptualizing their subject matter in the process of uncovering generativity. Still others found it useful to focus initially on the accessibility component of generative topics. Joan, a writing teacher, chose the topic "place" because she felt it provided her students with an accessible anchor from which to situate and develop their writing. Only later did she address larger issues of the discipline. However, Teaching for Understanding eventually pushes for some level of disciplinary reorganization and clarification that cannot be abdicated to a textbook, curriculum framework, or assigned theme. All teachers in the project found it useful to examine their own priorities, beliefs, and understanding of their subject matter.

Supporting Structures

Teachers make use of a variety of structures, mechanisms, and devices to support TfU. Lois posted her throughlines and a time line of the year. Bill, the math teacher described in Chapter Four, hung a poster stating "Geometry is the study of lawfully connected patterns in the world" to communicate the conception of geometry guiding his teaching. Eric devised a model of theory building to share with students. These displays of teachers' priorities made the learning agenda public; parents as well as students could see, question, and enter into a dialogue about the instructional emphasis.

These visual displays of their missions also served as constant reminders to teachers.

Assessment sheets, questions to consider, and assignment sheets have all been used extensively by TfU teachers to convey the goals of a unit, to structure students' performances, and to clarify assessment criteria. As Lois has noted, these structures focus students on the substance rather than the glitz of performances. Both Eric and Lois also used some type of student journal: process journals, log books, and reflection journals. These served as vehicles to promote reflection and aid ongoing assessment. Through regular use, they provided a written record of students' evolving thinking. On the basis of journal entries Lois and Eric provided individual students with the feedback and direction they needed. Lois and other teachers also used portfolios of student work as a means of documenting students' progress and providing a basis for both the teacher and the student to plan further learning.[8]

The Action: Application and Integration Moves

Teachers who work with the TfU framework find that they must articulate subgoals within their overarching goals and engage students in a progression of performances to help them ramp up to increasingly sophisticated performances of understanding.

Sequencing Instruction

Both Lois's and Eric's teaching sequences moved from an informal framed exploration stage to guided inquiry at the group level to a culminating phase that supported synthesis and connections in an integrative and more independent performance. Embedded in this sequence, both within each unit and across the year, was a gradual decrease in the outward guidance and structure provided for students, increasing explicitness about what students were expected to do, and an expectation of greater student autonomy.

Open-endedness, self-direction, and choice characterized the introductory messing-about stage. All Lois's students engaged in the process of reading a biography, but she permitted students to choose their selection and invited students' open-ended interpretations of this assignment. During the guided inquiry phase, as students researched influential Colonial figures collaboratively, a tight interdependence existed among students and between students and teacher. Lois used coaching and didactic teaching to prepare students for more complex and independent performances. Eric and Lois used the technique of appropriation frequently; through appropriation, an expert reinterprets the novices' actions, ascribing to them both intent and skill while providing domain specific connections and vocabulary.[9] Lois extracted general principles and introduced disciplinary language and processes through open-ended, analytic brainstorming sessions that resulted in guiding questions. To Rob's and Lelia's actions, Eric ascribed the purposeful intent of theory building and testing, though it was not clear to the students that this was what they were doing. To Rob's idea about the length of sides having something to do with leverage, Eric ascribed the principle of ratio, thus providing students concepts with which to move forward.

Although research has shown this sequence to be particularly effective, Teaching for Understanding need not be limited to project-based learning. In other TfU classrooms teachers used more incremental sequences of performances to build more sophisticated levels of understanding gradually. Some teachers who focused on developing understanding of abstract concepts emphasized the initial development of mental images followed by engagement in understanding performances. In some classrooms students worked more independently, returning to the group for feedback and guidance at regular intervals. This was particularly true in English classes where teachers asked students to engage in independent reading and writing activities. In addition some teachers have found focused observation, homework assignments, and short written understanding performances to be effective and somewhat more manageable forms of ongoing assessment.

Centering on Understanding

Central to TfU is maintaining the focus on understanding goals during this process so that the project does not become an end in itself. Lois and Eric always returned students' attention to their understandings rather than focusing on the logistics of the product. For example, Lois designed her understanding performance during the guided inquiry phase about the Founding Fathers so that the products themselves, students' bulletin board displays and presentations, would be teaching vehicles to develop greater understanding for the entire class.

Centering teaching on understanding calls for an ongoing dialogue with students in which teachers make their priorities and expectations clear, but all teachers in the project struggled with or resisted setting understanding goals. Lois initially felt that setting goals would limit students' inquiry and stagnate her teaching. Other teachers equated them with the textbook's objectives or worried about setting the right goals. Seeing the goals as flexible and evolving is helpful. Lois's conception of them as signposts that marked a direction rather than objectives to check off was a powerful realization for her. Her throughlines sparked a conversation that lasted throughout the year. Eric set the agenda with a few well-articulated understanding goals. He laid out his goals early in the unit in written form. Although students were initially confused by unfamiliar terms, the goals served as a reference point. Other teachers found it helpful to list specific goals on assignment sheets or to post them in the room for reference. Conversations about the meaning of goals and understanding are an important component of Teaching for Understanding.

Summary and Conclusions

The TfU framework offers guidance but makes many demands on teachers' knowledge and time in designing curriculum and pedagogy. Rather than dictating an outsider's set of procedures, the framework is an empowering instrument that allows teachers to address their own needs in designing curriculum while encouraging students to take control of their learning. Teachers consistently report that Teaching for Understanding is hard work but that the framework has "transformed my classroom," that they "are getting much more from kids," and that their classroom is "an exciting place to go." As one teacher expressed it after a year of wrestling with framework, "I'm exhausted. But the beauty is, once you've done all this, the class runs itself!"

Teaching for Understanding is neither a prescriptive nor a linear process. It is a subtle process requiring continual attention, support, and iteration. Teachers initiate work from their passions, interests, needs, and goals. They gradually integrate the framework with their practice through cycles of designing curriculum, engaging students in performances of understanding, assessing those performances, and planning curriculum in response to students' progress and problems. As teachers make their goals and assessment criteria explicit and public, students and other members of the school community join a dialogue to further clarify and refine understanding goals. As students engage in performances, teachers perceive more effective ways to support students and to refine assignments so that students increasingly devote their efforts to understanding, rather than to rote or trivial work. More information about students' responses to this kind of teaching may be found in Chapters Six through Nine.

The two teachers featured in this chapter were especially committed and able interpreters of the Teaching for Understanding framework who learned quickly how to integrate this approach into their classrooms. Although many other teachers have moved toward the kind of practices that Eric and Lois demonstrate, Eric's and Lois's stories raise questions about how teachers can be prepared and supported to teach for understanding. In Chapter Ten Vito Perrone addresses the process of preparing novice teachers. Alternative approaches to creating supportive contexts in schools are described in Chapter Eleven.

Part Three

Students' Understanding in the Classroom

Chapter Six

What Are the Qualities of Understanding?

Veronica Boix Mansilla
Howard Gardner

In Teaching for Understanding (TfU) classrooms students are invited to put their understanding into action. Their performances allow teachers to assess and orient their progress toward achieving understanding goals. As teachers confronted the challenge of assessing their students' work, we recognized the need for a more specific definition of understanding. What does it mean to understand a historical event in depth? What qualities of understanding can teachers expect from students who are investigating a natural phenomenon? In their questions we saw the need for more detailed guidance to assess students' understanding. Together we engaged in the process of developing a theoretically grounded yet practical conception of students' understanding within and across disciplines. We pondered the question, "What qualities are embodied in deep understanding?"

The authors would like to thank Rosario Jaramillo and Daniel Gray Wilson for their thoughtful contributions throughout the elaboration and testing of the Understanding framework, and Chris Unger, Lois Hetland, and Karen Hammerness for their comments on earlier versions of this chapter. We would also like to thank Theodore Sizer, whose inspiration and challenging critiques have helped us sharpen our views of disciplinary understanding.

In a climate of educational reform, debates around national standards, and cries to go back to the basics, multiple definitions of understanding live side by side. Some educators value the sophistication embodied in higher-order calculus operations; others stress the practical use of math to solve a problem of urban traffic. Some emphasize detail and precision in an account of the civil rights movement; others favor a critical analysis of the contrasting perspectives from which a story about the time may be told. Such different accents reflect the diverse interest groups in societies, the ways people interpret the world in which they live, and their diverse assumptions about the enculturation of youngsters.[1]

Despite such differences in emphasis, most educators hope that qualities such as disciplinary accuracy, social relevance, and critical spirit will indeed be embodied in students' performances. Presupposing such consensual goals, the TfU project has developed an Understanding framework to assess students' work and orient their development. This framework features four dimensions and four levels of understanding that can be discerned in students' performances. The main goal of this chapter is to introduce this reflective tool. To do so, we focus on two topics and ideal performances of understanding. Then we propose the Understanding framework as a tool to systematize the assessment of these exemplary performances. In the end we highlight some of the challenges that teachers may face in their efforts to use the framework in their classrooms.

Examining Students' Understanding

The quality of students' understanding rests on their ability to master and use bodies of knowledge that are valued by their culture. More specifically, it rests on their ability to make productive use of the concepts, theories, narratives, and procedures available in such disparate domains as biology, history, and the arts. Students should be able to understand the humanly constructed nature of this knowledge and to draw on it to solve problems, create products, make decisions, and in the end transform the world around them. Put differently, students should use knowledge to engage in a repertoire of performances valued by the societies in which they live.

Students may perform their understanding in areas such as trade, sports, or the arts as well as in more scholarly disciplines such as history, math, and science. Education in the former domains has historically focused on learners' performances (such as producing a piece of furniture, swimming a race, singing a song). In contrast, education in the disciplines has tended to emphasize accumulation of information in the student's mind. Drawing on the model that has long been favored in the crafts, our work supports its development in more scholarly domains. In light of the specific challenge educators face in reconceptualizing understanding in the disciplines, analysis in this chapter focuses on one example in history (U.S. industrialization in the nineteenth century) and one in science (genetic damage and cell growth). To illustrate such analysis we have created composite examples that bring together several students' most accomplished performances in TfU classrooms. Each composite was designed to represent the various dimensions of understanding portrayed in the Understanding framework and is occasionally enriched with features of performances portrayed in the developmental literature.

Understanding in History

Consider this example: the industrialization process that took place in the United States during the last half of the nineteenth century, transforming the modes of production and distribution of goods.

The Industrial Revolution: Disciplinary Background

Modern concepts of progress can be traced in part to the striking changes in transportation, manufacture, and communication brought about by the Industrial Revolution. This tumultuous process inspired abundant and often conflicting accounts of the period. Some authorities emphasize labor movements and working conditions; some highlight technological and macroeconomic growth; still others focus on the ideology underlying people's work ethics. These historical narratives also vary in their overall assessment of the development of industrial societies. Some portray it as a process of growth and progress; others characterize it in terms of long-term improvement of standards of living; still others construe it as a process of severe deprivation and profound social costs. In all cases historians' accounts of industrialization render homage to the complexity of this process. Usually they avoid linear or stereotyped representations and highlight continuities as well as changes over time.[2]

Knowledge about industrialization emerges from careful interpretations of texts and documents that remain from the period, levered by accounts or interpretations proposed by other disciplinarians in more recent times. Narratives about industrialization go beyond describing specific events (such as strikes, migrations, or policies); they explain them by scrutinizing people's worldviews and motivations for their actions. Such explanations would be incomplete if they disregarded the broader social and economic conditions that shaped and constrained these people's actions at the time. In most cases the richness of these explanations emerges from taking into account contrasting perspectives on the problem—for example, those of the industrialists and those of immigrant workers.

In the discipline of history, narratives organize and give meaning to isolated information about the past. They propose interpretive theses that lend coherence to events. For instance, factual information such as the tripling of American per capita income between 1870 and 1910 or the details of unhealthy working conditions are devoid of significance if detached from the broader theses they support—that industrialization resulted in a higher concentration of wealth toward the end of the century in the United States or that the country's leading role in the world economy in the early twentieth century was in part due to its macroeconomic growth. Conversely, these theses would not cohere without the examples that back them up.[3]

Accounts of industrialization vary not only in the way their authors go about investigating or interpreting the past but also in the purposes they serve. Some accounts aim to convince readers that values and worldviews such as class consciousness, for example, are shaped (or determined) by the social and economic circumstances in which people live, such as unemployment and economic recession in 1883. Another argument aims to orient individuals' behavior by highlighting the transformative power of a few industrial leaders at the time, portraying their attitudes, visions, and commitment as those of exemplary human beings. Historical accounts of one or another type do more than tell a story about the past;

they help individuals reinterpret their present and orient their future. Understanding these accounts in depth entails grasping their functional or pragmatic dimension as well.

Introducing Maria: A Portrait of Developing Understanding

Imagine a ninth-grade student, Maria. During a unit on industrialization, she carried out a project in which she studied the biography of a captain of industry, George Pullman. Her inquiry was motivated by a question of interest to her: "How does someone get to be an industrial leader?" Our imaginary student examined the personalities and visions of some captains of industry. In addition her class studied multiple aspects of the rapidly changing society, such as migration patterns, technological improvements, working conditions, and productivity. In her final essay Maria focused on the social, political, and economic conditions that led to the need for a strong and determined innovator. The following excerpt portrays Maria's understanding in her project.[4]

> You see, the books I read were making Pullman look like he was Mr. Perfect, like he never made mistakes. Only one book was different, because it was about the big [Pullman] strike. . . . You just couldn't believe these stories. When I was reading I thought that maybe writers write these books because they need some gods, some models to look up to. Maybe they want you to believe that the industrial leaders were great people, and expect you to respect all leaders.

> But I think you really needed to look at what was happening then to understand how somebody like Pullman got to be so important. . . . There were a lot of changes going on, a lot of new things started to happen, like the railroad and the factories with machines. You know, a lot of people thought that kind of a miracle was happening because of all these inventions and all the changes. But they were confused too. The cities were growing, life was fast, business was getting bigger. If somebody owned a little store, they could turn it into a factory or a big department store! They could send the stuff they made all over the country with the new railroads. People were getting excited and open minded. But not everything was so great! If you went to a factory at the time you wouldn't believe it. They were filthy; little kids had to work more than ten hours a day. It was really hot and the machines were dangerous! Farmers or people who made crafts or things had to move into the city slums. They had to work twelve hours a day just to survive.

I saw a book that had some pictures of real labor union pamphlets in it. The pamphlets showed and talked about how bad the factories were for the workers. The point of the essay I wrote is that Pullman was very successful when he started partly because he was generous. But mostly because he came up with the idea of the factory town when many people were looking for jobs and people were willing to try something new. It was also a time when people were very needed to work in the factories. Later, when the recession began to hit, business owners like him had to cut wages and fire a lot of people. The workers began to change their minds. They felt more united as workers and they organized the big Pullman strike in 1886 to force Pullman to cut their workday to eight hours. That was the beginning of the end of Pullman.

The Qualities of Maria's Understanding

Maria demonstrates important qualities of understanding. She has moved beyond stereotypical views of industrialization as a time of linear progress led by a few captains of industry that is usually perceived as the only leading force transforming American society. Instead, her account balances progress and conflict in ways that resemble a disciplinarian's practice. Maria demonstrates her ability to place individual facts, such as the creation of the factory town, within the broader framework of economic and lifestyle changes at the time. She is able to move flexibly between concrete examples (for instance, shop owners' and artisans' contrasting experiences) and broader, more conceptual interpretations (for example, industrialization as a complex process affecting different people in different ways).

By describing Pullman's success and failure, Maria demonstrates her ability to grasp continuities and changes over time—a central feature of historical inquiry. Furthermore, she demonstrates her ability to build historical explanations that involve human intentionality, such as people's openness to innovation and workers' growing class consciousness. Her explanation also involve broader related socioeconomic conditions, such as unemployment and economic recession. Maria enriches her account by considering multiple perspectives of the time, such as those of tradesmen, farmers, and artisans, although she does not recognize individual differences among people within these social groups. Her reference to pamphlets as sources of reliable evidence for her claims completes our picture of Maria as a student who has begun to understand how historical knowledge is built and validated.

Finally, it is worth noting that Maria appreciates that historical accounts are written with a purpose in mind—to create social myths, to validate certain social groups. She sees herself as writing an account of the past that conveys a message as well, that is, that individual actions like the creation of the Pullman town need to be seen in the broader context of the circumstances in which they occur.

Understanding in Science

Now consider a second story, this one drawn from the biological sciences.

Understanding Genetic Damage: Disciplinary Background

Genetic damage refers to the alteration of the information-carrying deoxyribonucleic acid in cells' genes. Such alterations can be caused by chemicals contained in drugs and food and by other environmental factors such as ultraviolet (UV) light or other forms of radiation. Some mutations are inconsequential, but others modify the cells' shape, metabolism, or growth cycle. Because the genetic information is altered, mutations also affect subsequent generations of the damaged cells.

Understanding genetic damage entails understanding that genetic information encodes enzymes that control most aspects of cell growth. In complex organisms, cells grow while in constant communication with other cells and their environment. Healthy cells maintain a very delicate balance between growing and ceasing growth. During finely tuned cycles of growth, new cells develop increasingly specialized functions, culminating in the formation of the mature tissues of an organism. In some cases a cell's genes are damaged in a way that causes uncontrolled cell growth, frequently resulting in a tumor. Because this phenomenon has been tied to cancer among adults and malformation in unborn infants, understanding the mechanisms of cellular growth under conditions of genetic damage has become a priority for biological researchers.

A central premise underlying the construction of scientific knowledge is that models and theories about phenomena such as genetic damage or cell growth are constructed and stand in relation to bodies of empirical evidence. Relatedly, scientific facts (for example, alteration of growth balance in a particular cell) stand in relation to, and are organized and interpreted by, one or more theories. In their attempts to explain the mechanisms of cell growth and genetic damage, scientists develop models of growth and damage that are validated by standards of adaptability, stability, and internal consistency—that is, whether these models account for phenomena in the world, maintain their structure in the face or persistent testing, and avoid contradictory assertions.

Scientific models or theories emerge throughout a process that entails generating hypotheses, testing them experimentally, and interpreting findings. They provide the basis to interpret new information, and reciprocally, new information is examined in order to test and revise these theories.[5]

Once sufficiently tested, models are often communicated in the form of diagrams that highlight particular structural and functional features of a process like genetic damage or cell growth. These diagrams convey powerful qualitative descriptions of the phenomenon. In contrast, changing patterns of growth are typically represented by graphs that summarize quantitative information about the process.

Introducing Charlotte and Andrew: A Portrait of Developing Understanding

Let us now introduce two other exemplary performances of understandings, those of ninth-graders Charlotte and Andrew. Imagine that their teacher detected their strong motivation to explore genetic damage and invited them to design an experiment to test the hypothesis that UV light causes cell mutation. In the following dialogue they discuss the design of an experiment to test the effects of UV light from the sun on living yeast cells.[6]

Charlotte: Let me see if we have the model right: when cells are mutated for some reason—radiation or chemicals or something like that—the genetic information in some of the cells gets damaged. So when these mutated cells reproduce, the new cells have features that the old healthy cells didn't have. Okay?

Andrew: Yeah. . . . But we wanna test something else. . . . Whether UV light makes mutations in our yeast cells.

Charlotte: Yeah, sure. The thing is that we gotta have a picture in our head to see what we can get—see?—to imagine what results we're gonna get. Let's say we give a lot of sun to this group of cells here, and let them grow colonies. We'll have to keep some cells in the dark too. So if the sun affects the genetic information, the cells in the colonies have to be different in some way from our controls in the dark. You know.

Andrew: So . . . if the light mutates some cells the colonies will get red, like we saw in the experiment on food preservatives. Remember?

Charlotte: You're right!

Andrew: You know, I'm thinking when we write the report for this whole thing someone may ask how we really know that the light was making a difference and that it wasn't just coincidence or another thing.

Charlotte: Hmm . . .

Andrew: Guess we've got to be careful and control all the variables . . . temperature, number of cells, the cells we pick and stuff.

Charlotte: We can also try different timing. Like we give different amounts of UV light time. So when we expose the colonies longer they should get more red than . . .

Andrew: I see . . . than the cells that are under the light just a little bit. We can make a two-entry chart. We can put "time under UV light" on one side and "number of red colonies" on the other.

Charlotte: Or maybe one of those curves would help! I'll make the graph when we're done.

Andrew: The other thing we can say in our report is that scientists study this not only because they want to know more about cells and how they get damaged, but also because they know that this is connected to cancer.

Charlotte: So, maybe we can find some of that and put in some piece about taking care of your skin and not letting UV light damage it too much!

The Qualities of Charlotte's and Andrew's Understanding

The dialogue just recounted reveals clear qualities of understanding. Both students demonstrate their ability to use a rich mental model of genetic damage. They describe some of the mechanisms involved in cell damage on the basis of which they are able to predict the effect of exposure to UV light. Although simple, their model of genetic damage mirrors those currently accepted in the discipline.

These students question their hunches with healthy skepticism and use methods of scientific inquiry such as variable control and experimental design to build warranted knowledge about mutation in yeast. Furthermore, they go beyond intuitive or *unschooled* inductivist-empiricist epistemologies of science, where knowledge is built through direct observation of the world. Instead, the students approach their empirical observations through the lens of a model of cell damage that will shape their interpretation of what they see. Collecting and classifying data is not a mechanical endeavor, nor is building hypotheses a matter of producing isolated guesses detached from the theories that organize their thinking.[7] Charlotte and Andrew's understanding goes beyond the algorithmic conception of the scientific method that dominates traditional science education.[8]

Charlotte and Andrew are attentive to the fact that scientific knowledge is made public and needs to convince its various audiences. Andrew puts himself in his readers' position and anticipates their skeptical concerns. The students reflect about distinctive ways to summarize their results. Furthermore, although they still draw unfounded implications from their limited experimental results to complex problems like cancer and skin care, these students are able to grasp the scientific and social relevance of studies in genetic damage (that is, to explain the mechanisms of damage and ultimately to contribute in part to the broader enterprise of preventing cancer and birth defects). They begin to understand science as a purposeful human endeavor.

Systematizing Qualities of Understanding

The composite performances of understanding just portrayed reveal sophisticated understandings. In each case the examples respond to distinct disciplinary endeavors: in history, interpretive inquiry and reliance on remnants of the past and primary sources; in science, experimental research and reliance on direct observation of highly controlled phenomena. Although bearing distinctive disciplinary traces, these performances also share some common patterns: students use a rich, detailed, and organized knowledge base; they draw on the methods and conventions of the disciplines to build and validate what they know; they attend to the social, scientific, or medical relevance of what they learn; and they care about the ways in which knowledge is shared with others. How can these qualities be systematized in a way that honors their disciplinary specificity but generates a language to talk about understanding across domains?

The Origins of a Framework

Identifying qualities of good understanding is not a new undertaking. Over time, disciplines like psychology and epistemology have sought to define such qualities in systematic ways. In a parallel fashion, communities of practitioners in disciplines, trades, and professions define and progressively refine the standards of quality for their products and practices. In so doing, these communities define the understanding that is available in a society at a given time. Capitalizing on this expertise, the Understanding framework introduced in this chapter has its roots in four principal sets of authorities.

First, disciplinary experts such as historians and biologists contributed detailed accounts of generative topics, such as, "Did industrialization mean progress?" and "How do cells grow?" Their work provided exemplary cases of rich, accurate, and organized knowledge bases and proficient use of forms of communication.

Second, philosophers of the disciplines, such as Thomas Kuhn and Joseph Schwab in science and David Carr, Jacques LeGoff, and Paul Ricoeur in history,[9] enriched understanding of the processes of inquiry in these domains—for example, designing experiments, controlling variables, and interpreting empirical evidence, as well as defining significant historical events, avoiding anachronism, and writing narratives that account for continuity and change in time. Their work underscores the role of healthy skepticism and methods in building warranted understanding.

Third, philosophers interested in knowledge more broadly, such as Jurgen Habermas and Agnes Heller,[10] and those specifically interested in curriculum, such as John Dewey, Paul Hirst, Philip Phenix, and (again) Joseph Schwab, informed our understanding of the organization of knowledge in various domains and the relationship between disciplinary knowledge and everyday life.[11] In most of these cases scholars emphasize the possible uses and limitations of knowledge for solving problems, making decisions, and reinterpreting and transforming the world and highlight the intentional and interest-driven nature of inquiry. Their work enriched the conception of understanding as a performance capacity.

Fourth, cognitive and developmental psychologists, such as Mario Carretero, Peter Lee, Peter Seixas, and Samuel Wineburg[12] in history and Susan Carey, Lawrence Kohlberg, and William Perry[13] in other domains informed our work by defining the obstacles and possibilities that students face when moving from unschooled toward *disciplinary* understanding.[14] Their studies were particularly relevant in formulating different levels of understanding.

The review of these sources allowed us to outline an initial conceptual portrait of qualities of understanding that we tested and enriched with an analysis of thirty-five students' reflections about understanding in four domains: English, math, science, and history. Our team of teachers and researchers assessed a series of students' videotaped reflections, identifying qualities of understanding that they valued, using some of the conceptual qualities originally portrayed, and reshaping them to accommodate the qualities emerging from the students' work. The TfU Understanding framework emerged as a result of this systematic dialogue between theory and data.

Four Dimensions of Understanding

To portray qualities of understanding systematically—in ways that are both respectful of disciplinary specificities and valid across domains—the Understanding framework highlights four dimensions of understanding: *knowledge, methods, purposes,* and *forms*. Within each dimension the framework describes four levels of understanding: *naive, novice, apprentice,* and *master*.

Knowledge

The knowledge dimension assesses the extent to which students have transcended intuitive or unschooled perspectives and the degree to which they can move flexibly between examples and generalizations in a coherent and rich conceptual web.

Early in life students build powerful theories about matter, about society, and about themselves. Though imaginative, these theories often conflict with the versions worked out over the centuries by knowledgeable people in domains like history, science, and the arts. Unschooled beliefs are robust even after years of schooling. In some cases they remain part of commonsense understanding of the world[15]—an understanding that is typically oriented to the practical, tied to the immediacy of the experience, local, egocentric, and validated by virtue of belonging to the generic collection of assumptions that a culture shares as "obvious."[16] Refining, transforming, or replacing these early intuitions is a central challenge students face when they aim at understanding the world around them in depth.

For example, in talking about industrialization, students like Maria naturally perceive the twelve-hour workdays, low wages, and poor conditions as unfair or inhumane. Because it resonates with experience in current postindustrial societies, few would question or problematize this commonsensical claim. However, to be more historically sound, a disciplinary revision describes the degree to which workers themselves envisioned their working conditions as inhumane and how their perceptions changed over time. Such a disciplinary approach considers the details of the workers' experience and places them in a broader interpretation of the period.

In the examples of students' performances Maria goes beyond oversimplified portraits of industrialization, moving flexibly among a variety of human experiences such as those of factory workers and farmers. She provides vivid examples to support a more general thesis that the impact of industrialization varied by social group. Similarly, in the science example Charlotte reviews her understanding of the process and phases of genetic damage prior to engaging in experimental design. In her review, concepts like mutation, genetic information, and cell reproduction are integrated in a flexible system that will orient her interpretation of results.

Summary of Knowledge Dimension Criteria

Transformed intuitive beliefs. To what degree do students' performances show that warranted theories and concepts in the domain have transformed their intuitive beliefs?

Coherent and rich conceptual webs. To what degree can students reason within richly organized conceptual webs moving flexibly between details and overviews, examples and generalizations?

Methods

The methods dimension recognizes that knowledge about the past, about nature or about society, contrasts with commonsense beliefs or mere information in that it is not readily available in the world to be picked up naturally and simply stored in individuals' minds. Knowledge results rather from a careful process of inquiry according to criteria that are publicly debated among communities of knowledgeable people in specific domains. Specifically, the methods dimension assesses students' ability to entertain healthy skepticism about what they know or what they are told as well as their use of reliable methods for building and validating claims and works as true, morally acceptable, or aesthetically valuable.

Over the years experts in various domains have developed methods and procedures that were tailored to build understanding of the specific kinds of phenomena they addressed. Like findings and theories, methods and validation criteria are publicly debated and agreed upon. They constitute individuals' most valid tools to build an understanding that goes beyond immediate and idiosyncratic experience and common sense. Understanding the foundations on which knowledge is constructed allows students to see why, amidst the infinite variety of accounts of problems like industrialization or genetic inheritance, only some are selected as fruitful, valid, and promising by knowledgeable people immersed in these issues.[17]

Experts in domain-specific cognitive development have documented the distinctive challenges students face in their attempts to grasp methods, procedures, and criteria to build knowledge in different domains. In science, for example, students often tend to equate experiments with recipe-like procedures that are followed to attain a certain result. When confronted with contrary evidence, students often deny it, holding on to their initial beliefs. The challenge these students face is to understand the logic of hypothesis testing that governs experimental design. They need to understand that experimental design is driven by theories about the phenomena they address and that experiments are designed to test whether their hypotheses are correct, not to prove that they are.

In contrast to biological phenomena, historical processes cannot be studied through experimentation and variable control. Understanding in history involves on one hand reconstructing people's motives and beliefs in a world that was different from ours but bears some resemblance to it and on the other hand reconstructing the institutions, social structures, and cultural practices in which they lived that defined the range of opportunities and constraints that guided, limited, and inspired their actions.[18] Understanding historical actors entails grasping the nuances in their beliefs, their internal contradictions, and the possible tensions between people and their contexts. This quality of understanding has proven to be a challenge for students, who often fall into the temptation of rendering past actions ludicrous or incomprehensible by projecting present values and worldviews on them.[19]

Accounts of industrialization or genetic inheritance are not "what really happened or happens" but rather people's current understanding of what is thought to have happened on the basis of specific modes of historical and biological inquiry. Accordingly, we claim that such topics cannot be detached from the modes of thinking and inquiry from which they emerge. Charlotte's and Andrew's understanding of genetic damage is deeply rooted in a process of experimental inquiry. They engage in such a process by designing experiments that involve hypothesis testing, control of variables, careful observation, and interpretation of results. They engage in a dialogue between theory and data whereby both the theory and the data are scrutinized and refined. Maria's performance embodies methods and procedures that are typically used in building historical knowledge, such as considering multiple perspectives on an event, building explanations that consider multiple causes, and identifying continuities and changes within a single process over time. In both cases rather than perceiving knowledge as unquestionable, easy-to-obtain information recorded in textbooks, students construct and validate trustworthy accounts.

Summary of the Methods Dimension

Healthy skepticism. To what degree do students display a healthy skepticism toward their own beliefs and the knowledge presented in sources such as textbooks, people's opinions, and messages in the media?

Building knowledge in the domain. To what degree do students use strategies, methods, techniques, and procedures to build reliable knowledge similar to those used by professional practitioners in the domain?

Validating knowledge in the domain. Are truth, good, and beauty dependent on authoritative assertions or rather on publicly agreed-upon criteria such as using systematic methods, providing rational arguments, weaving coherent explanations, or negotiating meanings through careful dialogue?

Purposes

The purposes dimension is grounded on the conviction that knowledge is a tool to explain, reinterpret, and operate on the world. This dimension assesses students' ability to recognize the purposes and interests that drive knowledge construction, their ability to use knowledge in multiple situations, and the consequences of doing so.

Knowledge in history and science, as well as in filmmaking or architecture, emerges from a dialectical relationship between human concerns and needs on the one hand and the bodies of knowledge and tools that are available to a society on the other. Far from being abstract formulations of unquestionable truths, knowledge in various domains emerges from essential questions about the world that are grounded on experience in everyday life (for example, Why do people get cancer, and how can it be prevented? How and why did the United States become a leading nation?). Inspired by these questions and interests, knowledge evolves through a process of reflection that satisfies publicly agreed-upon standards of validation. Completing a dialectic cycle, knowledge comes back to everyday life in the form of warranted frameworks or conceptual tools that people use to reinterpret and transform their world.[20] By exploring the essential questions that drive knowledge construction, teachers and students can reflect about the reasons why certain topics are worth studying in schools.

Accounts of U.S. industrialization, for instance, satisfy individuals' essential need to understand other people's lives and understand themselves. Where do city lifestyles come from? How have people dealt with rapid technological changes? Disciplinary answers to these questions respond to specific interests. Some explain the relationship between economic and population growth in a search for patterns that people may find in the future; others expand individuals' consciousness and experience by examining the increasing ambivalence women workers felt regarding child labor; still others focus on immigrants, women, or people of color in order to illuminate and legitimize previously silenced voices of the past, thus alerting people about important conflicts in societies today (such as gender, race, and labor).[21] In our examples Maria demonstrates her understanding of the Pullman biographies when she uncovers purposes underlying the idealized portraits of Pullman that she found: fostering a society's identity or validating a social group's authority. Charlotte and Andrew show their ability to relate their research on UV light and cell damage to broader social concerns about cancer that motivate scientific inquiry and are part of everyday life and the media.

When understanding ceases to be information accumulated in the students' mind and becomes a charter for action, new aspects of understanding need to be taken into account. For example, educators need to consider students' ability to find occasions to put knowledge into play and their critical assessment of the consequences of doing so. Students like Charlotte and Andrew may spontaneously critique a local newspaper's article on cancer by noticing that claims about causes for cancer are weakly grounded in correlational studies. Students like Maria may spontaneously use their understanding of working conditions among workers in the past to address issues of human rights in modern societies. Once students show the ability to engage spontaneously in these kinds of performances beyond the classroom environment, they demonstrate ownership over their understanding.

Summary of the Purposes Dimension

Awareness of the purposes of knowledge. To what degree do students see essential questions, purposes, and interests that drive inquiry in the domain?

Multiple uses of knowledge. To what degree do students recognize a variety of possible uses for what they learn?

To what degree do students consider the consequences of using this knowledge?

Ownership and autonomy. To what degree do students evidence ownership and autonomy to use what they know?

To what degree have students developed a personal position about what they learn?

Forms

Finally, a performance view of understanding pays special attention to the forms in which understanding is performed—the process by which it is communicated to others. The forms dimension assesses students' use of symbol systems (visual, verbal, mathematical, and bodily kinesthetic, for example) to express what they know within established genres or types of performances—for example, writing essays, performing a musical, giving a presentation, or explaining an algorithm. Because of its communicative nature, this dimension also emphasizes students' ability to consider audience and context as shaping forces in their performances.

Making knowledge public (as required by performances of understanding) necessarily involves the use of a language or symbol system.[22] The quality of a performance is determined in part by the effectiveness with which students use such symbols; for example, spatial arrangements of the elements in a cell that are relevant for its functioning call for graphic representations. Typically, models of cell growth are depicted in diagrams that require abstract representations of its mechanism. Using visual symbols this way is a challenge for students who tend to spontaneously depict elements in the cell as they appear under the microscope.[23]

Students' understanding is manifest in a variety of performances, such as writing an essay, giving a presentation, creating a song, or participating in a conversation. Each type or genre of performance requires that students use what they know according to the rules and criteria that govern that particular genre[24]—oral presentations need to be clearly enunciated, well organized, and smoothly paced; songs need to combine musical composition with lyrics in aesthetically appealing ways.

Finally, performing understanding for others requires that students take into account their audiences and contexts. Young or novice students' performances often contrast with those of masters in a domain because they communicate in egocentric ways, showing little flexibility to perceive and accommodate to different audiences. For example, students are often unaware of the degree to which their audience is or is not familiar with their topic and of social or ethnic backgrounds that will filter audience interpretation.

In our examples Charlotte and Andrew are planning to share their findings with a critical audience. They foresee critiques and address them in their work, and they select the modes of representation that suit the data to be presented: schematic graphs to illustrate their observations qualitatively, histograms and distributions to portray change over time. Because Maria's excerpt does not refer to the challenges she will face in writing a good story about industrialization or communicating her interpretations of the period to an audience, little inference can be made about the quality of the form dimension of her understanding.

Summary of the Forms Dimension

Mastery of performance genres. To what degree do students display mastery of the genres of performances they engage in, such as writing reports, giving presentations, or preparing the stage for a play?

Effective use of symbol systems. To what degree do students explore different symbol systems effectively and creatively to represent their knowledge—for example, using analogies and metaphors, colors and shapes, or movements?

Consideration of audience and context. To what degree do students' performances show an awareness of their audience—that is, the audience's interests, needs, cultural backgrounds, or expertise?
To what degree do they show awareness of the situation in which communication happens?

Four Levels of Understanding

The four dimensions illustrate the multidimensional nature of understanding. Whereas some dimensions may be more prominent than others in specific performances, deep understanding entails the ability to use knowledge in all the dimensions. Because the depth of understanding may vary within each dimension, distinguishing weaker from more accomplished performances is necessary. It was with this goal in mind that we characterized the four prototypical levels of understanding per dimension: naive, novice, apprentice, and master.

Performances of *naive understanding* are grounded on intuitive knowledge. They portray knowledge construction as an unproblematic process of grasping information that is directly available in the world. In these performances students do not see the relationship between what they learn in school and their everyday lives; they do not consider the purposes and uses of knowledge construction. At this level performances show no signs of students' ownership of what they know. Performances of naive understanding are unreflective about the ways that knowledge is expressed or communicated to others.

Let us revisit our industrialization example to illustrate. Students' performances at a naive level tend to report imaginative[25] but incorrect accounts of the process. The grounds and origins of such accounts remain unquestioned. Any reference to the significance of industrialization will seem irrelevant to students at this level; their narratives are likely to be incoherent or egocentric.

Performances of *novice understanding* are predominantly grounded on the rituals and mechanisms of testing and schooling. These performances begin to interject some disciplinary concepts or ideas and to establish simple, often rehearsed connections among them. They portray the nature and purposes of knowledge construction as well as its forms of expression and communication as step-by-step mechanistic procedures. The validation of these procedures depends on external authority rather than on rationally agreed-upon criteria developed within disciplines or domains.

At this level a story about industrialization mimics the textbook, incorporating concepts such as "captains of industry" or "labor unions." Prompted to justify the reliability of this account, students refer to their teacher's assessments, grades, or textbooks as unquestioned sources of validation. Essays at this level follow a structure that contains an introduction, body, and conclusion, but they still do so algorithmically, as steps in a protocol to be slavishly followed. When asked about the importance of understanding industrialization, students at this level tend to refer to its impact on their term grades and standardized test scores.

Performances of *apprentice understanding* are grounded in disciplinary knowledge and modes of thinking. They demonstrate flexible use of disciplinary concepts or ideas. Knowledge construction is seen as complex, following procedures and criteria that are typically used by experts in the domain. With support, performances at this level highlight the relationship between disciplinary knowledge and everyday life, examining opportunities and consequences of using this knowledge. Performances at this level show flexible and appropriate expression and communication of knowledge.

Certain aspects of Maria's performance in our example indicate that she has achieved at least an apprentice understanding of industrialization. She demonstrates her ability to perform within standards of good historical practice in ways appropriate to a child of her age. She describes industrialization from different points of view; she moves flexibly between detailed information and interpretive generalizations: she is aware of the purposeful nature of historical narratives. Her ability to consider both historical actors' intentions as well as the social, economic, and political circumstances in which they lived confirms her tendency to see knowledge construction as a problematic process.

Finally, performances of *master understanding* are predominantly integrative, creative, and critical. Students at this level are able to move flexibly across dimensions, relating the criteria by which knowledge is built and validated in a discipline to the nature of its object of study or the purposes of inquiry in the domain. Knowledge construction is seen as complex, driven by often conflicting frameworks and worldviews, and emerging as the result of public argumentation within communities of practitioners in various domains. Students can use knowledge to reinterpret and act upon the world around them. Knowledge is expressed and communicated to others in creative ways. Performances at this level often go beyond demonstrating disciplinary understanding; they may reflect students' critical awareness about the construction of knowledge in the domains. (That is, *metadisciplinary understanding* is the ability to combine disciplines in interdisciplinary performances of understanding.)

An important quality of Maria's performance of understanding is its integrated and critical nature. She goes beyond an apprentice level of understanding by drawing relationships across dimensions. For example, she notices that the purposes of certain biographies (proposing societal models or reaffirming the power of a few) may orient the selection of sources and the focus of attention of a writer's work. The critical spirit of her understanding is manifest when she reflects about knowledge construction explicitly and proposes that individual-centered histories must be complemented with broader historical analysis (such as a social, political, or economic history of the period).

The framework of dimensions and levels of understanding proposed in this chapter is not a rigid representation of disciplinary understanding. Instead, it constitutes a conceptual tool, a framework to examine students' understanding and orient their future work. As a working tool, it needs to be adapted to the specific content, contexts, and levels of instruction in which it is used. (Summaries of these dimensions and levels of understanding appear in Tables 6.1 through 6.5 in the appendix at the end of this chapter.)

Conclusions

The TfU performance view of understanding defines understanding as the ability to use knowledge in novel situations. In so doing, the TfU framework proposes that knowledge becomes a reflective tool for making products, telling stories, solving problems, making judgments, and transforming everyday life. This conception of knowledge and understanding contrasts with a widespread view of disciplinary knowledge in schools, where disciplines are usually seen as collections of certified facts arranged under such labels as "math" or "history"—where students need to master these facts as a sign of their cultural literacy.[26] In this tradition, American industrialization becomes a collection of events "that really happened," complemented with a list of causes and consequences and detached from its multiple interpretations as well as from its role in providing models of virtue and vice to shape national identity.

Reconceptualizing knowledge in the disciplines as tools entails four major shifts away from this factual epistemology. First, it requires a shift in focus from isolated facts about the world to broader, richly organized conceptual networks of examples and generalizations that are currently accepted as warranted in the domains taught. Second, it requires that individuals see these accounts as humanly constructed according to certain commonly agreed-upon methods and criteria that render them reliable (such as naturalistic observation, interpretation of sources, and empathic understanding). Third, it requires attention to the purposes that motivate inquiry around specific problems and the uses to which the resulting bodies of knowledge can be put (such as explaining, predicting, and controlling nature, or developing class consciousness or national identity). Fourth, it requires that individuals find appropriate ways to communicate and share knowledge (for example, by presenting supporting data for a claim, formulating an argument, or using the poetic power of a narrative). These four shifts embody the four dimensions of understanding presented in this chapter that far from being static and unrelated categories, interact dynamically in students' performances.

By proposing a four-dimensional Understanding framework, we invite teachers and students to ask new kinds of questions about topics like the Industrial Revolution or the mechanisms of genetic damage: What are the accounts of these phenomena that society holds as true? Why do people consider these accounts reliable? Why is it important to learn about this? How can students use what they know reflectively to orient their actions in everyday life and transform the world they live in? How can they best share what they understand? In Chapters Seven and Eight the dimensions and levels of the Understanding framework are used to shed light on these questions by revealing the qualities of understanding in students' work.

Appendix

Table 6.1. Four Dimensions of Understanding and Their Features.

Knowledge	Methods	Purposes	Forms
A. *Transformed intuitive beliefs* To what degree do students' performances show that warranted theories and concepts in the domain have transformed students' intuitive beliefs?	A. *Healthy skepticism* To what degree do students display a healthy skepticism toward their own beliefs and toward knowledge from such sources as their textbooks, people's opinions, and messages in the media?	A. *Awareness of the purposes of knowledge* To what degree do students see essential questions, purposes, and interests that drive inquiry in the domain?	A. *Mastery of performance genres* To what degree do students display mastery of the genres of performances they engage in, such as writing reports, giving presentations, or preparing the stage for a play?
B. *Coherent and rich conceptual webs* To what degree are students able to reason within richly organized conceptual webs, moving flexibly between details and overviews, examples and generalizations?	B. *Building knowledge in the domain* To what degree do students use strategies, methods, techniques, and procedures similar to those used by professionals in the domain to build reliable knowledge?	B. *Uses of knowledge* To what degree do students recognize a variety of possible uses of what they learn? To what degree do students consider the consequences of using their knowledge?	B. *Effective use of symbol systems* To what degree do students explore different symbol systems to represent their knowledge in effective and creative ways—for example, by using analogies and metaphors, colors and shapes, or movements?

C. *Validating knowledge in the domain*
Are truth, goodness, and beauty dependent on authoritative assertions, or rather on publicly agreed-upon criteria such as using systematic methods, providing rational arguments, weaving coherent explanations, and negotiating meanings through careful dialogue?

C. *Ownership and autonomy*
To what degree do students evidence ownership and the autonomy to use what they know?
To what degree have students developed a personal position around what they learn?

C. *Consideration of audience and context*
To what degree do students' performances show an awareness of the audience, such as the audience's interests, needs, ages, expertise, or cultural backgrounds?
To what degree do they show awareness of the context of the communication?

Table 6.2. The Knowledge Dimension: Its Features and Levels of Understanding.

Feature	Defining Questions for Feature	Level 1—Naïve	Level 2—Novice	Level 3—Apprentice	Level 4—Master
A. Transformed intuitive beliefs	To what degree do students' performances show that warranted theories and concepts in the domain have transformed students' intuitive beliefs?	Disciplinary concepts are missing; intuitive, folk, or mythical beliefs prevail.	Eclectic. Students mix intuitive beliefs with fragments of disciplinary knowledge, but intuitive views still dominate.	Disciplinary theories and concepts prevail. Some intuitive beliefs may appear. Disciplinary knowledge is still viewed as unrelated to common sense.	Disciplinary concepts and theories prevail. Students recognize the importance of disciplinary knowledge to refine commonsense beliefs and the importance of common sense to inspire, develop, and critique disciplinary knowledge.

B. Coherent and rich conceptual webs				
To what degree are students able to reason within richly organized conceptual webs, moving flexibly between details and overviews, examples and generalizations?	Bits or parts of knowledge seem dull, blurred, or undifferentiated. Examples and generalizations are unconnected. Even when prompted, students see problems either from the point of view of specific examples or broad generalizations.	Students state simple, fragile, or rehearsed connections between concepts or ideas. Students expand on examples but are unable to relate them to generalizations or frameworks in the domain. When prompted, students can move from specific examples to broad generalizations in rehearsed ways.	Students show fertile networks of ideas or points of view within a domain. Although some gaps or contradictions may appear, they move spontaneously between specific examples and generalizations in the discipline. Students still do not show the ability to reason creatively within these disciplinary frameworks.	Students show highly organized networks of ideas or points of view within a domain. Students show fluent movement between a rich variety of specific examples and broader disciplinary generalizations. Examples and generalizations are used thoughtfully to support each other. Students create new associations, examples, interpretations, or responses that are consistent with disciplinary frameworks and ideas.

Table 6.3. The Methods Dimension: Its Features and Levels of Understanding.

Feature	Defining Questions for Feature	Level 1—Naive	Level 2—Novice	Level 3—Apprentice	Level 4—Master
A. Healthy skepticism	To what degree do students display a healthy skepticism toward their own beliefs and toward knowledge from such sources as their textbooks, people's opinions, and messages in the media?	*Knowledge and world are undifferentiated.* It is unquestionable because it is the world. Students see the world as immediately apprehensible, therefore no specific methods are required to test claims—that is, to confirm or reject them.	*Knowledge is information about the world.* Skepticism is not very apparent. Students see a need for backing up their statements, yet that is a matter of proving that they are right, not finding out whether their beliefs are correct. Students also fail to show skepticism toward what they take to be disciplinary content They accept what they read or listen to as correct information.	*Knowledge is humanly constructed.* With support, students can doubt and be self-critical or skeptical about what they think, know, hear, read, and take to be disciplinary content. In most cases critiques are scattered or rehearsed. Students focus their skepticism on single methods or procedures. Contradictions or misconceptions may appear. Sometimes students' skepticism becomes nihilistic, thus putting any belief or disciplinary knowledge under question.	*Knowledge is humanly constructed, rationally arguable, framework driven, and provisional.* Students doubt and are self-critical or skeptical about what they think, know, hear, read, and take to be disciplinary content. Students' critiques generally refer to the basis on which disciplinary knowledge is built—that is, they perceive and use multiple methods and procedures in a domain and implicitly recognize the limitations of single methods.

B. Building knowledge in the domain			
To what degree do students use strategies, methods, techniques, and procedures similar to those used by professionals in the domain to build reliable knowledge?	No method for building knowledge is apparent beyond trial and error.	Students begin to understand that methods are helpful to build knowledge, but they apply procedures mechanically.	Students see the value of methods for building reliable knowledge. "Knowledge is humanly constructed through methods."	When presented with new evidence, theories, or interpretations, students may focus skepticism on the provisional nature of disciplinary knowledge, the purposes that drive knowledge construction, or the uses or consequences of knowledge.
			Students tend to use a single and simple method or procedure to build knowledge in the domain.	Students use a variety of methods effectively or use single methods in sophisticated ways.
				Some students perceive that methods emerge through public, rational argument.

Table 6.3. The Methods Dimension: Its Features and Levels of Understanding (*continued*).

Feature	Defining Questions for Feature	Level 1—Naive	Level 2—Novice	Level 3—Apprentice	Level 4—Master
C. Validating knowledge in the domain	Are truth, goodness, and beauty dependent on authoritative assertions, or rather on publicly agreed-upon criteria such as using systematic methods, providing rational arguments, weaving coherent explanations, and negotiating meanings through careful dialogue?	No validation criteria are apparent. Things are seen as self-evidently true, morally acceptable, or aesthetically pleasant "because it is so." Validation criteria are absent or still magical and mythical.	Students begin to see the importance of validating knowledge, moral values, or aesthetic judgments. Yet validity is grounded on external authority such as textbooks, experts, or teachers, who are seen as sources of correct information. Validation or justification tends to be based on immediate experience or authoritative assertions unrelated to rules or traditions in the domain.	Students see the importance of validating knowledge, moral values, or aesthetic judgments. They perceive single methods and validation procedures. When confronted with alternative methods valued in the domain, they easily fall into total relativism: "all claims are humanly made and therefore equally justifiable." Some students use validation standards and procedures in the domain but do so mechanically, without perceiving their relationship to broader frameworks or traditions in the domain. Validation procedures are seen as certain and unquestionable.	Students validate knowledge, moral values, and aesthetic judgments by referring to multiple methods or procedures and to the canons of validation in the domain. Some students go beyond their previous relativism to explain how methods and validation criteria relate to broader frameworks or view points. They see how some can be selected over others through rational argument. Students see validation criteria as open to questioning and revision over time.

Table 6.4. The Purposes Dimension: Its Features and Levels of Understanding.

Feature	Defining Questions for Feature	Level 1—Naive	Level 2—Novice	Level 3—Apprentice	Level 4—Master
A. Awareness of the purposes of knowledge	To what degree do students see essential questions, purposes, and interests that drive inquiry in the domain?	Students are unaware of essential questions and purposes that drive inquiry in the domain; that is, they are unaware of the point of learning what they are taught.	Students are aware that essential questions guide inquiry in the domain, but these questions and purposes are not clearly or are mechanically related to inquiry in the domain.	With support, students can identify essential questions and purposes that drive the construction of knowledge and use it to reflect on the relevance of what they learn in school.	Students spontaneously search for and identify essential questions and purposes that lead human inquiry and reflect about the relevance of what they learn. Some students recognize these questions as a significant part of their own lives. Other students question the purpose of knowledge construction in a domain because of potential negative consequences of its use.

Table 6.4. The Purposes Dimension: Its Features and Levels of Understanding (continued).

Feature	Defining Questions for Feature	Level 1—Naive	Level 2—Novice	Level 3—Apprentice	Level 4—Master
B. Multiple uses and consequences of knowledge	To what degree do students recognize a variety of possible uses of what they learn?	Students do not explore the potential of what they learn beyond prescribed tasks.	Students explore the potential of what they learn in school when they are supported. The uses of knowledge that they identify are closely tied to school rituals and tasks, such as making presentations or writing essays.	With support, students use what they learn in school in multiple and original ways in everyday life to solve practical problems, generate explanations, interpret themselves and others, and modify situations.	Students spontaneously use knowledge in multiple and novel ways. They clearly perceive knowledge as a tool to predict and control nature, orient human action, or improve their surrounding social or physical world.
	To what degree do students consider the consequences of using their knowledge?	Their performances show little or no relation between what they learn in school and everyday life experiences.	With support, students begin to connect what they learn in school to everyday life experiences. Connections may still be rehearsed.	Students spontaneously reinterpret daily experience through lenses learned in school; for example, the values that orient students' decisions are clearly informed by worldviews learned in school.	Students spontaneously reinterpret daily life experiences through lenses learned in school and use those experiences to interpret what they learn; for example, the values that orient students' decisions are clearly informed by worldviews learned in school.
			Students do not examine the consequences of using knowledge beyond school walls.	With support, some students examine practical, logical, social, and moral consequences of using knowledge by, for example, supporting a position or worldview and generating an unintentional reaction or change.	Some students spontaneously assess the practical, logical, social, and moral consequences of using knowledge: for example, by supporting a position or worldview and generating an unintentional reaction or change.

C. Ownership and autonomy				
To what degree do students evidence ownership and the autonomy to use what they know?	Students' use of knowledge requires considerable support and depends on authority's instruction. There is no evidence of long-lasting growth.	Initially students need support to use knowledge in novel situations but eventually are able to do so on their own.	Students use what they have learned freely, but their performances still do not take into account others' perspectives and interests.	Students demonstrate that they own what they have learned. They feel empowered to use knowledge independently of authoritative concerns or power relationships. They do so with careful consideration of multiple perspectives and concerns.
To what degree have students developed a personal position around what they learn?	Students do not see the point or the need for developing a personal position about what they learn.	When supported, students see authors' or disciplinarians' interests and positions. However, they still tend to see them as unrelated to a personal position on the topic they learn about.	Some students perceive how personal positions, purposes, and interests affect the way knowledge is constructed. They realize that, like experts, they too have interests and purposes for learning. They also realize that, like experts, they can develop personal positions about what they learn. Yet students still perceive these interests as capriciously driving people's motivations. Some students develop personal positions about what they learn but still do not take into account alternative points of view.	Some students perceive how personal positions, purposes, and interests affect the way knowledge is constructed. They realize that, like experts, they too have interests and purposes for learning. They also realize that, like experts, they can develop personal positions about what they learn. Interests and personal positions are no longer seen as capricious but as rooted in worldviews, frameworks, or backgrounds.

Table 6.5. The Forms Dimension: Its Features and Levels of Understanding.

Feature	Defining Questions for Feature	Level 1—Naive	Level 2—Novice	Level 3—Apprentice	Level 4—Master
A. Mastery of performance genres	To what degree do students display mastery of the genres of performances they engage in, such as writing reports, giving presentations, or preparing the stage for a play?	The genres or types of performances by which students communicate their ideas appear as irrelevant to them. Students are unaware that genres have specific rules.	Students follow the canons of specific performances ritualistically; for example, presentations are a matter of following certain tips and instructions. When prompted, students can successfully follow instructions to perform in the new genre.	Students engage in rich, understanding performances and move flexibly and expressively within the genre or type of performance in question. Students show awareness of rules when they begin to explore new genres.	Students engage in rich understanding performances and move flexibly and expressively within the genre or type of performance in question. Some students produce novel and acceptable changes to prototypical ways of performing in each genre or they successfully combine genres in acceptable ways. Some students demonstrate ownership of the genre by eliciting a clear personal style or voice in performing in this genre. When exploring new genres, students spontaneously attend to and engage in performing within the rules.

B. Effective use of symbol systems	To what degree do students explore different symbol systems to represent their knowledge in effective and creative ways—for example, by using analogies and metaphors, colors and shapes, or movements?	Symbol systems are used nonreflectively, resulting in flat and unclear representations. No communicative or aesthetic intention is apparent.	Students show initial familiarity with the symbol system in question: for example, by using commonplace metaphors, simple movements, or balanced designs.	Students show flexible and graceful mastery of a symbol system—expressive metaphors and analogies or careful body movement, for example.	Students show easy access and flexible or graceful mastery with different forms of representation of what they know or high mastery of one specific symbol system.
			These students tend to use only one symbol system to express what they have learned.	The focus of attention is on the symbol system itself; students explore colors, terms, and movements but with a focus that often interferes with the performance's representative purpose.	Students show aesthetic awareness in their use of symbol systems, such as compelling use of metaphors and analogies, originality, parsimony, or elegance. In each case they purposefully use symbols to support representational goals.
				When prompted, students use more than one symbol system, although they are still not able flexibly and aesthetically to alternate among symbol systems and decide which is the most powerful for the purpose at hand.	When necessary, students spontaneously use more than one symbol system, integrating them flexibly and aesthetically in ways that serve the purpose at hand.

Table 6.5. The Forms Dimension: Its Features and Levels of Understanding (*continued*).

Feature	Defining Questions for Feature	Level 1—Naïve	Level 2—Novice	Level 3—Apprentice	Level 4—Master
C. Consideration of audience and context	To what degree do students' performances show an awareness of the audience, such as the audience's interests, needs, ages, expertise, or cultural backgrounds? To what degree do they show awareness of the context of the communication?	Communication is egocentric. Audiences and contexts are not taken into account. No awareness of possible miscommunication is apparent.	Audience is taken into account but through egocentric lenses; the audience is expected to accommodate the presentation and to assume any burden for understanding it. Communication equals transmission. No attention is paid to specific ways in which the context may be shaping communication. Miscommunications are seen as lack of attention on the part of the audience or as technicalities of communication, such as terms or illustrations used without being understood.	With support, students take audiences into account—that is, they are sensitive to such differences as gender, interests, needs, level of expertise, and cultural backgrounds. Yet they still do not perceive themselves as audiences for others. Students show initial awareness of some ways in which contexts may affect communication but manage contextual factors mechanically if at all. Students still do not have a realistic sense of the difficulties of communication. To them, communication is a matter of intention; wanting to communicate is thought to make it happen.	Students take audiences into account by being sensitive to such differences as gender, interests, needs, level of expertise, and cultural background. They also see themselves as audience for others and are able to provide thoughtful feedback. Some students are also aware of the various demands that contexts may impose on communication and can gracefully use contextual factors to enhance communication. Students are clearly aware of the difficulties of communication. Communicating with others often entails understanding and affecting other people's worldviews, frames of reference, and beliefs.

Chapter Seven

How Do Students Demonstrate Understanding?

Lois Hetland
Karen Hammerness
Chris Unger
Daniel Gray Wilson

What does Kathy understand about the Renaissance? How well does Janice understand Newton's laws? Does Sam understand character development in *The Color Purple*? Does Manuel understand the cost of warming his bedroom by five degrees? In attempting to assess students' work during the last years of the Teaching for Understanding (TfU) project, both teachers and researchers repeatedly faced questions such as these. How can we recognize deeper or better understanding? The Understanding framework described in Chapter Six (see Tables 6.1 to 6.5 in the chapter appendix) was developed in response to these needs.

Readers will recall that the Understanding framework defines four dimensions of understanding: knowledge, methods, purposes, and forms. Each dimension has two to three features, framed as questions, that describe its components (see Table 7.1).

For each feature there are four levels of understanding—naive (level one), novice (level two), apprentice (level three), and master (level four). The generic descriptions of these levels from Chapter Six are presented in Table 7.2.

This chapter uses the Understanding framework to analyze selected examples of student work to address three research questions:

Table 7.1. The Dimensions and Their Features.

Knowledge	Methods	Purposes	Forms
A. Transformed intuitive beliefs	A. Healthy skepticism	A. Awareness of the purposes of knowledge	A. Mastery of performance genres
B. Coherent and rich conceptual webs	B. Building knowledge in the domain	B. Uses of knowledge	B. Effective use of symbol systems
	C. Validating knowledge in the domain	C. Ownership and autonomy	C. Consideration of audience and context

What does student understanding look like in TfU classrooms? How can we assess student work for deep understanding? How might teachers use assessments of student work to promote even deeper understanding?

Consider the puzzles of assessment posed by the work students produce in complex understanding performances. For example, to demonstrate her understanding of evolution, Tomoko, like other students in her class, has written an essay illustrated with schematic drawings. Her graphic work is detailed, indicating, for example, that mammals such as herself, her dog, and a giraffe she saw in the zoo all have seven bones in their necks, but that long-necked birds such as the goose on the farm next door have seventeen. These representations suggest an understanding of patterns in species—the same patterns from which Darwin developed his theory of evolution.

Unfortunately, the concepts in the essay itself are not as powerful: she describes natural selection as an intentional process of adaptation to an environment, and she misinterprets evolution as a scientific fact rather than a humanly constructed and therefore fallible theory. Because Tomoko is in a Teaching for Understanding classroom where assessment is ongoing, she will have opportunities to revisit these ideas. But how can her teacher evaluate what she does and does not understand and help her move from her current understanding toward a richer and deeper one?

Table 7.2. Levels of Understanding.

Naive Understanding	Novice Understanding	Apprentice Understanding	Master Understanding
Performances are grounded on intuitive knowledge.	Performances are grounded on the rituals of testing and schooling.	Performances are grounded on disciplinary knowledge and modes of thinking.	Performances are predominantly integrative, creative, and critical.
Students portray knowledge construction as an unproblematic process of grasping information that is directly available in the world.	Students begin to interject some disciplinary concepts or ideas and to establish simple, often rehearsed connections among them.	Students demonstrate flexible use of disciplinary concepts or ideas.	Students are able to move flexibly across dimensions, relating the criteria by which knowledge is built and validated in a discipline to its object of study or the purposes of inquiry.
Students do not see the relationship between what they learn in school and their everyday lives. They do not consider purposes and uses of knowledge.	Students portray the nature and purposes of knowledge construction, as well as its forms of expression and communication, as step-by-step mechanistic procedures.	Students see the construction of knowledge as complex, following procedures and criteria that are typically used by experts in the domain.	Students see the construction of knowledge as complex, driven by often conflicting frameworks and worldviews, and emerging as the result of public
		With support, performances highlight the relationship between disciplinary knowledge	

Table 7.2. Levels of Understanding (*continued*).

Naive Understanding	Novice Understanding	Apprentice Understanding	Master Understanding
Performances show no signs of students' ownership of what they know. Performances are unreflective about the ways in which knowledge is expressed or communicated to others.	The validation of knowledge construction procedures depends on external authority rather than on rationally agreed-upon criteria developed within disciplines or domains.	and everyday life, examining opportunities and consequences of using this knowledge. Performances show flexible and appropriate expression and communication of knowledge.	argumentation within communities of practitioners in various domains. Students can use knowledge to reinterpret and act upon the world around them. Knowledge is expressed and communicated to others in creative ways. Performances often go beyond demonstrating disciplinary understanding to reflect students' critical awareness about the construction of knowledge in the domains (for example, metadisciplinary understanding) or students' ability to combine disciplines in their tasks (for example, interdisciplinary understanding).

Tomoko's products are partial demonstrations of her understanding, and assessing them should indicate ways to help her deepen her understanding of evolution. But do her drawings demonstrate a fundamental grasp of the ideas, even though important concepts expressed in writing are problematic? Or does the writing convey that the essence of what she has learned is misunderstanding, despite the insight so artfully represented through the drawings? Neither response feels quite right: the first risks confirming misconceptions that could affect Tomoko's ability to use information appropriately in the future, but the second risks discouraging an engaged, able student. Too often teachers feel that they have to make a choice, and that may be because they lack an assessment tool that helps them acknowledge both depth and limitations in understanding.

The Understanding framework can help resolve the puzzle of Tomoko's work. Her drawings reveal sophistication along two dimensions—purposes and forms—because they convey compelling personal and real-world connections and because they clearly, creatively, and accurately communicate her knowledge about evolution: different biological classes on the evolutionary tree *have* evolved differing skeletal structures. However, her writing demonstrates flaws along two other dimensions, knowledge and methods: her web of information is missing some key concepts and relationships about the theory of evolution, and her assumptions about the ways theories are used by scientists are still naive.

Tomoko's teacher does not need to convey to her either that she grasps evolution (when she does not fully) or that she has failed hopelessly (when in fact she understands a great deal). The Understanding framework provides a tool for assessing both strengths that can be used as the foundation for deeper understanding and weaknesses that further instruction can challenge. By identifying levels of competence along these four dimensions of understanding, teachers draw a step closer to designing further instruction to promote the development of understanding.

This chapter illustrates how the Understanding framework can reveal dimensions of understanding in student work. We examine work from four disciplines—science, English, mathematics, and history—that was created by students in four TfU classrooms. This work represents neither the best nor the worst from these classrooms but shows how students with varying motivations and abilities from a range of school and disciplinary contexts performed in sustained inquiries. Each portrait begins with a brief snapshot of the understanding performance itself, followed by an analysis of the work using the Understanding framework. After the examples, we address the third research question by speculating about possible ways teachers could use their assessments to redesign instruction toward promoting deeper understanding.

Like teachers who might use the Understanding framework, initially several of the chapter authors learned it through using it. Our method was to first read over both the selections of student work to be assessed and the dimensions, features, and levels until we developed familiarity with them. Next we read the student work again as we looked for examples of each dimension in turn—knowledge, methods, purposes, and forms. At each potential match between a student's performance and one of the dimensions, we checked the features for that dimension to confirm which were being addressed. Usually only some features were represented in any sample of student work; those that were missing were often as informative as those that were present. Then we read through the levels for each identified feature to find a match with what the student had said. After assessing each match, we counted the number of matches at each level within a dimension. Generally the level with the most matches in each dimension became the assigned level for that dimension, but sometimes one statement exemplified one level or another so well that we assigned that level. If there were few or no consequential matches for a dimension in a selection of student work, we rated the dimension's level as "not applicable" for lack of evidence.

Clearly, coding is both science and art. Raters' expertise with disciplinary concepts and standards contributes to the assessment, as do the specific understanding goals of the students' classrooms. Because of the potential for variation in ratings that these factors introduce, each work was read by at least three raters. The final assignment of level emerged from a discussion among the coders, at which time disagreements were resolved based on evidence in the work. Despite the number of variables contributing to the coding, raters never differed by more than one level.

An important caveat must also be noted: the work examined here for each student only begins to demonstrate that student's understanding. TfU teachers attend to a collection of student performances and develop evolving profiles of each student's understanding. Teachers examine understanding performances both as they occur and retroactively, looking not only at final products or performances but also at drafts, process journals, peer feedback sheets, learning logs, and comments from class discussions and individual conferences. Detailed portraits illustrating how teachers might examine and analyze entire portfolios of student work using the Understanding framework cannot be presented here. What this analysis intends to provide is a glimpse into the potential of the framework as a tool for analyzing an array of work that can direct decisions about next steps for the students' efforts.

Physics: Understanding Mechanical Advantage

> After much thought the one thing I feel I really learned in physics was not really a specific unit we covered but the idea of observation of the world around me and questioning why and how. . . . To me physics has taught me to be aware of things and how they work or how things happen more than anything. I may not know the exact measurements or causes of some of the things, but I feel I have gained the desire and more knowledge to figure things out like [electrical] shocks and how everyday objects work.

The twelfth-grade physics student who wrote this passage beautifully captures the spirit of inquiry that Eric Buchovecky sought to cultivate in his students. As described in Chapter Five, Eric taught physics for middle- to upper-track eleventh- and twelfth-grade public school students at Belmont High near Boston. He struggled with the challenge of making physics valuable and meaningful for all students—not only the budding physicists and engineers but also those who were merely putting in their time with little sense of direction beyond high school graduation. Eric's students spanned the entire range.

In this unit Eric wanted students to see where "mechanical advantage" existed in the world and to appreciate its utility and power. Specifically, two of his understanding goals for the unit were the following:

> Students will understand and appreciate how the principle of conservation of energy applies to and can be used to analyze simple machines.

> Students will understand and appreciate how the principles of conservation of energy, mechanical advantage, and efficiency apply to more complicated machines and how to recognize and analyze simple machines in the everyday world.

As described in Chapter Five, Eric had students do informal relatively unstructured investigations with levers and pulleys early in the unit. Then the class discussed and Eric demonstrated the principles they had discovered, followed by small-group explorations of those concepts. For the final project, Eric asked each student to select a common mechanical device and describe its utility and how it uses mechanical advantage to fulfill its function. The work presented here samples the culminating understanding performances of two students, Marta and Hank.

Marta's Work Viewed Through the Understanding Framework

Marta's final project is shown in Figure 7.1. Analysis of her understanding performances follows.

Knowledge: Apprentice

Marta's analysis gets to the heart of the matter, applying the concept of conservation of energy to deduce that a greater force is exerted by the clipper blade than is applied to the lever arm: "The lever arm allows the user to apply less force than is needed to close the clippers by making you push the lever arm a greater distance down than the distance the clipper travels." She coherently and fluently uses both disciplinary terms such as force and concepts such as quantification of the clipper's gain of 10.92 Newtons when only 2.1 Newtons is applied. Marta evidences an understanding of the central disciplinary idea of creating more force out of less force via leverage, exposing the essential mechanism in her analysis. She was not scored at the master level, however, because there is little

Figure 7.1. Marta's Nailclippers.

Individual Machine Project

① Nail Clipper

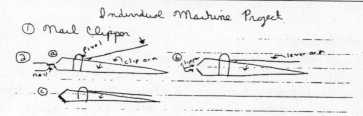

② ⓐ ... pivot ... clip arm ... nail

ⓑ clipper ... lever arm

ⓒ

③ - By pressing your finger down on the lever arm, you force the clippers to close, and clip your nail.

- There is a lever arm, which makes it easier to close the clippers and clip your nail. The lever arm allows the user to apply less force than is needed to close the clippers by making you push the lever arm a greater distance down than the distance the clipper travels.

Ex

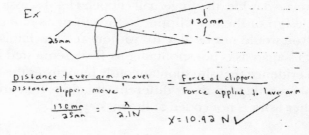

25mm 130mm

$$\frac{\text{Distance lever arm moves}}{\text{Distance clipper moves}} = \frac{\text{Force of clippers}}{\text{Force applied to lever arm}}$$

$$\frac{130mm}{25mm} = \frac{X}{2.1N} \qquad X = 10.92 \ N$$

This equation shows that the amount of force needed to push the clippers together is substantially less than the force needed to close the clippers

④

lever ... lever arm ... pivot

The lever in the nail clipper facilitates the closing of the clippers by making less force needed to be applied to close them. If no lever were involved, you would not be able to apply enough force with your finger to close the clipper.

extension or broader generalization of the principles beyond their direct application to the nail clippers.

Methods: Apprentice

Marta uses several disciplinary procedures to make sense of and analyze the mechanism of the nail clipper. She analyzes it narratively by relating the differences in applied forces to the differing distances traveled by the lever arm and the clipper, and she supports her case mathematically. She also supports her case by stating a rival hypothesis: "If no lever were involved, you would not be able to apply enough force with your finger to close the clipper." She is not scored at the master level because there is no evidence of being skeptical of or testing the basic disciplinary idea of mechanical advantage in levers.

Purposes: Apprentice

Marta found and explained an illustration of mechanical advantage in her everyday life: the fingernail clipper. Her discussion connects the design of the nail clipper to the clipper's nail-cutting function: "you would not be able to" without the mechanism. Because Marta's analysis is not spontaneous (Eric requested it) and there is no evidence that she spontaneously recognizes the uses of mechanical advantage in many different situations that are helpful to her, her work is not coded at the master level.

Forms: Master

Marta provides three different genres and symbol systems used by physicists in her explanation of the nail clipper: schematic drawings, narrative descriptions and explanations, and numerical quantification. She provides the reader several labeled illustrations of the nail clipper and its mechanism, highlighting different points with each. In the first case she illustrates the mechanism; in the second she highlights the quantitative differences in distance traveled by lever arm and clippers. In addition, she provides both a qualitative and quantitative analysis of the mechanism in text and mathematical symbols. This flexibility in the use of genres and symbol systems suggests her awareness of the needs of a physics audience, who would take different types of information from each representation. Marta is given a full score of master on forms.

Hank's Work Viewed Through the Understanding Framework

Hank's final project is shown in Figure 7.2. Analysis of his understanding performances follows.

Knowledge: Novice

Hank does little more than identify the critical parts of the mechanism that may affect mechanical advantage in a push lawn mower. In his drawings he simply illustrates and labels. His text offers descriptive details with little analysis: "When the lawnmower is pushed part A spins and while it spins the gear that is part of it turns the wheel. . . . There are more teeth on part B than C, that is why there is a one to four ratio of revolutions." Hank connects the ratio of revolutions between the two cogs with mechanical advantage, but he never explicitly states how it results in mechanical advantage either qualitatively or quantitatively. His analysis lacks an explanation that generalizes the central disciplinary idea, instead staying tied to the particular context of this simple machine. Consequently, he is coded as a novice.

Methods: Novice

Hank's performance only partially reveals how he constructed or validated his claims about the lawn mower's mechanism. However, by identifying the variables involved and suggesting some possible causal mechanisms, he demonstrates an early understanding of the process of building a scientific explanation. Perhaps most interesting here is Hank's note, in which he analyzes the mechanical advantage lost by standing up while pushing the lawn mower. He argues that full efficiency would probably be gained by pushing the lawn mower from directly behind, which would align the applied force with the direction of motion. His use of "about" in the statement that one's efficiency is "probably about 50 percent" signals some skepticism about how well his figure depicts an exact quantitative relationship between the angle of the lawn mower arm and the loss in efficiency.

Purposes: Apprentice

Hank too has found a novel application for the idea of mechanical advantage in the world. However, his description of the lawn mower makes no reference to his personal purpose for analyzing

Figure 7.2. Hank's Lawn Mower.

1. A Push Lawnmower.
2. Diagrams

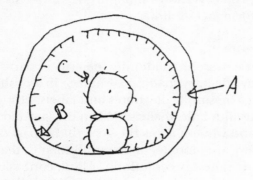

A. Wheel. B. Wheel's Gear. C. Blade's Gear.

(For every on revolution of the wheel, the blade has four revolutions)

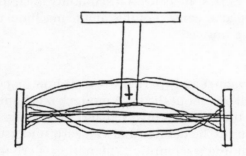

When the lawnmower is pushed part A spins and while it spins the gear that is part of it turns with the wheel. The gears have teeth that help interlock one gear to another. Part B is attached to part A. Part B's teeth are interlocked with part C, the blades gear. There are more teeth on part B than C, that is why there is a one to four ratio of revolutions. Part B has four times as many teeth as part C. C is attached to the blade, so the blade also turns with part C in a ratio of four revolutions to part A's one revolution.

When the lawn mower is being pushed the spinning blades pass a stationary bar that allows the grass to be cut, when the grass is in-between the blade and the bar there is a scissors like motion that snips the grass.

Note: When one is pushing on the mowers handle, that person is almost at a 45 degree angle, so your efficiency is probably about 50%. The reason why is ideally, you would be getting a 100% efficiency if you were pushing directly behind the lawnmower components themselves. There is only one problem, the human body would be uncomfortable to crawl and push at the same time, besides it is easier and more time efficient to be standing up while you push.

this particular case and never ventures a hypothesis for the function of such a lawn mower design—for example, that the gearing mechanism produces the necessary high rotational speed of the blade from the relatively slow rotation of the wheels. He does, however, spontaneously present the case of losing advantage when mowing standing up, venturing that the ideal situation would be to push the lawn mower from directly behind it. He goes on to point out that realistically "the human body would be uncomfortable to crawl and push at the same time," and further adds, "Besides it is easier and more time efficient to be standing up while you push." This commentary suggests his understanding of an important purpose of scientific inquiry: to control the natural environment efficiently. He uses the purposes of advantage in the design of simple machines and understands the realistic design constraints that affect what one could or would want to do to gain ideal mechanical advantage. For these reasons, we scored him at the higher of the two levels he was straddling.

Forms: Novice

Hank presents two diagrams: one depicting a front view of the lawn mower, the other showing the gears that link the wheel of the mower to the blade shaft. The front view is descriptive and orients the reader to the exact type of mower under consideration. The other diagram is more technical, showing the elements of the machine that Hank has identified as essential to its operation. Hank illustrates the main components of the lawn mower mechanism; however, he does not illustrate how that mechanism results in mechanical advantage. His drawings therefore do not fully achieve the purpose of the genre of scientific illustration, despite their clarity and precision. Doing so would require that he go beyond analogical portraits of elements in the machine and toward schematic graphs of their functioning. Further, his labels use ordinary language rather than technical terminology for referring to the wheel and gears. In his text about the gear mechanism there is straightforward description and no explanation, which also makes it lack disciplinary form: he explains the components but not the connection to mechanical advantage as a result of design. Once again, we coded him as a novice.

English: Understanding Autobiographical Essays

Joan Soble of the Pilot School at Cambridge Rindge and Latin High School taught a freshman writing course around the topic "writing about place," described in Chapter Four. The students wrote autobiographical pieces about how meaningful places—their homes, neighborhoods, communities, and cities—had shaped their lives. The students were not confident writers and were often reluctant to write more than a few sentences in the beginning of the course. Many students did not speak English as a first language, and most were unable to construct paragraphs, write introductory sentences, or capitalize words appropriately. These students were required to take Joan's course to develop their fundamental writing skills.

The course was organized around the following overarching understanding goal: students will understand that writing is a process; good writing comes as a result of drafting, seeking feedback, reflecting, revising, and editing. This particular unit, called Metaphorical Places, had five unit-level understanding goals, as listed in Chapter Four. We focus here on two: students will understand that place can be used metaphorically in one's writing, and students will understand that the act of writing about one's understanding of one's place in society is empowering.

During the unit students created essays describing their *life roads*. They selected a goal that they hoped to attain, such as becoming a jazz musician, running a small business, or going to college or trade school, and wrote about their journey toward achieving that goal. Joan asked them to create metaphorical places along the path that represented particular obstacles, challenges, supports, or decisions that they might encounter. Here we examine examples of life roads created by two students, Rick and Maria.

Rick's Life Road

Rick presented a careful and reflective three-page discussion of his journey toward becoming a saxophone player. His introduction read:

> When I was in kindergarten, many years ago, my goal in life, much like every five-year old across America, was to become a fireman.

Firemen seemed cool, they're heroes, life savers, and the best part to me of being a fireman was the long pole in the firehouse they got to slide down. A fireman seemed to be the thing to be when I was younger. As I have grown older my goals have changed, over and over again, from a fireman, to a basketball player in the NBA, to a rapper, to a jazz musician. My latest goal, and the profession I would like to enter when I am older, is a jazz musician. Jazz is exciting, difficult, tricky and interesting. It would be so much fun to play my sax as a job.

In the body of his paper, which began, "The road to becoming a sax player will be hard, and has been already," Rick told about his struggle to commit to daily practice.

That following summer I didn't touch the sax at all. When school started up, I came to a crossroad. To quit or to play, those were my options. I decided to quit, which led me directly into a dead end. It seemed as if my saxophone career was over. Deep into November my parents finally convinced me to take a few lessons to decide whether or not I really wanted to quit. For the following month, I walked the road traveling straight up the face of a mountain that seemed to be equal in height to Mt. Everest. I worked hard from then on and it has definitely paid off. I have already passed the obstacles that confronted me only to reach the foot of the hardest part of my journey, where even harder work is needed.

Rick's final section was the weakest part of his paper. He concluded in two sentences: "My goal is now firmly planted in my mind, and I plan to work hard to fulfill it. And although over the past year I have worked extremely hard and become a good solid jazz musician for my age, the road goes on."

Rick's Work Viewed Through the Understanding Framework

Analysis of his understanding performances places Rick at the following levels.

Knowledge: Apprentice

In the knowledge dimension Rick displayed the characteristics of an apprentice because disciplinary concepts about essay structure generally prevailed in his writing. The essay's introduction and body were coherently organized and followed a set of criteria the class had developed about the elements of good writing: his introduction explained the subject of his essay, which was his goal in life; established a mood—reflective and somewhat light-hearted; and gave background information to his audience about his past goals. The body of Rick's essay gave facts and reasons to support his subject and explained his opinions and attitudes through details—all disciplinary moves in writing, as well as part of the class's criteria. His conclusion, however, was weak and revealed some naive beliefs about writing—a sense that one should tell everything on one's mind was apparent in his excessive detail, which is why we did not place him at a master level.

Methods: Not Applicable

It is not clear from this essay alone how Rick built and validated his disciplinary knowledge about writing. Other class performances, such as Rick's reflective journal entries about process writing, his iterative drafts, his group dialogues in which students shared feedback around their writing, and class discussions in which Rick built arguments for particular literary interpretations, lend more insight to his understanding of methods.

Purposes: Novice

In the purposes dimension Rick was coded at the novice level. He shared an important personal interest in his piece, yet the essay did not express the power of an author who writes as a way to understand himself or the world. This does not mean that Rick needed to express more intimate or personal thoughts. Rather, it means that his writing could express more interesting and unique rationales and ideas for his choices. It is clear that he wrote his piece as a school assignment, and the connection of such writing to his life—his sense of the purposes of writing—is a bit mechanical. His weak conclusion is an indication of his need to develop a clearer sense of the purpose of writing. A more powerful or reflective conclusion to his essay would have shown a deeper sense of writing as an expression of the self.

Forms: Novice

In the forms dimension Rick also scored at the novice level. Although he shows some apprentice-level qualities, he followed the instructions of the assignment ritualistically. His "crossroad" and "dead end" were not particularly original, but these metaphors did suggest his feelings and represent the events. He was also fairly expressive in this genre and showed a developing sense of the rules of autobiographical essay: he traced a path from his past to his future, a trademark of autobiographical writing. His metaphors were woven fairly well into his essay and added a sense of visual imagery and color to the paper. Joan commented that Rick revealed some understanding of the drama of language, noting this sentence: "From there, my road was filled with uphills, downhills, potholes, bumps, fallen trees and floods." She found a poetic lilt in this sentence, expressed through the alliteration and rhythm of the catalogued obstacles.

Maria's Life Road

In her life road Maria wrote about her goal to become a famous singer. She began, "My goals occupy my thoughts every day of my life. For as long as I can remember the one main goal that I've set for myself is to be a famous singer. When I was younger, my grandfather and I used to sing together. We would sing 'Tomorrow' from the movie 'Annie.' My grandparents would have me promise them that one day I would be famous and have lots of concerts, and they'd be sitting in the front row every time."

This introduction continued for over a page and moved away from the main subject of becoming a singer to other goals. The body of Maria's paper was lengthy and included too much irrelevant detail. However, she described her journey from elementary school to high school and forward to the future. She wrote of difficulties: "Then came the river. That was when my cousin was on trial. But even though the high rapids at some times became unbearable, with the strength of one another, my family and I were able to find some way to cross the river."

Maria's conclusion rambled a bit but was more fully developed than Rick's: "If my goals come true, I will be so proud of myself. I will be proud that I was able to challenge myself and meet the standards of that challenge and not settle for less. I think everyone should have goals for themselves, whether the goal is passing your hardest class or graduating from college and going on to medical school. What's the point of living if you don't make expectations for yourself? I think that people can do anything they want to do, as long as they apply enough hard work and time."

Maria's Work Viewed Through the Understanding Framework

Analysis of her understanding performances places Maria at the following levels.

Knowledge: Novice

Maria's understanding of essay structure was not as strong as Rick's; we placed her at the novice level. She demonstrated the disciplinary concept of structure through her introduction, body, and conclusion. As Joan noted, however, Maria tended to tell readers everything she thought or felt about a subject even more than Rick did, without much attention to organizing ideas around particular themes.

Methods: Not Applicable

As with Rick's essay, it was difficult to ascertain Maria's understanding of the methods dimension based solely on her essay. Again, other class performances such as reflective process journals that document the evolution of her ideas, group writing discussions in which she gave and received feedback, and class contributions in which she raised and defended her own literary interpretations would lend more insight to our understanding of how Maria saw the processes of building and validating literary knowledge.

Purposes: Apprentice

In the purposes dimension we scored Maria at the apprentice level. She used writing as a form of self-expression in a way that Rick did not. Joan remarked that this piece revealed much of Maria's voice—her determination, strength, and vulnerability. Although her conclusion lost the thread of her original subject of becoming a singer, it still posed a thoughtful and important question about what inspires and presses people to develop and grow in their lives. Maria saw writing as a form in which to pose important questions such as, "What's the point of living if you don't make goals for yourself?" Joan also noted that Maria "used writing as a way to work things out," pointing to the passage about her family's troubles and to her strong sense of her goals in the conclusion.

Forms: Novice

In the forms dimension, too, we scored Maria at the novice level, despite strong leanings toward apprentice. She seemed to understand the genre of autobiographical writing, although she did not follow all the rules of the genre as completely as Rick did. Like Rick, she traced a path from past to future, and she also considered the future thoughtfully in her conclusion. Maria demonstrated a strong command of metaphor; she wove the metaphors smoothly into her texts. As Joan says, "Maria uses [metaphors] to serve her end"—she actually expressed ideas and emotions through them—as opposed to the way Rick used them as additional description.

Mathematics: Understanding Ratios and Similarity

Bill Kendall, the geometry teacher at Braintree Public High School described in Chapter Four, organized his sophomore class around his overarching goal: "Geometry is the study of lawfully connected patterns in the world." In the class, students explored real-world phenomena through geometrical ideas. For example, students designed floor plans of their homes and other buildings using geometrical relationships and shapes, and they measured distances and heights of objects around the school using concepts from the class. This section presents student work from a unit exploring similarity and ratios by using mirrors.

Following a unit on similarity, Bill designed a four-day project around three understanding goals: students will understand ratios and proportions to solve algebraic problems; students will understand the definition of similarity as it relates to polygons and triangles; and students will understand how to use similar triangle patterns in solving and understanding real-world problems. The project engaged students by posing the problem shown in Figure 7.3.

Bill asked students to keep journals to record their developing ideas as they worked in groups with a small mirror, a yardstick, and an eight-stage worksheet to guide their investigations of the

Figure 7.3. Mirror Project.

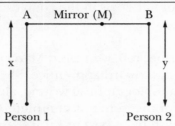

Two people face a smooth wall. Calculate where to place a small mirror so that they can both see each other in the mirror. What patterns emerge if the people stand in different places? What mathematical conclusions can you make?

mathematical patterns and connections embedded in these understanding performances. In the first performances students ran nine informal experiments to get a feel for the problem. Next they ran a series of experiments designed by Bill to reveal the patterns and relationships at work. The students then wrote their first reflections, noting progress and emerging patterns and speculating about why they occurred. To test their conjectures, they ran nine more experiments and reflected a second time on why their ideas did or did not work. If their explanations were not supported by their tests, the students came up with different conjectures that could be verified experimentally. If their explanations were supported, then they completed a worksheet aimed to test their ability to find missing lengths and ratios of similar triangles. In conclusion the students wrote a third and final reflection explaining and giving examples of the connections between this project and the mathematical notion of similarity.

Evelyn's Mirror Project

Evelyn was an average student who had often expressed her hatred of math until this year. Figure 7.4 shows her responses to the reflection assignments at the three points just described.

Figure 7.4. Evelyn's Mirror Project.

Early Reflection
I think the pattern between *X* and *AM* has to be the same as between Y and *MB*. Another pattern that is forming is *AM* + *MB* = *AB*. Some examples are [see chart]

Midproject Reflection
I think what is happining is that the sides are in the same ratio. See, $y = 3x$ and $MB = 3AM$ because our experiments proved this over and over again. Also $y = 2x$ then $MB = 2AM$. In our first try, we noticed that $y = x$ and $MB = AM$. Some examples are [see chart]. This is happening because the distance from the wall corresponds to the distance of the mirror to the point on either side of the mirror.

Final Reflection
The Mirror Project is connected to similar triangles because if you look at the diagram you see the figures form two similar triangles. All triangles are similar by the two sides being the same ratio and their angle being the same (*SAS*) or by all three sides being the same ratio (*SSS*) because the 3rd side is forced into being similar. And *AA* because of vertical angles [see drawings].

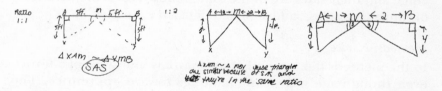

Evelyn's Work Viewed Through the Understanding Framework

Analysis of her understanding performances places Evelyn at the following levels.

Knowledge: Apprentice

The connections between what Evelyn observed and her mathematical knowledge steadily increased in coherence and specificity, for which we assessed her final reflection at the apprentice level.

She was not scored at the master level, however, because her final conclusion contained some ambiguous references.

In her first reflection Evelyn was vague about what pattern she observed and stated the very simplistic mathematical relationship of $AM + MB = AB$. Her explanation of the pattern became more sophisticated in her second reflection, in which she identified the mathematical concept of ratios and gave specific examples. However, at this point the nature of the problem was still fuzzy—she did not, for example, connect the central concept of this unit, similarity, to her work. In the final reflection her explanation is more explicit and detailed. She indicated the connections between similarity, similar triangle patterns, and ratios. But her incorrect reference to vertical angles and her questionable use of SAS and SSS raises suspicions about the coherence of her connections.

Evelyn's mathematical connections were more articulate and specific than those of some students. For example, after going through the same performance a fellow classmate who was coded at the novice level simply wrote: "All of the distances are in the same ratio. If x is bigger than y, then AM is greater than MB. And if y is greater than x, then MB is greater than AM." Other students scored at the master level demonstrated more explicitness in their ability to generalize and specify the mathematics. For example, one student wrote, "the triangles are similar because their angles are equal and their sides are in the same ratios. This is the definition of similar triangles," and supplied detailed examples.

Methods: Novice

In the methods dimension Evelyn's work is indicative of a novice even though she has strong leanings toward apprentice. The process by which she built her understanding was conjecture, experimentation, reflection, and revision, all vital procedures of disciplinary inquiry in mathematics; however, this process was embedded in the structure of the project, and she seems to have followed it in a recipe-like manner. Nonetheless, not all students adhered to this method. Some students did not keep reflective journals; others simply fudged their data to sustain their erroneous conjectures.

The most telling indication of a novice level is in Evelyn's method of verifying her results. In all her reflections she describes what she sees happening but does not move past empirical verification toward more abstract axiomatic reasoning, a central feature of disciplinary understanding in mathematics. Even in her final reflection she did not ground her reasoning about similar triangles on any mathematical definition or proof but still only on what she saw. Students coded at the apprentice level reasoned that their connections were true because of the definition of similar triangles. In further contrast a student scoring at the master level justified the nature of this phenomenon with a general proof of where the mirror would be found given any two distances that the people stood apart from each other and the wall.

Purposes: Not Applicable

We do not have much evidence from this work to assess Evelyn's understanding in the purposes dimension. Because of the structure of the project, she kept a journal and regularly reflected on how she was making sense of the problem. But nowhere did she indicate any personal valuing or speculate about any disciplinary uses of this knowledge. In fact, no student included any evidence of such connections. We are left to wonder if Evelyn (or the other students) made personal connections to this knowledge or could extend it meaningfully into their own experience.

Forms: Apprentice

Evelyn scored at the apprentice level in the forms dimension. She used variables, equations, data displays, and drawings to illustrate her knowledge about the phenomenon's relationships and general trends. Although parts of her meanings were left unclear (in her final reflection, for example, we are left to wonder what she means by "vertical angles" and question her use of the symbols for the congruence patterns *SAS* and *SSS*), her coherent use of visual and linguistic symbol systems suggests important understanding. Nevertheless, the ambiguities indicate room for growth.

Evelyn used algebraic symbols to clarify her meanings more effectively than her peers. Even in her midproject reflection she was able to create equations to describe the relationships in her data, rather than just using language to say "x is twice y" or "x is greater than y," which is what many students did. For example, one student scoring at the naive level did not supply any pictures or diagrams to clarify his final reflection, which read: "The mirror project and the similar triangles are the same because they both use SAS." Meanwhile, other students coded at the novice level provided a few diagrams but did not explain what they meant.

History: Understanding the Historian's Process

Lois Hetland's seventh-grade interdisciplinary course centered on history and also addressed aspects of anthropology, English, and the arts. As described in Chapter Five, her course focused students' learning around twelve open-ended questions she called *throughlines* (see Exhibit 5.3, p. 139) that were displayed in her classroom and referred to regularly throughout the year. Lois's students wrote reflectively about the throughlines at three points during the year: October, March, and June. In addition to the understanding revealed by ongoing assessment of her six generative topics, the technique illustrated here helped her and her students to see how understanding about the past developed over time. For that reason the understandings revealed in this case are slightly different from the previous cases; they are less specific to a given generative topic. What follows are comparisons of two students' responses to the throughline question: "How do we find out the truth about things that happened long ago and/or far away?"

Renee's Throughline Responses

Renee, an able student who was successful in school, seemed to Lois to lack deep, personal engagement and motivation. As her responses show, her investment increased as her understanding of the throughline question developed over the year.

Initial Response from October 1993

We find info about things far away and long ago because after a certain time they wrote things down. And when they didn't we have archaeology.

Midyear Response from March 1994

We can find out about things that happened long ago by not only looking at records of time gone by but looking at land, too. One example of this is cave paintings and another is the mounds built by the Indian mound builders in the south. If we dig in the land, we can find bones, artifacts, and pieces of things. These are sort of "pieces of time." Time is kept in the land. These questions all seem to relate, don't they?

Year-End Response from June 1994

These history questions . . . I think they both mean the same thing. They are both asking "Is there bias in historical sources? Can you see through the bias? What will you do so that you aren't biased, too?" I don't think my thinking ever changed on these questions. I think I first started to know the answers when we had our first discussion on the subject. I think it was when we were doing our life albums. We named all of the different ways you could get the clearest picture of your person's life. . . . I think you can only partly understand what a question is until you have answered it.

In addition to this text Renee spontaneously created a schematic diagram (see Figure 7.5) to further clarify her thinking about the process of understanding throughlines. She included this diagram as part of the final reflection.

Renee's Work Viewed Through the Understanding Framework

Analysis of her understanding performances places Renee at the following levels.

Knowledge: Not Applicable

Renee's throughline response does not offer enough information to make a useful analysis or accurate rating regarding the degree of complexity or coherence of the knowledge dimension. However, her drawing does suggest that by year's end she is making more connections within a web of concepts, a central feature of the knowledge dimension.

Methods: Apprentice

Renee's initial understanding within the methods dimension was coded at a naive level but grew to a score of apprentice that approached mastery. Her initial response revealed an implicit belief

Figure 7.5. Renee's Schematic Diagram.

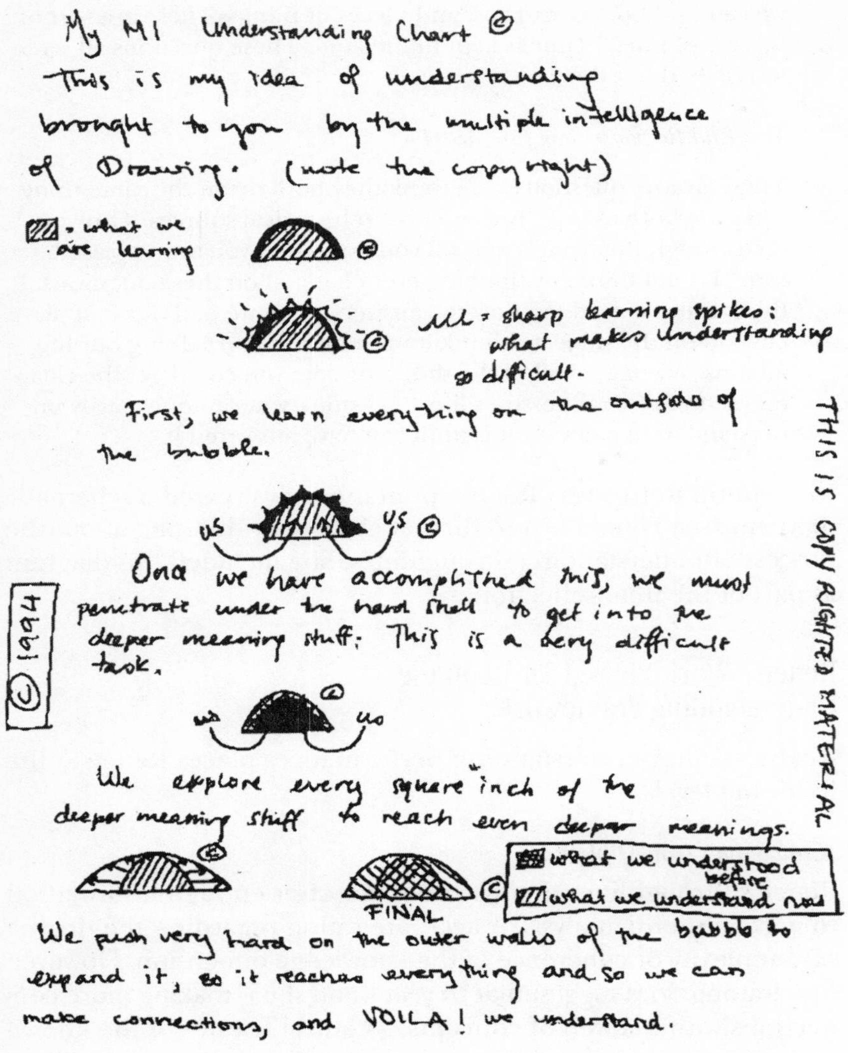

My MI Understanding Chart ©
This is my idea of understanding
brought to you by the multiple intelligence
of Drawing. (note the copyright)

▨ = what we
are learning

▨ ©

ﻨﻨﻨ = sharp learning spikes:
what makes understanding
so difficult.

First, we learn everything on the outside of
the bubble.

us ﻨﻨﻨ us ©

Once we have accomplished this, we must
penetrate under the hard shell to get into the
deeper meaning stuff; This is a very difficult
task.

© 1994

us © us

We explore every "square" inch of the
deeper meaning stuff to reach even deeper meanings.

▨ © ▨ ©
FINAL

▨ what we understood before
▨ what we understand now

We push very hard on the outer walls of the bubble to
expand it, so it reaches everything and so we can
make connections, and VOILA! we understand.

THIS IS COPYRIGHTED MATERIAL

that finding out about the truth is a simple task, because the past is just what people wrote down. She exhibited no skepticism in her response and no sense of the complex methods involved in building or validating knowledge in history. Her midyear performance shows growth; she used examples to support her point that there are two ways to learn about the past (through "records of time gone by" and by "looking at land"), but her effort backed her belief that she was right more than it explored whether she actually was right. Her approach seemed mechanical and resembled a recipe more than a demonstration of deep thinking about the historian's role as interpreter. She was, however, beginning to be speculative ("These questions all seem to relate, don't they?").

In her year-end responses Renee demonstrated her belief that by engaging fully with details while trying to answer overarching questions people come to understand and even expand their questions. Her statements about bias suggest that she is considering sources skeptically, a conclusion further supported by the diagram's emphasis on multiple approaches. Unlike many seventh-graders, Renee considers multiple perspectives in her efforts to construct knowledge about the past, pointing to "all the different ways you could get the clearest picture of your person's life." The dynamic quality of methods and learning procedures depicted by Renee suggests that she may be ready to understand that in history, truth is provisional and humanly constructed.

Purposes: Master

By year's end Renee's understanding evolved to be coded at a master level. Her initial responses lacked attention to the ways knowledge can be used. What she wrote sounds rehearsed, almost as if somebody told it to her once. Her midyear response combines ideas from the course with her personal interests; the cave paintings were something she found interesting outside of class. But she did not explore the consequences of a "dig in the land" for these "pieces of time," nor tell us how that might be useful beyond school walls.

However, in her year-end response she spontaneously reinterpreted the question itself into several subquestions about bias and its effect on authors and interpreters of sources, including herself. Her sense of ownership over the ideas reveals further master-level understanding in this dimension through her strong personal voice in both examples ("Voila!"), her purposeful use of originality and aesthetics, and the ownership she asserted ("I don't think my thinking . . ."; "I think I first started to know . . ."; "I think you can only partly understand . . ."). Even more distinct are the ten references to copyright on the diagram. Renee was not asked to conceptualize the process of achieving understanding in the throughlines assignment, but she chose to do so. Although she did not offer compelling evidence in this assignment that she acted on the world in this way, the performance is a powerful demonstration of ownership of and personal commitment to her classwork.

Forms: Master

By year's end Renee's understanding evolved to be scored at the master level in the dimension of forms. Her initial response had very little evidence for this dimension beyond some implicit consideration of audience: she utilized the schooled convention of restating the question in answers to essay questions. Similarly, the midyear response repeated that canonical orientation toward audience. However, she did use a lovely metaphor ("pieces of time") and the question at the end seemed intended to engage her audience more directly.

In her final response she competently introduced, defined, supported, and raised further questions while maintaining an expressive flow—a sophisticated use of the genre of short-answer essay. In addition her spontaneous choice of the schematic diagram as part of her response to the throughline assignment gracefully combined graphic and verbal symbol systems. Finally, she clearly adapted her forms for her audience—her teacher—who had repeatedly demonstrated that she valued visual representations of thought.

Dan's Throughline Responses

Dan had received tutorial help throughout his schooling. Although popular and athletic, he expressed frustration about schoolwork. Despite their considerable difference in learning profiles, needs, and development over the year, Dan, like Renee, demonstrated growth as assessed through his throughline reflections.

Initial Response from October 1993

The truth is found out by reading foreign letters and poems.

Midyear Response from March 1994

We can read them in books or maybe dig up clues.

Year-End Response from June 1994

I thought [in the fall] it was very easy to find the truth about things that happened a long time ago and far away. I thought the part about bias was a strange question. . . . To find out the truth about Zenger, I used an autobiography, magazine, encyclopedia, and books. . . . I now knew [sic] you have to look at more than one source to find the truth. I think autobiographies are the best way to find out the truth. Reading many different sources will give you everyone's point of view on the matter and helps you. If you read three books and two say the same thing and one doesn't then you can think the third book has a bias. When I do research in the future, I know I should read more than one book to find out different opinions.

Dan's Work Viewed Through the Understanding Framework

Analysis of his understanding performances places Dan at the following levels.

Knowledge: Not Applicable

Similar to Renee, Dan did not demonstrate enough about this dimension for a valid assessment. In his year-end reflection, he suggests concepts such as bias, opinion, point of view, and truth, which indicate that his web of historical issues is richer than it was at the start of the year, but the performance still reveals too little evidence for making even a tentative evaluation of level.

Methods: Novice

Dan's initial responses indicate that he thought historical knowledge was constructed through an unproblematic process: just by finding it somewhere. This is coded as a naive-level performance, where knowledge cannot be questioned because it *is* the world. His reference to "clues" in the midyear answer suggests that he may have begun to understand that interpretation of sources is not literal.

However, his year-end reflection demonstrates the leap toward understanding that causes us to score him at the novice level: "When I do research in the future, I know I should read more than one book to find out different opinions." He attributes this growth to his work on a biography project about Peter Zenger. However, it is still not clear whether he understood that history is an interpretive discipline—his assertions that "you need to look in more than one source to find the truth" and that "reading many different sources will give you everyone's point of view on the matter and helps you" seem somewhat mechanical. His validation technique of comparing sources for agreement is a good start on a valid disciplinary method, but the external authority of the books themselves is maintained, not his own interpretation based on evidence.

Purposes: Novice

The first two responses offer almost nothing by which to assess Dan's understanding in the purposes dimension. Evidence in the year-end entry is also scanty, but it suggests that Dan has come to see history as more than a collection of facts, events, and dates. He is aware that opinions vary and that truth is not "very easy to find." It seems that the question has scaffolded his thinking toward a new view of the uses of historical knowledge. This idea can serve as a foundation from which to learn that history can be written to validate some social groups over others. In addition he relates this to his own work and opinions: "I thought the part about bias . . . I now knew . . . I think autobiographies . . . When I do research in the future, I know I should . . ." The increased investment in his final throughlines reflection in and of itself suggests that Dan has grown in his appreciation of the value of history, at least in school. All of this suggests scoring at a novice level in the dimension of purposes.

Forms: Novice

Once again, we see enough information to make an assessment of the forms dimension only in the year-end response. Here, Dan demonstrates some understanding of the genre of historical essays: he introduces his earlier thoughts, shows how his ideas developed, and closes with a statement about how he will use this knowledge in the future. This form was scaffolded by the assignment sheet, but he had not used such scaffolding in previous assignments. Doing so might indicate an increase in his understanding about either the canons of this type of performance or the importance of addressing his teacher as an audience or both. Either way, the final performance reflects growth in the forms dimension worth scoring at the novice level.

Implications for Instruction

How might teachers use assessments such as these to guide students toward even deeper understanding? The answer to this research question is the conjecture of the authors, because the Understanding framework was developed after the field work in classrooms was complete. Nevertheless, the preceding analyses suggest many potential uses of the Understanding framework. Two seem central: using the framework as a comprehensive guide for assessing program toward planning more focused instruction, and using it to help students do self- and peer assessment and help teachers assess individual students.

The Understanding Framework as a Guide for Assessing Program

In history Lois noticed that she did not obtain much information about the knowledge dimension from the throughline reflections, even though the intricate conceptual webs and understanding of history that her students had built over the year were well represented in the students' portfolios of work from their various projects.

Knowledge

Lois commented that the dimensions could have been useful in helping her assess and revise her throughlines because she could have considered whether knowledge was as strongly emphasized by them as she wanted it to be.

Lois also could reconfigure her program slightly to gather a more complete picture of the knowledge dimension. First, the Understanding framework might help her to identify dimensions with which many students struggled, allowing her to redesign sequences of understanding performances to address those weaknesses. Second, seeing the lack of evidence for the knowledge dimension in her throughlines might have inclined her to restructure an aspect of her ongoing assessment. She might have combined assessment of throughlines with assessment of the students' project portfolios. She might have asked her students to design a portfolio selection of various unit materials—journals, reflections, drafts, sketches, photographs, audio- and videotapes, and final products—to demonstrate their understanding of specific throughlines. Such a selection of student work with explanatory reflections about how students thought the work demonstrated understanding would certainly present a much richer image of the conceptual knowledge webs students were using. The Understanding framework might have helped her see the need for that improvement.

Methods

In English Joan noticed that many of her students were scored as novices who simply adjusted their drafts because of what their peers or teachers told them, sometimes even when they disagreed with the suggestions. They accepted the idea of revision without really understanding how the changes improved their writing. To increase her students' understanding of the procedures of expert writers, Joan might revise her program's understanding performances to guide students to compare and contrast drafts with final pieces or expert models. She might also emphasize the importance of personally meaningful revisions and help students consider their revisions more seriously by raising a question such as the following: How could you use critical responses to retain both personal voice *and* meaningful ideas?

Purposes

Joan might also have used the dimensions to revise her program's ongoing assessment to focus her feedback and comments toward the needs of individual students. For example, in purposes Rick's reflections were still a bit mechanical. He seemed to understand how writing could be used to narrate a story or share his thoughts about a topic, but he was not yet able to use it as a tool to reflect upon important and formative experiences in his life, which is what students scored at an apprentice or master level might have done in autobiographical essays. With the Understanding framework Joan could have seen the need to focus Rick on using his own experiences in his writing—conjecturing about why he struggled to commit to practicing the saxophone, or why he agreed to return to playing, or what his goal to become a jazz musician reflects about him as a person.

Forms

In physics some students would have benefited from more attention to their use of symbol systems, a component of the forms dimension. Hank, for example, simply drew an illustration of the lawn mower without linking the drawing clearly to the concept of mechanical advantage. One way that Eric might have redesigned his program to help Hank develop more facility with the forms used to communicate knowledge in science might have been by designing understanding performances in which students searched, analyzed, and critiqued a variety of resources—texts, reference books, museum displays, Internet sources, popular media articles, journal articles—regarding the different representations used, and comparing them. Such pointed understanding performances could help students reflect on both the multitude of representations possible for particular disciplinary concepts and on the links among genre, symbol, audience, and meaning. With the Understanding framework, Eric might have been better able to identify this need.

The Understanding Framework as a Guide for Self-, Peer, and Teacher Assessments

The dimensions could be shared with students as a guide for reflecting upon their own work. Had the dimensions been available, Lois says that she might have explained them to her students directly from the outset or during the year; other teachers of older students are now experimenting with using the Understanding framework this way. She might, for example, have shown Renee and Dan which aspects of their work mapped onto which dimensions, allowing both teacher and students to acknowledge successes and focus effort on weaknesses.

Marta and Hank, in Eric's class, might have benefited from using the dimensions to review each other's and other students' analyses. Hank might then have gained more insight into how mechanical advantage is achieved, and how several means of expression (illustration, charts with captions or titles, algorithms, and narrative explanations and descriptions) convey that understanding. At the same time Marta may have developed an increased awareness of the issue through considering what mechanical advantage is gained or lost by others' designs.

In mathematics Bill thought that Evelyn would probably have benefited from one additional cycle of practice, reflection, and assessment. If the Understanding framework had been part of that additional reflection and she had considered her own work in relation to it, she might well have wondered about and discovered ways to use mathematical knowledge for her own purposes.

Conclusion

Let us return to the research questions on which this chapter is based.

What does student understanding look like in TfU classrooms? As our examples illustrate, understanding is often difficult to recognize. It reveals itself in fragments, looking more like a case built from evidence than a conclusive fact. It looks like a dynamic system in the process of change, not a static judgment stamped upon a student as an identity. Most important, it looks multifaceted— more a profile of strengths and weaknesses than the simple numerical composites of traditional evaluations.

Understanding looks varied, both because it has different dimensions and because it is revealed in a range of planned and spontaneous situations. Although the examples assessed in this chapter are mainly planned and formal, we wish to reiterate the need to look for student understanding in a variety of performance and assessment types. Across the classes teachers noted that spontaneous and informal performances and reflections were valuable additions to the evidence about understanding gathered from planned and formal performances. Informal performances and assessments offered opportunity for students to demonstrate novel connections between disciplinary and personal contexts. They also allowed students to use the forms most natural to them, offering those with different intelligence profiles a chance to demonstrate important understandings they might otherwise have been unable to express. All of this implies a need for teachers to examine an array of student products gathered over time.

How can we assess students' products for deep understanding? These cases suggest that the Understanding framework is an effective tool for assessing student work for deep understanding because it helps to delineate both points of conceptual clarity and misconceptions. For each dimension students show various levels of expertise that can serve as foundations for next efforts or as targets to be challenged.

With the variety and complexity of student products produced in TfU classrooms, the levels of naive, novice, apprentice, and master—used for the dimensions of knowledge, methods, purposes, and forms and their component features—solved some of the limitations found in summative assessments: traditional evaluation effectively compares one student to another but is less valuable as a guide for next steps in learning. By considering dimensions of student work relative to the dimensions of academic disciplines, the researchers were able to respect and value students' strengths while identifying areas for more attention. Assured that they already understand a great deal, students may be more willing to tackle areas of limitation—a necessary habit for lifelong work toward developing deep understanding.

How might teachers use assessments of student work to promote even deeper understanding? Evidence of the value of the Understanding framework for teachers is speculative; it has been useful for researchers, but teachers are only now beginning to experiment with it in classrooms. In part this is because the Understanding framework was evolved near the end of the research project. In part it seems to be because the framework is complex; to use it with facility, busy teachers would need great familiarity with it, requiring a time-consuming learning process. However, although few teachers have begun using the framework for assessment as illustrated in this chapter, some have started to use it to design and assess understanding goals to encompass the full breadth of understanding that the dimensions suggest.

Our analyses suggest that teachers could find it useful, as researchers did, for identifying directions students, either individually or as a class, could pursue to deepen their understanding. Such a mapping of the terrain may make next steps seem more possible to students, offering directions for thinking, for effort, and for critique. Students in the classrooms where the research was conducted expressed appreciation for the clarity provided by other elements of the TfU framework, such as understanding goals and criteria for ongoing assessment (see Chapter Nine), and it is reasonable to expect that they would be equally thankful for the explicitness the dimensions offer. The task seems to be finding ways to make the tool efficient for busy teachers with many students. Further research examining how teachers solve this dilemma will be a valuable contribution to teaching for understanding.

Chapter Eight

What Do Students in Teaching for Understanding Classrooms Understand?

Karen Hammerness
Rosario Jaramillo
Chris Unger
Daniel Gray Wilson

Renee understood historical texts to be informed by the beliefs, values, and experiences of their authors. Dan recognized how mechanical advantage helped him in everyday tasks. Rick understood how to construct a personal essay supported by facts and reasons. Evelyn appreciated the roles of ratios and similarity in the mirrors experiment. In addition to illuminating the assessment of understanding, these portraits from the previous chapter give us some ideas about what understanding looks like for several students. They convey with some intimacy the character of individual understanding.

But questions remain. How representative are these students? How many students achieved these kinds of understandings? An analysis of a much larger group of students from all of the Teaching for Understanding (TfU) classes may help to situate the understandings of Renee, Dan, Rick, and Evelyn in a broader context. Building on the instruments used to assess these four students' understanding, in this chapter we examine the understandings of a cross section of students from these classes. Three central questions guide our analysis:

- How well did students achieve the understanding goals their teachers set out?
- Did students in some classes develop deeper understandings than others? If so, how do the classes compare?
- What might account for any differences in student performances within and across classrooms?

The bulk of the analysis is based upon an interview conducted with students at the end of a Teaching for Understanding unit (see Exhibit 8.1 in the chapter appendix for the interview protocol). For this interview, students brought their own work from the selected unit and were asked to tell us about the work, as well as to respond to questions such as, "What have you learned from doing this project?" "What do you think your teacher wanted you to understand?" and "What do you think was the purpose of doing this project?" Students from all four classrooms responded to the same questions, although the interviews varied in that students from each class brought the representative materials or products from their particular unit.

Students were selected by asking the four teachers to choose a group of nine or ten students representing the top, middle, and low range of achievement in their class. Additional data was drawn from a second interview that took place several weeks after the unit was completed (see Chapter Nine for a full consideration of the purpose and results of this interview). The same students were involved in both interviews.

Using the Understanding framework described in Chapter Six, we scored students' discussions in these interviews at one of the four levels (naive, novice, apprentice, or master) within each of the four dimensions (knowledge, methods, purpose, and forms).[1]

Following are the results of the interviews from each of the four classrooms. The results from each classroom are described in three parts: a brief summary of the understanding performance around which the students were interviewed; a summary by dimension that describes the nature of students' responses at each level; and a figure that indicates the number of students scored at each level by dimension. Next we consider possible influences on students' understandings—such as the teacher's level of experience, the discipline, student population, and school culture—and how such factors might have shaped both the practice and the results of Teaching for Understanding. We conclude with some suggestions for future explorations of understanding.

History: Understanding Biography as History

In Lois Hetland's humanities class, twenty-two seventh-grade students were engaged in a focused study of Colonial America. Lois had identified a set of overarching throughlines for this course around the study of history and literature, such as "How do we find the truth about things that happened long ago and/or far away?" "How do we look at a culture?" and "How do we discover central themes?"; these guided the design of each of the units in her year-long class. (See Chapter Five for more on her curriculum.) In one particular unit, groups of students investigated those overarching questions by studying one of the thirteen colonies and presenting their research in both a written report and a display about the colony at a "Colonies Fair" (similar to a living museum). The students also prepared a biography, in the form of a life album of a person who lived during the Colonial period. This unit served as the focus of our interviews with Lois's students.

A representative set of ten of the twenty-two students were asked to bring their life albums and colony reports to this interview in order to answer questions about how those projects had helped them understand Colonial America and, more generally, historical inquiry. In Figure 8.1 we present the numbers of students as we characterized them across the levels and dimensions of understanding.

Knowledge

Students who demonstrated that they had a rich map of the past were scored at the master level. These four students provided a fairly well-connected web of details about the time periods they studied. They also linked the particular colony or historical figure they had investigated to disciplinary concepts or theories. Students whose conceptual understandings were not as detailed and who were less adept at linking examples with broader generalizations were identified as apprentices. These five students recalled some details of Colonial history but had particular difficulty connecting

Figure 8.1. Distribution of Students' Understanding in History.

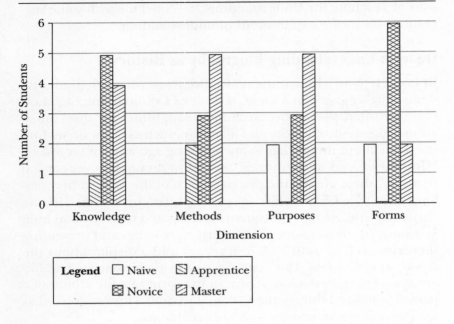

events or individuals to disciplinary themes or concepts. The one student who did not mention how the information he had learned related to historical ideas was scored at the novice level. None of the students described information about the past in a disconnected and unorganized way or revealed misconceptions or stereotypical views of the past. If they had, those responses would have been considered at the naive level.

Methods

Linda described the importance of understanding a historical event from more than one point of view and even went as far as mentioning the importance of interpreting missing information in historical accounts, noting the necessity of what she called "reading between the lines." She recalled reading historical accounts of Colonial America, wondering about the Native American and female perspectives.

Curtis commented upon the importance of putting himself "in the shoes" of historical actors, recognizing that the different perspectives and values of people in the past may have caused them to act in ways that would not be accepted or condoned today. Both Curtis's and Linda's responses are strong examples of the master level in methods.

Students who discussed at length the impact of bias or point of view in the practice of historical thinking were scored at the master level in methods. These five students emphasized the necessity of taking several perspectives when interpreting a historical event. They appeared to understand historical texts as one point of view of an event; they did not describe history as an account of the truth about what happened long ago. They also referred to the use of several methods in examining a historical event or period. For example, they noted the understanding they gained of history by taking the perspective of a particular historical figure or by examining the views of the ordinary rather than the famous figures of history. They further indicated that one historical event may produce a variety of interpretations and points of view.

Students who also described the importance of critically considering the sources and obtaining several different perspectives of an event but who did not discuss the use or importance of other methods with detail or much substance were scored at the apprentice level. These three students, as opposed to students scored at the master level, suggested that a variety of sources can be used together to gain an understanding of history. They did not explain that some claims may be more valid than others, nor were they as articulate about the influence that different perspectives may have upon historical accounts.

Students who described the necessity of examining several sources but did not explain the methodological reasons for such multiple sources were scored at the novice level. One of those two students, for example, said that his process involved looking in several historical sources for ideas that "matched." None of the students said that they obtained their information exclusively from a book or that their teacher explained what had happened, which would suggest a belief that everything one needed to know about history could be learned from a single source. Such a response would have been scored at the naive level.

Purposes

Martha's discussion of her work in the history class provides a powerful example of master level understanding in the purposes dimension. Martha explained that she recognized the current historical emphasis upon examining previously unheard voices as important to her own identity as a Native American. She said that she had tried to incorporate this approach to history in her group presentation on the colonies and had convinced her group to present the Native American perspective of the colonization of Massachusetts. Martha clearly developed a personal position regarding what she had learned in class, which now informed her coursework.

Students who talked substantively about how they applied what they had learned in school to make sense of their own life experiences were scored at the master level. These five students said they considered the purposes and questions of history to be personally important. For example, several students talked about the nature of bias and the ability to "look at a culture" as being helpful in their own lives. Master students also tended to extend those personal connections a step further by linking their individual knowledge back to the classroom again—just as Martha did in the previous example.

Students who connected their understanding of the big ideas in history to their own lives but who did not connect that experience back to school or to the discipline were scored at the apprentice level. These three students did find that their understanding helped them make sense of their own or other's actions but were unable to make use of that insight in their work. For example, one student said he now used his understanding of the existence of different perspectives to interpret the arguments of friends and family members, but he did not talk about how that experience, in turn, informed his understanding of history.

None of the students identified the big questions driving the curriculum, nor did they talk about how and why those overarching questions might be important outside of class. Such responses would have been scored at the novice level. Students who did not talk about or identify any of the purposes of studying history were scored at the naive level. Two students were scored at this level.

Forms

Students who demonstrated a deep understanding of the genres used in the unit (biographies, oral reports, and research papers) were scored at the master level. These two students demonstrated an extremely rich exploration of a person's life through their biography project or their colonies reports. They explained that they had purposefully selected symbols, language, and visuals to best represent their understanding of the colony or historical figure to others, and their selections or presentations were beyond ordinary—they were creative and a bit unusual. As one student said, "I selected this theme because it made sense to me. The books didn't do this. I did!" These two students also commented upon the importance of attending to audience; for instance, they discussed how to edit their writing to be as clear as possible to readers.

Students who similarly revealed a rich understanding of the genres, but who appeared less intentional or purposeful regarding their work were characterized at the apprentice level in understanding. Six students were scored at this level. None of the students followed the rules of the genre mechanically, selected simple or commonplace representations, or failed to follow all the rules of the genre. Such responses would have been scored at the novice level.

Students who created presentations that lacked intentionality in selecting particular symbol systems were scored at the naive level. For example, one of these two students painted a series of watercolors to accompany her report, but they were not supported by any direct intention beyond illustration of events in her report. "I made them blurry," she explained, "because they were blurry in the book I read."

Physics: Understanding Electricity and Simple Circuits

In Eric Buchovecky's physics class, sixty-eight junior and sophomore students engaged in a variety of performances intended to help them understand and develop scientific ideas. Over the course of the year students completed group and individual projects in which they conducted their own investigations and developed and supported their own ideas about the relevant concepts and processes. They were also consistently asked to apply these ideas to novel real-world situations (see Chapter Five for a detailed account of Eric's class). In a spring unit, Eric's students explored the topic of electricity through a series of experiments designed to build their understanding of concepts such as electrons, electrical flow, circuits, and static electricity.

In the interviews a representative set of ten students talked about their understanding of electricity. To facilitate this conversation, students were given the materials (including batteries, wire, capacitors, light bulbs, Styrofoam, metal pie plates, and wool socks) that they had used in exploratory experiments so that if they wished, they could use them to demonstrate their understanding. Figure 8.2 presents the numbers of students as we characterized them across the levels and dimensions of understanding.

Figure 8.2. Distribution of Students' Understanding in Physics.

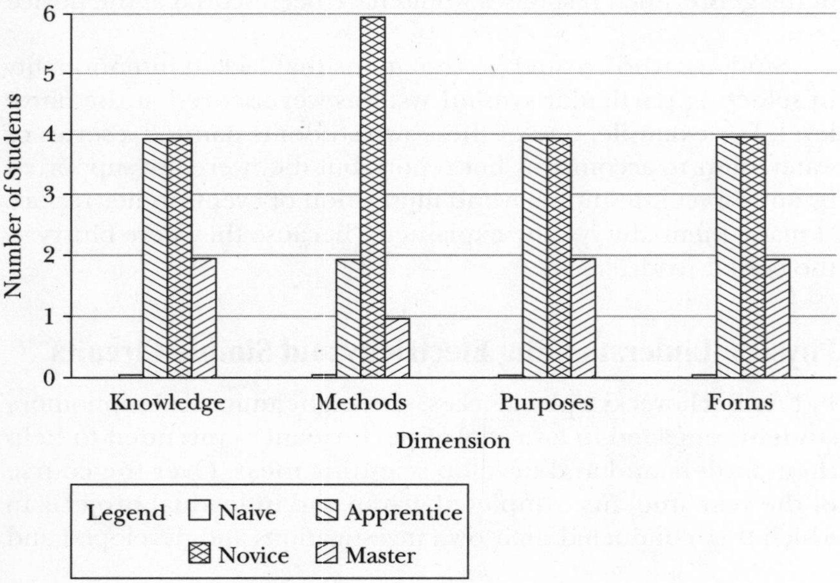

Knowledge

Students who spoke articulately about the disciplinary conceptions of electricity, power, and electrons were scored at the master level. These two students gave organized, specific examples of electricity and its properties and used a variety of disciplinary terms fluently in their discussion. For example, using materials from their labs as props, they explained the notion of excess charge and the flow of electricity. They explained why, for example, rubbing a sock on Styrofoam resulted in excess charge, and they described how the excess of negative charge resulted in a metal flag being repelled by a pie plate rim. They were also able to detail how the discharge of electrons from the pie plate resulted both in an "electric shock" to someone holding it and in a lack of electrons, which then resulted in the repulsion of the metal flag from the pie plate rim.

Students who also discussed the flow of electrons but were less sophisticated in their explanations were scored at the apprentice level. These four students used some disciplinary language but did not organize their specific ideas as explicitly within the larger ideas of the unit. In addition, though these students explained the phenomenon by using some disciplinary theories, they could not give the examples that characterized the students at the master level.

Students who talked about electrons but did not support their discussion with any specific examples were scored at the novice level. These four students' language and explanations appeared to be more fragile and sometimes contained a mixture of disciplinary ideas and intuitions. For example, one student at this level explained the movement of the electrons in the following manner: "Well, they need to move because they have a great desire to get over there. I mean, you added some heat, or energy or friction, by rubbing it."

None of the students failed to describe the phenomenon at all or neglected to use specific terms, such as electron flow or result of excess or lack of electrons in an object. Nor did any of the students reveal intuitions about the notion of electricity not yet reconciled with disciplinary ideas. Such responses would have been scored at the naive level.

Methods

The one student who said that scientific knowledge was gained through observations of events, through generating hypotheses, and by gathering evidence to support or contradict such hypotheses was scored at the master level. This student explained that he checked the validity of his knowledge by conducting both thought and real-world experiments. In the context of the unit on electricity he offered detailed explanations of the nature of electricity by using examples such as why a live electric cable "flops" around on the ground.

Students who mentioned that they built their knowledge through class experiments with the lab materials but who were not as explicit about the process of the scientific method were scored as apprentices. These six students did, however, demonstrate a thorough understanding, particularly when the validity of their knowledge was in question (sometimes the batteries, light bulbs, and capacitor would not respond as they had predicted). These six students correctly held to the theory and looked to other variables that may have influenced the outcome; a wire not connected, a capacitor not fully discharged, or a burned-out bulb.

Students who remarked in the interviews that they built their knowledge through working with the materials but did not mention the role of observation, hypothesizing, and verification were scored as novices. When circumstances such as a surprising or contradictory result challenged these three students, they did not defend their conclusions through empirical examples as the apprentices did. Rather they became perplexed, defended a conclusion's merit by saying, "Well, that is what the teacher told me," or simply responded that this was what they had learned in class. Unlike the apprentices, they were not able to engage immediately in a physical or mental exploration to explain the unexpected outcome.

None revealed a lack of understanding regarding how they built their knowledge of electricity beyond merely conducting the experiments in class. Nor did any of these students verify their knowledge by simply suggesting that laboratory results represented solutions or answers to our questions. Such responses would have been scored at the naive level.

Purposes

Students who talked at length about the usefulness of their scientific knowledge to interpret and reflect upon phenomena in the everyday world were characterized at the master level. One of these two students said, "[This is] what science is all about—looking at phenomena, then coming up with a theory which works and can help people with all types of problems." These two students said they saw potential and possible future applications in their lives. For example, one student talked in detail about how his understanding of electricity as the flow or abundance of electrons could serve as a tool to help him think about rewiring the electricity in houses. Both these students also connected their understanding of personal applications back to their understanding of the discipline.

Students who talked about how they could connect their understanding of electricity to their own lives or the world but who presented scantier explanations were scored at the apprentice level. These four students described possible applications, such as radios and lightning, but they did not articulate a more personal sense of the meaning of that knowledge. More important, they did not connect these applications back to the purposes of the discipline.

Students who gave rehearsed or simplistic connections of this knowledge in the real world were characterized at the novice level. These four students talked about the importance of understanding electricity as the flow of electrons through wires and the different outcomes of their labs depending on whether light bulbs were hooked up in series or parallel, and how that could be related to house wiring or how working with pie plates could explain what it means to get a shock. However, they did not discuss the value of their understanding as a tool for explaining and making sense of a variety of everyday phenomena nor did they relate it back into the purpose of the discipline. None of the students we interviewed failed to refer to the usefulness or purposes of the knowledge in any respect, which would have been characterized as a naive response.

Forms

Students who took the audience (in this case the interviewer) into account when explaining and clarifying their understandings were scored at the master level. These two students used the class and other materials in a variety of ways. They developed original analogies or metaphors, rephrased their ideas, and drew diagrams in order to help the interviewer understand their explanations. Students who showed some fluency with symbol systems and sense of audience but whose analogies or diagrams seemed more rehearsed or based on sketches and explanations made in class were scored at the apprentice level. Four students were scored at this level.

Students who did not manipulate and use any materials (visuals, analogies, or others) to demonstrate or illustrate their points were scored at the novice level. These four students relied mainly on simple verbal explanations that were at times unclear. None of the students failed to use any symbol systems at all to help illustrate their ideas to their audience; such responses would have been scored as naive.

English: Understanding Reading and Writing Short Stories

In Joan Soble's semester-long literature class, ninth- through twelfth-grade students were involved in exploring short stories as representations and investigations of human experience. Understanding the elements of the short story, such as plot, character, setting, mood, and tone, and recognizing how authors use those elements to convey themes about people's lives and experiences was a related overarching goal. Students read short stories such as Gilman's "The Yellow Wallpaper," Chekhov's "The Beggar," and Poe's "The Tell-Tale Heart" and considered how the era might have influenced beliefs about human experience. They read contemporary stories as comparisons. After reading a series of short stories the class developed criteria for a "good" short story and used them to interpret stories they read for class, as well to write their own short stories.

Of the class of twenty-six students, a representative set of ten were interviewed. Students brought short stories they had written to discuss in the interview. Figure 8.3 shows the numbers of students as we characterized them across the levels and dimensions of understanding.

Figure 8.3. Distribution of Students' Understanding in English.

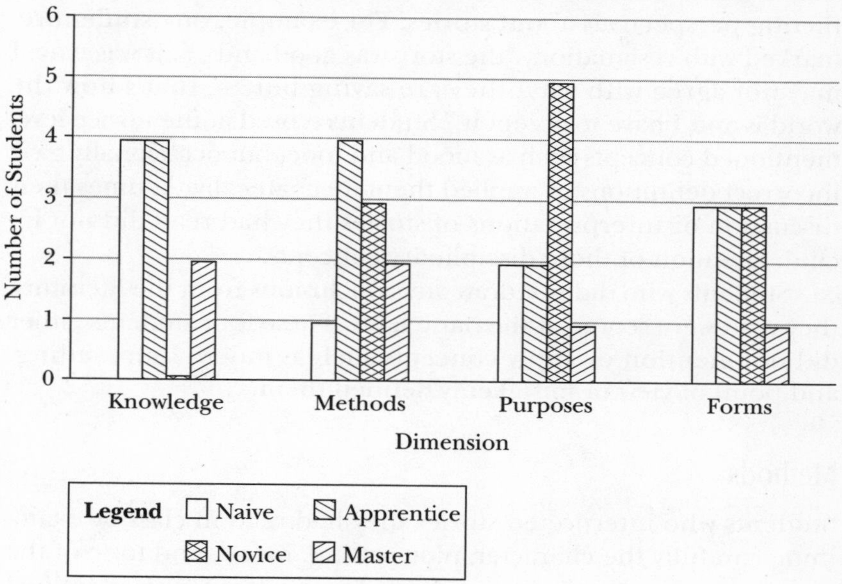

Knowledge

Students who shared story interpretations that went beyond a literal interpretation were characterized at the master level. These two students indicated that they understood that authors were trying to convey an impression or point of view about human experience and not just telling a good or compelling story. These students also defined the elements of the short story (plot, mood, characters, setting, and so on) with some detail and gave examples from the short stories they had read.

None of the students who indicated an understanding of stories as representing more than the literal account of an event gave a sparser and more rehearsed discussion of the symbolic meaning of the stories. Such a response would have been scored at the apprentice level.

Students who appeared to hold the intuitive belief that stories told the truth about life were scored at the novice level. These four students did not show that they recognized that stories are told from a point of view or that they understood the possibility of conflicting perspectives about stories. For example, one student remarked with resignation, "the story was good and . . . it was true. I may not agree with what they are saying but . . . that's how the world is and I have to accept it." Students scored at the novice level mentioned concepts such as mood and tone, but occasionally gave incorrect definitions or applied them mechanically. At times their discussion or interpretations of stories they had read did not include mention of those disciplinary concepts.

Students who did not draw any conclusions from the literature they read were scored at the naive level. These four students either did not mention or apply concepts such as mood, tone, setting, and point of view or mistakenly defined them.

Methods

Students who interpreted stories they had read in class by examining carefully the character, plot, setting, mood, and tone of the story were scored at the master level. These two students identified themes about human experience in the stories they read. They emphasized that their classmates might have come to different interpretations of stories and that such differences were valuable to hear in order to reflect upon one's own ideas; they demonstrated that an understanding of the meaning of a story was built through discussion and even disagreement.

Students who referred to just one element of story—often describing only the main character's motivations—in developing an interpretation were scored at the apprentice level. These three students examined the plot, setting, tone, and mood less frequently in their interpretations. They sometimes referred to the importance of understanding other students' points of view about stories. They did not mention, however, that the purpose of such a discussion is for constructing meaning or that alternate interpretations could be provisionally valid. One student, for example, said he liked hearing other perspectives because he increased the validity of his own interpretation by "adding" their interpretations to his own.

Students who rarely referred to story elements in their interpretations were scored at the novice level. These four students emphasized the importance of class discussion as a way to get to know classmates or express their own feelings, rather than as a method of developing a richer appreciation of the story. The one student who did not connect the elements of story to her interpretation was scored at the naive level. This student also did not give any reasons for, or appreciation of, sharing stories with others or listening to other's interpretations.

Purposes

Carter provides an excellent example of understanding purpose at the master level. He connected his understanding of historical and cultural influences of literary meaning to his own actions as a short story author. He explained that if he had lived in an earlier time his story would have been different, and he explained in some detail how and why. He also identified themes, such as loneliness and community, in stories he had read in class, discussed the presence of those themes in his life, and described how he addressed them in his course writing. Carter was the only student scored at the master level in the purposes dimension of understanding.

Students who identified the meanings of short stories but who failed to connect such knowledge back to their work or to the discipline were scored at the apprentice level. These five students described how such ideas helped them gain insight into their own or other's actions but did not bring those insights to bear upon their work. For example, one student remarked that reading "The Beggar" helped her see that "if you wanted to change your life around there is a way you could do it."

Students who did not discuss how stories related to their own experiences or to the world around them were scored at the novice level. However, these two students did suggest that what they were learning in class would help them in school. Students who did not talk about the connections between themselves or the world and the literature they read were scored at the naive level. These two students did not describe any purpose in reading literature beyond completion of school assignments. As one student expressed: "I don't know what [my teacher] wants. She gives us stories about people and asks us to answer questions."

Forms

Carter also provides an excellent example of the master level in forms—he indicated a deeper understanding of the symbolic nature of elements in stories by describing how his own story could be interpreted as a story about literal as well as figurative madness. He also described how he had purposefully created details and events that would best convey the withdrawal and isolation felt by the protagonist. Furthermore, he tried to understand his audience by imagining what he himself might find interesting. He even critiqued his story for leaving out some important insights experienced by his main character, explaining that such information might have helped his readers understand the story even better. Carter was the only student scored at the master level in forms.

Students who indicated the reasons for their choices of characters or the ideas they wanted to express but who did not express the same rich intentional selection of details and ideas were scored at the apprentice level. These three students also showed that they took audience into account by describing the importance of incorporating the feedback of their peers into later drafts of their stories.

Students who talked less clearly about the audience were scored at the novice level. One of these three students, for example, maintained that he wanted "to interest people" but did not say how he could do so. These three students described writing stories in order to complete an assignment but often did not mention wanting to express a particular idea or meaning in their pieces. Novices also used more commonplace metaphors and characters and simple representations in their stories. Students who showed some aesthetic intention but who indicated no understanding of audience were scored at the naive level. These three students revealed only fragile understandings—if any— of the symbolic natures of the elements in stories.

Mathematics: Understanding Shapes and Areas

Over the year, the forty-nine students in Bill Kendall's two sopho-more geometry classes engaged in a variety of performances to ex-plore the following overarching understanding goal: "Geometry is the study of lawfully connected patterns in the world." In March, Bill assigned the "community center project," which required his students to create a scaled floor plan of a fictitious community cen-ter for their town. Students were asked to create the floor plan keeping in mind three concepts they had encountered in class: shapes (triangles, circles, quadrilaterals, hexagons), their areas, and ratios.

From the two classes a representative set of nine students were chosen. In the interviews students were asked to talk about their understanding of the shapes and areas they used in the project. To facilitate this conversation, the students brought in their floor plan and all other work they had done around the project. Figure 8.4 presents the numbers of students as we characterized them across the levels and dimensions of understanding.

Knowledge

None of the students interviewed was able to make rich and orga-nized connections between the overarching disciplinary idea and specific examples of area formulas. Such responses would have been scored at the master level. However, students who made con-nections between the shapes, their formulas, and specific exam-ples of how the formulas worked were scored at the apprentice level. These two students also were able to explain how such shapes and formulas were deduced. For example, one student showed how she used trapezoids in her project and talked fairly fluently about how the formula for a trapezoid is related to triangles and quadrilaterals. The other student at this level described how the larger disciplinary idea of patterns was involved in the project and gave a few simple examples.

Students who discussed a number of shapes and formulas but made few connections between them as shapes or described their relationship to formulas were scored as novices. These three

Figure 8.4. Distribution of Students' Understanding in Math.

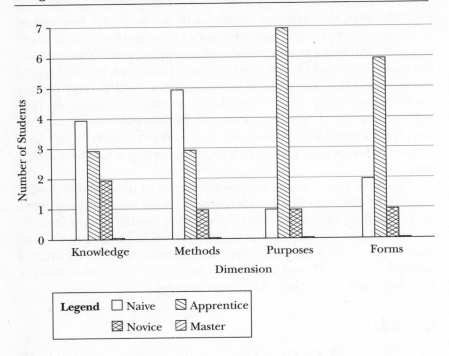

students sometimes stated the larger ideas, such as ratios, shapes, patterns, and problem solving, but they did not connect them to specific examples. Students who mentioned fewer shapes and formulas for their areas but tended to refer to them incorrectly were scored at the naive level. These four students did not make any connections with this knowledge to other larger disciplinary ideas such as pattern, shape, or ratios.

Methods

None of the students interviewed verified their knowledge, deduced formulas from other formulas, or created new formulas. Nor did any of the students we interviewed describe how the process of mathematical inquiry involves both problem solving and generalizing beyond specific instances. Had there been any such responses they would have been scored as master level. The one student who said he built his knowledge of the areas of shapes through trying out ideas, observing the results, and revising his approach was scored at the apprentice level. He also suggested that he believed his knowledge of the area formulas to be valid because he could deduce these formulas from other formulas he knew to be true.

Students who said that they built their knowledge by simply doing the project and following the procedures were scored at the novice level. These three students explained that they used a process of application but could not articulate more about what this process was. They also maintained that their knowledge was valid either because the teacher told them so or because it agreed with the textbook. These students did not refer to mathematical methods of supporting their knowledge.

Students who could not indicate a process by which they built their knowledge were scored as naive. These five students suggested that they developed knowledge by, as one student put it, "just doing the work." Furthermore, characteristic of the naive level in methods, these students did not question the validity of their knowledge, indicating that whatever they had learned was unquestionable and true.

Purposes

None of the students described what they saw as the larger purposes of the mathematics, nor did any students forge rich connections between the mathematical concepts and their own lives. Such responses would have been considered at the master level in purposes. Students who made some personal connections between the ideas and their lives but failed to clearly articulate reasons to study these concepts were scored at the apprentice level. These two students discussed the course concepts in terms of technical applications. For example, one student related how she transferred what she had learned by talking with her dad about areas and shapes in buildings that he built. When asked about the purpose of her knowledge, she remarked that if she were to pursue a similar career such knowledge certainly would be important. She did not describe any wider applications of her knowledge.

Students who articulated some personal connection to the knowledge by describing real-world applications but whose discussions sounded more rehearsed or simplistic were scored as novices. When asked about the point of studying areas, these seven students tended to suggest that the concepts would definitely be useful but did not give strong examples. The one student who indicated little personal connection to the concepts in the course and who remarked that she did not know the point of studying areas was scored at the naive level. She did remark that she might find such mathematical concepts useful if she became a carpenter, but at the same time she expressed serious doubts as to whether that would be a career she would select.

Forms

None of the students interviewed used multiple means of expression, such as diagrams, objects, metaphors, similes, examples, or other illustrations, in describing their understanding. Such responses would have been scored at the master level. The one student who explained his understandings verbally and used diagrams to illustrate meanings without being prompted was scored at the apprentice level. His community center project indicated an awareness for a larger audience: he had selected particular shapes and sizes in order to create a space that would be most functional for a diverse community. This student also rephrased his understandings when asked and asked clarifying questions so that he could respond correctly to the interviewer's inquiries.

Students who described their understandings occasionally making use of diagrams or other means of communication but who gave thinner or muddier explanations were scored at the novice level. These six students also had difficulty rephrasing their understandings, and they revealed a weaker awareness of audience: they constructed their projects and adhered to the criteria but made no personal tailoring in their project for a larger audience beyond the teacher.

The students who talked about their understandings in unclear ways and offered no diagrams, pictures, or metaphors for clarification were scored at the naive level. These two students indicated no sense of an audience for their work, explaining that they were just "following the directions" in their projects. When asked to rephrase their understandings, they were unable to do so.

Making Sense of Understanding

These findings convey the range of understandings achieved in these four classes. They also begin to reveal some of the subtle differences in understanding among classes and within classes and raise some interesting hypotheses that we can begin to explore.

Differences in Students' Overall Understanding by Classroom

One of the questions we wondered about was whether students' understanding scores would be different in different classrooms. Indeed, we found some interesting variations. To compare students' levels of understanding across classrooms, we analyzed each student's level in each of the four dimensions (see Exhibit 8.2 in the chapter appendix for the resulting ratings). Then we assigned a value to each level (naive = 1, novice = 2, apprentice = 3, master = 4) and calculated each student's overall score of understanding in each dimension. Students' scores for overall understanding were distributed on a scale from 4 to 16.

Students whose sum fell between 4 and 6 were assigned an overall score of naive understanding. Students with summed scores between 7 and 10 were assigned an overall score of novice understanding. Those with summed scores between 11 and 14 were assigned an overall score of apprentice understanding, and those with summed scores of 15 or 16 were assigned an overall score of master level understanding. (To see the distribution of overall understanding scores across classes, see Exhibit 8.3 in the chapter appendix.) Table 8.1 shows the number of students within each classroom who scored at the various levels of master, apprentice, novice, and naive.

The history class had the highest number of students who were scored at the master level: three. History also had a larger number of students scored at the apprentice level—five—than the other three classes. Only one history student scored at each of the novice and naive levels. In the physics class two students were scored at the master level, five at the apprentice level, and four at the novice level. None of the physics students was scored at the naive level. One English student scored at the master level, and three were scored at each of the apprentice, novice, and naive levels. In mathematics, none of the students was scored at the master level and just one at the apprentice level. Four students were scored at the novice level, and three were scored as naive.

Differences among the classrooms can also be illustrated by the percentages of students scoring at or above the apprentice level in all dimensions. Table 8.2 shows that 40 percent of the history students scored at the master level in all dimensions, as did 18 percent of the physics students and 15 percent of the English students; none of the mathematics students scored at the master level in all dimensions, however.

To determine whether the variations across classrooms were significant, we used the Mann-Whitney U-test to make pairwise comparisons of the ranked scores of overall understanding for students in each class. This test showed that students in the history class scored significantly higher than those in the English and math classes, and students in the physics class scored significantly higher than those in the math class. Exhibit 8.4 in the chapter appendix displays these results. The other pairwise comparisons (his-

Table 8.1. Students' Overall Understanding Scores by Classroom.

	History	Physics	English	Math
Master	3	2	1	0
Apprentice	5	4	3	1
Novice	1	4	3	4
Naive	1	0	3	3

Table 8.2. Percentage of Students Scoring at or Above Apprentice Level by Class.

	History	Physics	English	Math
Master	40 percent	18 percent	15 percent	0 percent
Apprentice or master	83	63	43	14

tory with physics, physics with English, and English with math) did not show significant differences.

Association Among the Dimensions

We also wondered whether, within classrooms, individual students' understanding might vary among the various dimensions of knowledge, methods, purposes, and forms. Did some students develop deeper levels of understanding in one dimension, such as methods, while developing thinner levels of understanding in another?

We found that students' attainments in different dimensions were highly associated. As illustrated in Table 8.3, the level of association among the dimensions is shown by the high percentage of students who scored at the same levels in pairs of dimensions. Furthermore, students tended to score at one level, or within two neighboring levels, in all four dimensions: 95 percent (thirty-seven of thirty-nine) ranged at most within two neighboring levels across the four dimensions, and 33 percent (thirteen of thirty-nine) scored consistently within one level among all four dimensions. In other words, if Marco scored at the master level in methods, he also tended to score at the master level in forms.

Exhibit 8.5 in the chapter appendix displays the numbers of students who scored either within the levels of naive or novice or within the levels of apprentice or master on different dimensions of understanding. A chi-square analysis of these results demonstrated a significant association between students' levels of understanding across dimensions ($p < .001$).

What can we take away from these findings? The trends and patterns of understanding across the four different classrooms raise a number of questions. For instance, why did more of the history

Table 8.3. Percentage of Students Scoring at the Same Level in Different Dimensions.

	Knowledge	*Methods*	*Purposes*
Forms	67 percent	54 percent	74 percent
Purposes	51	56	—
Methods	62	—	—

students give responses that were scored at the master level? Why did none of the mathematics students do so? Next we consider some possible explanations for our results, focusing upon variations in teachers' experience with the TfU framework, in student population, in school context, in the nature of the discipline, and in aspects of the research project itself.

History

A series of factors may have influenced the high scores of student understanding in history. First, Lois Hetland had worked with the framework for two years. During that period she focused on articulating, shaping, and refining her pedagogical goals. Throughout her two years with the project she had designed and gradually implemented TfU in her classroom so that by the time we conducted these student interviews she was teaching a yearlong TfU course. None of the other three teachers had such rich practical and theoretical experience with the framework.

The student population and school may also have affected the results: the students came mostly from middle-or upper-middle-class families and attended private school. In addition many of the classes that students attended at this school had features of an inquiry-based approach to learning. Thus students had many opportunities to gain some familiarity with the process of inquiry into generative questions.

For Lois herself the school setting may also have been important in supporting the development of a powerful TfU curriculum. In allowing her to have some time to think about her practice, to develop new curriculum, and to experiment with the TfU approach to teaching, her school may have provided the kind of support one needs to reform or reshape one's practice in substantive ways.

Beyond the school context it could be that the discipline of history in general seems more consistent with the philosophies and practices of TfU. It may not be as much of a leap for history students to think about history in terms of generative questions as it is for mathematics students, for example. Finally, aspects of the research project itself may have shaped the students' scores: Lois's research partner, Martha Stone Wiske, was an experienced educational researcher who had worked with the TfU project since its inception.

Physics

Although students in physics did not receive as many high scores as the history students, they still performed quite well. At some level this result might seem surprising. Eric Buchovecky was less familiar with the TfU framework: the year we worked with his students was his first year with the project. However, his student teaching program at Harvard addressed approaches to teaching and learning consistent with Teaching for Understanding.[2] Indeed, Eric was able to take courses with some of the researchers involved in the project and thus was somewhat conversant with the TfU principles and practices.

In addition, though Eric's school is a large public school and may not have had an expressed philosophy consistent with TfU, his students were enrolled in a college preparatory class and, like Lois's students, came from mostly middle- and upper-middle-class backgrounds.

Furthermore, the way students have typically been taught science, with a focus upon conducting class labs, may have some features consistent with TfU. The task the students were asked to discuss in their interviews might not have seemed all that different or unusual to Eric's students, therefore, and may have enabled them to feel more comfortable and more confident in their work. Finally, Eric's partner, Chris Unger, was also an experienced educational researcher; his support may have contributed to a curriculum that was particularly consistent with TfU goals and approaches.

English

The English students did not perform as well as either the history or physics classes. These results may also have been influenced by the teachers' experience and by the school context. Joan taught at an alternative school that expressed a philosophy in many ways consistent with TfU approaches; it emphasized personal responsibility and academic engagement and attempted to provide a close supportive atmosphere for its students. However, though the courses offered at Joan's school may have been more consistent with an inquiry-based approach (thus enabling Joan's students some level of comfort with her teaching), the English students were an extremely diverse group academically, economically, and culturally. In addition a number of students in this particular class were

considered "at risk" for academic failure by the school administration and were struggling to be academically successful.

Although Joan was an experienced teacher and had encountered ideas similar to TfU in professional development seminars
and other programs, she had not had the sort of previous experience Eric had with the project; this was her first year with it. Also,
Joan's research partner, Karen, was in her second year with the TfU
project and was less experienced in developing TfU curriculum
than some of the other researchers.

Mathematics

The mathematics students performed the least well of the four
classes. This result seems surprising given Bill's longer involvement
with the project: like Lois, he was in his second year with the project. However, Bill's school context and the discipline itself may
have together contributed to some constraints upon Bill's curriculum development and his ability to implement Teaching for
Understanding approaches.

Bill's school context—a large public school serving middle-
income suburban students—was not a deeply supportive atmosphere for innovation. The school did not take an approach to
teaching and learning that emphasized ideas consistent with TfU,
such as performance assessments or developing curriculum around
generative topics. In fact, Bill felt he had considerably less freedom
in terms of implementing TfU curriculum and—in contrast with
Lois, who was able to gradually shift her pedagogy to become more
and more consistent with TfU—Bill taught only one TfU unit the
previous year. Furthermore, the math students were on a rotating
block schedule that allowed Bill to teach them for only forty-five
minutes per day, limiting the amount of time students and teacher
could dedicate to in-depth understanding performances and reflection upon goals. Finally, Bill's students were "lower-track" tenth-
graders from diverse economic and social backgrounds.

Mathematics itself—as seen as a school discipline, or perhaps
as shaped by Bill's department, school, or district—may also have
contributed to the results of his class. Bill was concerned that he
develop curriculum consistent with the mathematics text he was
required to teach; this constraint likely shaped the kind of course
he was able to design and teach.

Bill is not unique in feeling this way about his discipline. Grossman and Stodolsky[3] conducted research on teachers' conceptions of their discipline and found much variation across subject matters. They discovered that though English teachers tended to describe their discipline as "permissive," mathematics teachers spoke of the "constraints of the content"—referring to the linearity of the subject matter and the necessity of coverage. Math teachers also rated their subject as more "defined" and "static" than did science teachers, but English teachers strongly disagreed with the description of their subject as static.

Finally, factors within the research project may have contributed to the results. Bill's research partner, Daniel, was new to the TfU project and was learning about the ideas of Teaching for Understanding himself.

Conclusion

This chapter has attempted to convey what a broad range of students' understandings looked like in four Teaching for Understanding classrooms. We cannot claim a cause-and-effect relationship between TfU pedagogy and student performances, but our analysis reveals findings that we hope will prompt further exploration. First, these results suggest that even in very different—and in some cases difficult—circumstances a number of students in Teaching for Understanding classrooms achieved a master level of understanding. Second, students' performances in the different classrooms indicate how such factors as teachers' experience, student population, school context, and the nature of the subject matter may influence the levels of understandings attained by TfU students. These factors warrant deeper investigation. Finally, our analysis shows that an examination of understanding in terms of methods, forms, knowledge, and purposes is a fruitful way of thinking about student understanding. Beyond the specific goals of research, such an approach may allow educators to note strengths and weaknesses of the performances of their students and in the levels of understanding attained by the whole class. This kind of information may enable teachers to reflect on and improve their curriculum and practice.

Appendix

Exhibit 8.1. Initial Student Interview Protocol.

1. Tell me about the work you have or the project you recently completed. Is there something you really like about it? Are there things you don't like about it?
2. What have you learned, if anything, from doing this?
3. Did something the teacher did help you learn that, or did you pick that up on your own from other classes?
4. Did something you did in class help you learn that?
5. What do you think the teacher wanted you to learn from doing this project? What was the point of doing this?
6. Are there things that you think the teacher wants you to understand in this project? Throughout the class so far?
7. The teacher had these understanding goals (show the student both the unit-level and yearlong goals). Do you recognize them? Some people feel that knowing the understanding goals of a class is useful, and others feel they are not as helpful. What do you think?
8. Select a goal you feel you understand. Tell me about your understanding of it. Select another goal you would like to talk about, and tell me about your understanding of it. Select a goal you feel you don't understand well, and talk about why you do not understand it.

Exhibit 8.2. Students' Levels of Understanding in the Four Dimensions.

Name	Class	Knowledge	Methods	Purposes	Forms
1	History	Apprentice	Apprentice	Master	Apprentice
2	History	Apprentice	Master	Master	Apprentice
3	History	Apprentice	Master	Apprentice	Apprentice
4	History	Apprentice	Novice	Naive	Naive
5	History	Master	Apprentice	Apprentice	Apprentice
6	History	Apprentice	Apprentice	Apprentice	Apprentice
7	History	Master	Master	Master	Apprentice
8	History	Novice	Novice	Naive	Naive
9	History	Master	Master	Master	Master
10	History	Master	Master	Master	Master
11	Physics	Novice	Novice	Novice	Novice
12	Physics	Novice	Novice	Novice	Novice
13	Physics	Novice	Apprentice	Apprentice	Novice
14	Physics	Apprentice	Apprentice	Apprentice	Apprentice
15	Physics	Novice	Novice	Novice	Novice
16	Physics	Apprentice	Apprentice	Novice	Master
17	Physics	Apprentice	Apprentice	Apprentice	Apprentice
18	Physics	Apprentice	Apprentice	Apprentice	Apprentice
19	Physics	Master	Master	Master	Apprentice
20	Physics	Master	Apprentice	Master	Master
21	English	Novice	Apprentice	Apprentice	Novice
22	English	Naive	Novice	Naive	Naive
23	English	Master	Master	Apprentice	Apprentice
24	English	Novice	Apprentice	Apprentice	Apprentice
25	English	Naive	Novice	Novice	Novice
26	English	Master	Master	Master	Master
27	English	Naive	Novice	Naive	Naive
28	English	Novice	Novice	Apprentice	Novice
29	English	Naive	Naive	Novice	Naive
30	English	Novice	Apprentice	Apprentice	Apprentice
31	Math	Naive	Naive	Novice	Novice
32	Math	Novice	Naive	Novice	Novice
33	Math	Naive	Naive	Naive	Naive
34	Math	Novice	Novice	Novice	Novice
35	Math	Naive	Naive	Novice	Naive
36	Math	Apprentice	Novice	Apprentice	Apprentice
37	Math	Naive	Naive	Novice	Novice
38	Math	Novice	Novice	Novice	Novice
39	Math	Apprentice	Apprentice	Novice	Novice

Exhibit 8.3. Students' Overall Understanding by Classroom.

Overall Score		Number of Students			
Level	Sum	History	Physics	English	Math
	16	2	—	1	—
Master	15	1	2	—	—
	14	1	—	1	—
	13	3	—	—	—
Apprentice	12	1	4	—	—
	11	—	—	2	1
	10	—	1	1	1
	9	—	—	1	—
Novice	8	—	3	—	2
	7	1	—	1	1
Naive	6	1	—	—	2
	5	—	—	3	1
	4	—	—	—	1

Note: Overall score sum = the students' knowledge + methods + purposes + forms scores; letting naive = 1, novice = 2, apprentice = 3, master = 4.

Exhibit 8.4. Comparison of Differences in Students' Overall Understanding Across Classrooms: Results of Mann-Whitney U-Test.

History		English			History		Math			Physics		Math	
Score	Rank	Score	Rank		Score	Rank	Score	Rank		Score	Rank	Score	Rank
6	4	5	3		6	4	4	1		8	8	4	1
7	5.5	5	3		7	6.5	5	2		8	8	5	2
12	11	5	3		12	12	6	4		8	8	6	3.5
13	13	7	5.5		13	14	6	4		10	11.5	6	3.5
13	13	9	7		13	14	7	6.5		12	15.5	7	5
13	13	10	8		13	14	8	8.5		12	15.5	8	8
14	16	11	9.5		14	16	8	8.5		12	15.5	8	8
15	17	11	9.5		15	17	10	10		12	15.5	8	8
16	19	14	16		16	18.5	11	11		15	18.5	10	11.5
16	19	16	19		16	18.5				15	18.5	11	13
r_1	130	r_2	83		r_1	134.5	r_2	55.5		r_1	134.5	r_2	55.5
n_1	10	n_2	10		n_1	10	n_2	9		n_1	10	n_2	9

$U_1 = 25$ $U_1 = 10.5$ $U_1 = 10.5$

Exhibit 8.5. Association of Students' Levels of Understanding Across Dimensions.

	Methods	
	Naive or Novice	Apprentice or Master
Knowledge Naive or Novice	16	4
Knowledge Apprentice or Master	2	17

	Purposes	
	Naive or Novice	Apprentice or Master
Knowledge Naive or Novice	15	5
Knowledge Apprentice or Master	2	16

	Forms	
	Naive or Novice	Apprentice or Master
Knowledge Naive or Novice	18	2
Knowledge Apprentice or Master	2	17

Purposes

Methods

	Naive or Novice	Apprentice or Master
Naive or Novice	16	2
Apprentice or Master	2	19

Forms

Methods

	Naive or Novice	Apprentice or Master
Naive or Novice	17	1
Apprentice or Master	3	18

Forms

Purposes

	Naive or Novice	Apprentice or Master
Naive or Novice	17	1
Apprentice or Master	3	18

Chapter Nine

What Do Students Think About Understanding?

Chris Unger
Daniel Gray Wilson
with Rosario Jaramillo
Roger Dempsey

Teaching for Understanding (TfU) requires students to shoulder more responsibility than is customary in many classrooms. The TfU framework is based on a belief that students build and demonstrate understanding through creative and novel applications of their knowledge. To perform their understandings, students must become actively involved in their learning. In TfU classrooms students are aware of the goals toward which their efforts are bent. They assess their own work and their peers' performances by applying criteria and standards based on those goals. As Eric Buchovecky noted (see Chapter Five), integrating the elements of TfU into his practice entailed a significant change in the usual classroom culture, including new kinds of goals and altered roles for students as well as teachers.

Do students who notice and value such changes perform better than those who do not? Do students who share a performance view of understanding demonstrate more success in TfU classrooms than those whose beliefs are more consistent with the traditional view of academic achievement as accumulation of facts? Prior research has demonstrated a robust link between students' ideas about understanding and their level of understanding.[1] Such correlations suggested that students' conceptions about the TfU framework might influence the level of understanding they develop in TfU classrooms.

With these concerns in mind the TfU project researchers and teachers decided to investigate students' ideas about teaching and learning in TfU classrooms. This research did not attempt to analyze how students' conceptions changed as a result of Teaching for Understanding. Instead, the purpose was to learn how students in these classrooms thought about understanding and TfU and to determine whether these conceptions were related to students' understandings, as described in Chapters Seven and Eight.

As described in Chapter Eight, each of the four teachers who worked closely with the TfU project selected a sample of eight to ten students to represent the top, middle, and lower range of perceived understanding in their class. Researchers interviewed these students twice near the end of the academic year. The first interview took place at the beginning of a curriculum unit designed with the TfU framework and the second occurred about two or three weeks after the unit ended. Because four students were not available, the total number of students interviewed was thirty-five. The video-interview format, used in place of written instruments, gave students an easier and richer means to share their views. It also allowed the researchers to ask additional questions for greater clarification or elaboration of a student's answers.

The interview consisted of two parts in order to ensure both comparability in results and specificity about the different experiences with TfU across classrooms. The first part consisted of a set of questions to elicit students' conceptions of understanding and how understanding is developed. These questions, shown in Exhibit 9.1, were posed in all the interviews. The interviewers encouraged students to discuss differences in how they were taught and how they learned in the TfU class versus their non-TfU classes. In the second part interviewers attempted to learn whether students perceived the elements of teaching for understanding as helpful to their understanding. Questions in this second part varied across classrooms to highlight the specific moves each teacher made with the four elements of the TfU framework in the target unit. Some questions elicited information pertaining to more than one element of the framework (see Table 9.1).

Exhibit 9.1. Common Interview Questions.

---

1. Tell me about something you understand really well from this class.
2. How did you get or build that understanding?
3. How do you know you understand that?
4. What did your teacher do to help you understand that?
5. What did you do to help yourself understand that?
6. Is this class taught any differently from your other classes? If yes, how so?
7. Did you learn any differently in this class from your other classes? If yes, how so?

The interviews were transcribed; researchers attempted to sort similar kinds of students' responses into initial categories along a continuum, attending to the nature of students' perceptions and the reasons they offered. Prior research on students' conceptions of understanding and learning informed the refinement of these categories. For example, variations in students' responses about understanding were compared to Entwistle's "surface" versus "deep" approaches and Dweck's "incremental vs. entity" learning.[2]

With these conceptions in mind, researchers analyzed student responses within each classroom and discipline (recall that each teacher taught a different subject). Further analysis led to the definition of categories that could be applied regardless of subject matter. The interviews were then coded and scored according to these categories. Members of the research team checked the reliability of their process by comparing independently scored interviews. If a student's response fell into more than one category, the researchers made a decision as to which of the student's various conceptions seemed to have the greatest influence.

In the following section we present the results of this analysis. The subsequent discussion analyzes these findings in relation to our original questions. Finally, we suggest some implications for enhancing students' understanding.

Table 9.1. Interview Questions Related to Each Aspect of the Framework in Each Class.

	History	Math	Physics	English
Understanding performances	Engagement in long-term projects? Class conversations?	Did the projects and other activities help?	Finding and analyzing real-world problems?	Did the freewrites about the big ideas help? Did long-term projects help?
Ongoing assessments	Did reflecting with the process journals help? Did using the assessment sheet as a guide help? Did peer feedback help? Did individual conferences help? Did class conversations help? Did working in groups help?	Did handling it in stages help? Did peer and group assessments help? Did talking with the teacher help? Did the self-reflection sheets help?	Did logbooks help? Did completing your own grade sheets help? Did working in groups help?	Did student feedback help with your revisions? Did the reflection sheets help? Did peer feedback help?
Understanding goals	Were the throughlines helpful?	Did the understanding goals help?	Were the understanding goals helpful?	Did the understanding goals help?
Generative topics	Did connecting to your own life, passions, and interests help?	Did working with real-world problems help?	Did finding and analyzing real-world problems help?	Did discussion about how stories reflect real life help? Did talking about your personal reactions help?

Results

Students' responses to the interviews were analyzed to address the questions posed at the beginning of this chapter. First, we explain students' ideas about each element of the TfU framework and its educational effects. Then we display students' conceptions of understanding and analyze these results. Finally, we present the correlations of students' conceptions with their levels of subject matter understanding.

Students' Conceptions of the Generative Curriculum

Although the TfU framework focuses on the identification and development of generative topics, students tended to discuss the helpfulness of generativity beyond the topics of inquiry alone. Many said that particular kinds of projects, objects, specific performances, and even goals were especially generative for them and engaged them in the development of "important" understandings. Given the wealth of student comments regarding the generativity of the TfU classrooms not merely in the selected topics of inquiry but also in these other areas of their learning, we decided to analyze students' responses to the generative curriculum rather than the more narrow element of generative topics. The generative curriculum includes any component of the curriculum—topics, performances, goals, materials—that helped to engage students in deep inquiry into the understanding goals that teachers identified.

Did students perceive that curriculum rich with connections to their personal interests and to other disciplinary ideas was helpful to their learning and understanding? The categories of responses and the number of students within each category are displayed in Table 9.2.

Three of the thirty-five students either did not recognize or did not value generative connections. Either they did not see such connections in their teacher's teaching, or they did not think that such connections were useful to their learning. For example, one student in history remarked that the connections to their own lives made it harder to understand because "you can get carried away." He noted that history is "carved in stone" and that it doesn't make sense to relate things that have already happened to what is happening today.

Table 9.2. How Students Perceive the Role of Generativity in Building Understanding.

	History	Physics	English	Math	Total
Not helpful	1	0	2	0	3
"Looking at [real-world problems] is different . . . but I don't think it helped more."					
"[Talking about our personal reactions and how stories relate to life] is not helpful. We need to know what the story is about."					
Helpful because the connections were fun or interesting to me	2	0	3	3	8
"Yeah, [real-world projects and working in groups] is fun. . . . We actually got to do it in groups and we would help each other out. We went beyond the book. We went into the hallway and saw how it worked. More hands-on. More than just hearing about it. I don't think that it is more helpful, though. I don't think I learned more."					
"I like talking about how stories reflect real life because I just like it. It is more interesting than other things."					
Helpful because the connections were meaningful and relevant to me	3	6	3	5	17
"Seeing how it was used in real life, outside the math class, was helpful. . . . The more interesting it is the more I learn, the more I stay in tune. So I think that he made it all more interesting. Going outside, we thought that it was great and we paid more attention to it. . . . It is better for the students because it is more hands-on and it's better than falling asleep in class. . . . I think making it fun is important, but also we had to be able to do it. So I think that it is a balance of both. If you could do it, that means that you understand it. And if you could understand it, then it got more fun and interesting as you went along."					
"In this class you are dealing with it in terms of life, and how it deals with people and stuff like that. So you remember it. It just sort of clicks with you because it applies more to you. Like you will remember something that applies to you."					
Helpful because I see the connections as directly useful in my life	2	4	1	0	7
"Being able to apply ideas into other areas besides what you learned is important. . . . [Real-world connections] help me to see how it applies to me. . . . Like with a piano and levers, when you press a key it is more complex than I had thought. And I play the piano and sing, so knowing how an instrument works that I use is very useful to me."					

A second group of students (eight of thirty-five) noted that personal connections made the work engaging, but they did not recognize the centrality of the curricular topic to the discipline. These students mentioned that the techniques the teacher used (such as group work, projects, and the like) were enjoyable, but did not indicate that these techniques caused them to think more about what they were learning. In math, for example, students noted that the real-world projects were fun, but did not say that they learned more through such connections.

A third cluster of responses, from seventeen students, indicated that personal connections were not just fun but gave more meaning and reason for the knowledge students learned. Some of these students added that knowing the central disciplinary ideas or relationships was helpful in fostering personal connections. Others added that the techniques engaged them and gave them authority in their learning, which was generative in itself. In math, for example, students indicated that rich connections between topics helped them understand and that working independently in groups and on projects helped them think for themselves. Students from the physics class said that organizing the course around central themes helped them focus their learning of the discipline and that hands-on projects that dealt with real-world illustrations of physical concepts gave more reason for learning. And in English, students noted that activities that connected the stories and topics to their lives made them think about issues they had not thought about before.

Finally, seven students noted that generative connections were crucial to the understanding process. The connections between the student and the discipline were so richly relevant that these students often indicated they had "merged" with the disciplinary ideas and could freely use them outside of class. In history, for example, students noted that the throughlines were so generative that they could use them in other classes and could "see them everywhere" in such everyday activities as watching television. In physics, students said that the connections made in class to their own questions were so rich that they could use the teacher's scientific models to explain the workings of things in their daily environment, such as pianos, power lines, lawn mowers, and friction on a basketball court.

Students' Conceptions of Understanding Goals

Did students perceive publicly presented understanding goals as helpful to their understanding? The interviews investigated both unit-level understanding goals and more overarching goals (the ones called throughlines in some classes) that were the focus for an entire year or term. Categories of student responses and the number of students within each category are displayed in Table 9.3.

Seven of the total group of thirty-five students indicated that understanding goals were not helpful at all in their understanding. Some remarked that they had never seen the yearlong understanding goals before and could not think of how they or the unit-level goals could be useful to their understanding. Others remarked that they were aware of both of these types of goals but never understood what the goals were for or never really used the goals to help their understanding.

Fourteen students noted that the yearlong and unit-level understanding goals were helpful because they told them what to learn and do. Across disciplines, students remarked that knowing what to learn and do is important so that they can do what is expected for a good grade. The goals were helpful because they told the students exactly this: what to do, what to learn, what to achieve.

A third group of eleven students also indicated that both types of understanding goals were helpful because they outlined what to do and know. In addition this group went on to say that understanding goals, particularly the yearlong goals, provided students with a model that they used as they did work in the class. Besides just telling these students what to do and what to know, the goals helped them focus on what was important and acted as a checklist or map of central ideas and relationships that students should keep in mind. For example, some students in the history class said that the yearlong goals were helpful because they constantly related their work to these goals to see its significance. Similarly, in English a student indicated that the goals were useful as models around which he could organize his ideas and create a "more insightful" story.

Finally, three students noted that understanding goals were helpful because these goals acted as a guide to their understanding, both in and outside of class. They said that the yearlong

Table 9.3. How Students Perceive the Role of Explicit Understanding Goals (Yearlong and Unit-Level) in Building Understanding.

	History	Physics	English	Math	Total
Not helpful					
"No, I don't think that [throughlines] are useful. I never thought about them 'til the end of the year. . . . Using them doesn't tell you what you have to do."	2	0	2	3	7
"No, not at all. I never used [the overarching theme]. I am not sure what they are for. . . . I suppose that knowing [the unit-level goals] could be helpful. But I never really thought about it."					
Helpful because they told me what to do and learn					
"The [yearlong and unit goals] help. . . . It tells us what we have to learn so it helps us to learn. We know what we have to do, and that is our goal, so that helps us to know it."	0	7	2	5	14
"[The unit goals] are good because the teacher tells you what she wants out of you, what she expects, what the course expects."					
Helpful because they served as a disciplinary guide in my learning					
"It did help me learn. It helped me focus because you connect why you were doing all of these things with those questions."	3	3	5	0	11
"It is kinda like basically what to look for. What the important parts [are] in the lecture or in the labs. It is kinda like looking for the basic things that we should keep in mind as we go through the units. . . . They helped me learn. They helped me separate the other things from the important things, so you're not going to remember everything in a unit. So you might as well look for and understand the most important things about the subject."					
Helpful because they gave me a way I could use my learning in the world					
"Everything we did made sense in relation to the throughlines. They gave us an idea of how to use a couple of intelligences, a basis of information, in other things in your life. Like social or academic [areas]. In other classes we basically learned, but we didn't learn for the future. This class was designed to have us learn differently. It is a different structure. It is based on these few topics. That in itself will make us learn differently. That will lead us to the idea that classes should be taught that way. . . . This will be something that we can carry with us into other classes and later. We'll know that there is always a theme and biases and all the things that we learned here. Instead of learning by just filtering information and just listening."	3	0	0	0	3

understanding goals were helpful not only because they provided a model of the central ideas and questions in the discipline but also because they altered student perspectives.

Students' Conceptions of Understanding Performances

How did students perceive understanding performances that asked them to use and creatively apply the knowledge they built in class? The categories of responses and the number of students within each category are displayed in Table 9.4.

In keeping with the other analyses, we defined a category for responses indicating that no activities or performances were helpful to student learning in any way, but no students were scored in this category. Nine of the thirty-five students said their understanding was helped through activities that enabled them to better "get" the information, but they did not see such activities as useful for other purposes. These students did not cite the helpfulness of the understanding performances designed by their teachers. Instead, these students felt that their understanding was built solely through such things as teachers' lectures, notes, homework, paying attention in class, drills, worksheets, quizzes, and tests. As one English student said, "When she explains it to us it helps it get into our heads." On the whole, answers in this category lacked a sense of reflection and thinking about the activities.

Many students indicated that understanding performances and "hands-on" activities were extremely helpful to their understanding. Across the disciplines students often noted that both smaller activities and larger projects were helpful because they asked the students to apply their knowledge to problems. For example, math students noted that the mirror project was helpful because it got them involved in seeing and using the concept of similarity. In English, students remarked that their stories and weekly freewrites were helpful because they required the students to use ideas such as mood.

Finally, a group of five students noted that understanding performances were crucial to their understanding. Such performances asked them to think about the ideas, solve unique problems on their own, and apply and connect the knowledge both in and out of class. For example, students in the history class said that the

Table 9.4. How Students Perceive the Value of Understanding Performances in Building Understanding.

	History	Physics	English	Math	Total
Not helpful	0	0	0	0	0
Helpful because they gave me knowledge	1	1	5	2	9
Helpful because we applied our knowledge in hands-on activities	5	7	4	5	21
Helpful because they made me think about applying my knowledge in creative ways in and outside the classroom	2	2	0	1	5

Helpful because they gave me knowledge

"I just paid attention and took notes. That's what it means to learn."

"I understood it when she wrote it on the board and we took notes. . . . When she explained it, it clicked in my head."

Helpful because we applied our knowledge in hands-on activities

"We had to use what we knew for the Community Center Project. . . . If we wouldn't have done the project I would have got it. He would have just gone over it in class and I thought I would have understood."

"[I understood electric circuits] by trying different things [so that] I could see if it worked out. And that is what I did. I tried parallel, series, and different things to see if it worked. . . . It was better when you did it, you understand it more clearly. . . . You can understand what you are doing. You have a better idea of what you are doing, and that is better than when someone else just tells you."

Helpful because they made me think about applying my knowledge in creative ways in and outside the classroom

"[I understood] all the deep ends of all the time periods that we have been studying. Like if there is a prejudice of a certain group of people at the time [of the Revolutionary War], you want to look at how everybody views that prejudice. And not only white males. You sift through the differences and compare them. . . . I use it a lot in arguments, like when someone knocks [over] a glass of milk and they blame someone. I hear both sides of the argument and one will make more sense. So it is things in everyday life that you do."

"Well, in order to get [electricity] I had to understand how charge worked in general. I have seen charge in action when you rub a balloon and you stick it to the wall. But I had to have someone explain to me how that works before I understood why it was that it did that. And when using that I can apply it [to] situations in which it might not be so obvious. . . . But this is the whole basic idea: I have taken simple examples and basic core facts and I have managed to use them to apply to other situations—sometimes several of them. Sometimes it only takes one. The fact that I can answer questions that are of interest to me, that makes it all the more worthwhile."

biography project helped them relate the experiences of people in colonial times to their throughlines and to see how prejudice exists everywhere in the world. In physics, students reported that the levers and pulleys project was valuable both because they applied their ideas in explaining the inner workings of a machine of their choice and because they began to see how levers and pulleys are used all around them.

Students' Conceptions of Ongoing Assessment

In general, teachers used three types of ongoing assessments in their classrooms: self-assessments (reflection sheets, journals, and the like), peer assessments (for example, small- and large-group discussions), and teacher assessments (such as formal grading, informal discussions, and the like). Did students perceive these ongoing assessments as helpful to their understanding? Categories of responses and the number of students within each category are displayed in Table 9.5.

Only one student indicated that none of the three types of ongoing assessments was helpful to her understanding. She remarked that feedback about her performances from her teacher and other students was a waste of time. Moreover, she said that opportunities for self-reflection were also not helpful.

Ten students noted that some ongoing assessments were helpful. These students said that feedback from the teacher or from other students about their work was helpful because it informed them if they had the right answers or had the right information. Such feedback gave them the chance to change their answers to get a better grade. Moreover, these students said that working with others was helpful, as others could help them "get it" if they did not understand. Many of these students, however, did not see the point in self-reflection sheets because these sheets gave them "no more information" than they "already knew." These students thought feedback was helpful only if it came from authorities who knew the right answers, and they ascribed little value to their peers' perspectives.

Another group, eighteen students, also indicated that ongoing assessments were helpful because they told the students if they were "right or wrong." But these students went on to cite the value

Table 9.5. How Students Perceive the Role of Ongoing Assessments in Building Understanding.

	History	Physics	English	Math	Total
Not helpful except for the teacher's final assessment	0	0	0	1	1

"[Peer feedback] wasn't helpful. I didn't get much from other people. . . . [Thought sheets] weren't helpful because I already knew what I was thinking, so I just had to write it down again. It didn't help me that much because some of things that I was thinking were hard to put . . . on paper."

	History	Physics	English	Math	Total
Helpful because it tells me if I got the right or wrong answer	3	0	3	4	10

"[Peer feedback] is good because they helped you out and [told] you if you didn't understand it."

"It is good to hear what other people say about your work so you can change it if it is wrong. . . . It is good to see your mistakes in your story so you can fix it."

	History	Physics	English	Math	Total
Helpful because it provides me with feedback on how to improve my work	3	6	6	3	18

"[Peer feedback] helped me because we got to know what other people thought of my work and how I could improve myself."

"Yeah, [peer feedback and freewrites] are very helpful because they helped my process. . . . I was able to look back at my process and say 'this worked last time, maybe I will do it again.'"

	History	Physics	English	Math	Total
Helpful because it provides me with a means to deepen my understanding	2	4	0	0	6

"Getting [peer feedback] was extremely helpful. . . . A problem I had was understanding that my opinion may not be necessarily the answer. [Group work] has helped me get a different view of how these ideas might work—that is very important! The ability to get other people's ideas and opinions [is important]."

of other people's opinions in informing them about how to improve their work or improve their process. Most of these students valued self-assessments because they informed them about how their learning process evolved over time. In English, students often remarked that peer feedback was helpful because through it they could hear other peoples' ideas about their stories and think of better ways to create stories. In physics, students remarked that the journal helped them review how their understanding of concepts and processes was changing.

Finally, six students noted that such ongoing assessments were helpful because they created a dialogue among themselves, other students, and the teacher. This allowed them to understand other people's opinions and develop their own opinions about what they were learning. They said that ongoing assessments were more than just feedback sessions for creating right or wrong products or better processes. Rather, assessments created opportunities for deepening their own understanding through talking with others and self-reflection. Helpful feedback was not centered on authority; these students had a deep appreciation for other students' perspectives. In English, for example, students in this group noted that peer and group feedback allowed them opportunities to understand other people's ideas, which enabled them to develop deeper understandings.

Student's Overall Conceptions of Understanding

Besides investigating students' perceptions of the elements of Teaching for Understanding in their classrooms, we also studied students' ideas about understanding itself. How did students perceive the nature of understanding? What ideas did they hold about building and having understanding? The categories and the number of students within each category are displayed in Table 9.6.

Eight of the thirty-five students indicated that understanding is the ability to acquire facts and simple concepts for rote purposes. In history, for example, students at this level understood such things as historical characters. In math they understood such things as the formula for a trapezoid. In English they understood what a story, character, or mood is. And in physics they understood things such as mechanical advantage. These students added that an important

Table 9.6. How Students Perceive Understanding.

	History	Physics	English	Math	Total
Understanding is the acquisition of facts and the ability to recall them	2	1	3	2	8
"I understand area. . . . I know I understand it because I remember most of it for the test."					
"I know that I understand [what mood is] because I did well on the test."					
Understanding is the ability to apply and use knowledge in designed ways in the classroom	2	4	5	5	16
"I understand levers, pulleys, and machines. . . . I know I understand because I did the projects and labs and could help others in my group figure it out."					
"I understand mood because I could use it when I made my comic book."					
Understanding is the ability to creatively and competently apply and use knowledge in novel ways in everyday life	4	5	1	1	11
"I know I understand [themes] because I can bring themes to my mind and go through them. For example, I can think of the economics. It is when you ask the questions. For instance, you say, 'maybe this happened because . . .' 'If you can connect it to religion, to economics, daily events, that's when you understand. If you can connect all of it you have a pretty good understanding."					
"Earlier we did displacement because we were interested in it. [I understand it] because I can apply the knowledge to things that I enjoy."					

feature of understanding is that "you get it" through remembering these facts accurately and quickly for tests and homework.

Nearly half the students talked about understanding as the ability to apply or connect facts and concepts during class activities. In math, for example, these students equated understanding with such classroom applications as using area formulas to solve an assigned problem, such as designing floor plans for houses. Likewise, in English, students described understanding as the process of using the criteria for what makes a good story to create stories. And in physics, students said they understood concepts such as machines, levers, and pulleys because they could do the projects and help their peers. Across disciplines, students in this group noted that a sign of understanding is the ability to help, show, or explain to others how to do these applications and that understanding is built in class through designed activities.

Finally, a group of eleven students described understanding as the ability to connect creatively what they were learning with other ideas both in and outside of class. They noted that it is important to be able to use what they were learning in different and novel ways to explain new things outside of class in the real world. Moreover, many of them indicated that such connections altered their points of view, perspectives, attitudes, and beliefs about what they were learning. These students expressed a deep sense of ownership of the knowledge. In history, for example, students cited understanding the concept of throughlines and how they related to various aspects of their life. Other students understood the way the teacher had been teaching them with TfU and could see how it could apply in other subjects. In physics, students indicated that they not only understood why and how levers and pulleys worked but could apply this knowledge on their own to their interests such as music and pianos.

These results are interesting when compared to earlier research by Chris Unger and Noel White, who investigated a broad spectrum of secondary students' conceptions of understanding throughout the Boston area.[3] In their study they interviewed thirty-five secondary students, using an almost identical set of questions to that shown in Exhibit 9.1. They asked students to tell them about something the students understood really well in school, how they got it, and how they knew they understood it. The researchers also probed students about what they did that helped them and what their teacher did that helped them. In addition the researchers asked the same students to tell about what they understood really well in nonschool contexts, how they got it, and how they knew they understood it.

Interestingly, none of the thirty-five students Unger and White interviewed was scored as having a performance-based view of understanding in school. Only five students had a performance-based view of understanding in a nonschool setting. For example, one student discussed her understanding of cross-country skiing and the development of that understanding through ongoing training, competition, and reflection. Another student discussed understanding how to run a business his father owned. *Within the context of school, however, no student was scored as having a performance-based view of understanding nor mentioned teaching or learning moves that signaled a performance-based view of teaching or learning.*

Correlation of Students' Conceptions to Their Understanding

How do students' conceptions of the TfU framework correlate with their understandings of subject matter as presented in Chapter Eight? To answer this, we ranked the conception categories of the TfU elements in the order they appear in Tables 9.2 through 9.5. Similarly, we ranked the categories of understanding in the order shown in Table 9.6. Students were assigned scores according to the categories of their responses. These ratings were then compared with students' understanding of subject matter as scored according to the Understanding framework presented in Chapter Eight (see Table 9.7).

In every case students' conceptions were strongly correlated to their understanding as presented in Chapter Eight. Spearman rank correlation analysis (see Table 9.8 in the chapter appendix for presentation of the data) was conducted to rank students in the compared categories (accounting for ties) and to compare their differences. This analysis revealed that students' conception of generative topics, understanding performances, understanding goals, and ongoing assessments were all significantly correlated with their level of understanding. That is, the level of sophistication in students' beliefs about the helpfulness of these elements

Table 9.7. Ranked Correlations Between Students' Conceptions and Their Understanding.

Ranked Correlations	Spearman r_s	t-value (df = 33)	Significance
Overall understanding X Conception of generativity	0.431	2.7697	$p < .01$
Overall understanding X Conception of understanding goals	0.6651	5.1164	$p < .001$
Overall understanding X Conception of understanding performances	0.5353	3.6406	$p < .001$
Overall understanding X Conception of ongoing assessment	0.6292	4.6553	$p < .001$
Overall understanding X Conception of understanding	0.7069	5.7412	$p < .001$

was correlated to the level of subject matter understanding they exhibited. This analysis also revealed that students' conceptions of understanding were correlated to their level of understanding. That is, students' sophistication in beliefs about understanding (rated in increasing order according to the categories shown in Table 9.6) was correlated to the levels of subject matter understanding they exhibited. Table 9.7 displays these correlations accompanied by their related Spearman rank correlational coefficients (r_s) and their computed t-values.

These correlations were further illustrated through the recurring patterns in individual students' scores. For example, Burt, a student in history, scored at level 3 or 4 in his conceptions of all four elements of the framework. He also held a performance-based view of understanding. His understanding of subject matter, as analyzed with the Understanding framework, was scored at the master level. In contrast, Jenny, a math student, scored at level 1 or 2 in her conceptions of the framework elements and held a level 1 nonperformance view of understanding. Her understanding, as scored with the Understanding framework, was naive. These examples are just two of many that exemplify the same trend in correlations of students' conceptions of both TfU and understanding with their understandings of subject matter.

Discussion

In this section we relate these findings to the overarching questions posed at the beginning of this chapter. The implications of these answers for teachers who are interested in Teaching for Understanding are presented in the following section.

Did students in these classrooms perceive the four elements of the Teaching for Understanding framework as helpful for their learning?

In short, yes. As the data indicate, the majority of students (69 percent) found that generative curriculum was meaningful, relevant, and helpful. A greater majority of students (80 percent) said that clearly stated and explicit goals were helpful because they told the students what they were supposed to do and learn. Half of this group (40 percent of the total) noted that these goals were also helpful because they served as disciplinary guides in the students' learning. As for understanding performances, the majority of students (74 percent) found that direct application of their knowledge was helpful. Of these students, a small group (14 percent of the total) also recognized the importance of the creative application of their knowledge outside the classrooms. The majority of students (69 percent) noted that ongoing assessments were quite helpful because they allowed for dialogue and reflection on the students' growing understanding.

Although the ratings of students' responses varied across classrooms, the majority of students recognized and appreciated the Teaching for Understanding elements when they were clearly put into practice as an integral part of the learning environment. Though the main focus of this chapter is not to discuss the differences in conceptions between classes, it is worth noting that students' conceptions about particular elements of the TfU framework were more sophisticated in the classes where the teacher's enactment of the elements was more complete and public. For example, history students' ideas about understanding goals may have been influenced by this teacher's unique use of overarching understanding goals, which she called throughlines. No other teacher in this study employed such a tool.

What were students' conceptions of what it means to understand?

The data from interviews indicate that the majority of students (77 percent) in these classrooms viewed understanding as beyond simply the acquisition of facts and the ability to recall them. Nearly one-third of the students in this study conceived understanding as "the ability to creatively and competently apply and use that knowledge in novel ways in everyday life"—the performance-based view.

This is striking in contrast to the earlier study of secondary students throughout the Boston area in which none of the thirty-five students was scored as having a performance-based view of understanding in school. Although the interview protocol was slightly different for the two studies, these results suggest that enacting the elements of Teaching for Understanding in the classroom may influence students' conceptions of understanding.

Are these conceptions correlated with students' understanding?

The sophistication of students' conceptions about TfU and about understanding was consistently and strongly correlated with their understanding as rated by the Understanding framework described in Chapter Eight. Those students who discerned and valued the elements of the TfU framework—generative topics, clear understanding goals, performances of understanding, and ongoing assessment—demonstrated higher levels of understanding subject matter. Similarly, students who viewed understanding as the acquisition of facts tended to demonstrate lower levels of understanding than those who perceived understanding as the ability to apply knowledge to classroom tasks or, better yet, to use knowledge creatively in many settings, including everyday life outside of school. That is, students' sophistication in beliefs about what understanding is correlated to the levels of understanding they exhibited. These correlations were apparent when individual students' scores were analyzed, as well as in the comparisons of group scores.

Possible Implications

The results demonstrate that for students in Teaching for Understanding classrooms, conceptions of understanding and of the TfU elements were correlated to their understanding. Because the research described here did not consist of formal experiments with control groups, we are conservative in our conjectures about the causes of these correlations and await further research.

The most cautious view, which incorporates the findings of Chapter Eight, suggests that students with greater ability and in the most supportive environments (both loosely defined) simply developed greater understanding and more sophisticated conceptions of the TfU elements and understanding, with no causal links among these different accomplishments. An alternative view asserts that students who recognized and appreciated the TfU elements in practice as helpful to their learning benefited more from this approach because they tended to notice and value the teaching moves. Students who equated understanding with performance could take advantage of the kinds of teaching moves that fostered performance-based understandings. They may have been more likely to see the opportunity and apply learning strategies that helped them build their own understandings.

There is much literature on student learning that supports the latter view. The review by Pintrich, Marx, and Boyle of the conceptual change literature and argument for the importance of "hot cognition" in learning suggests that a curriculum based on generative topics would be helpful because it draws on students' interests and builds on their experiences, making their learning meaningful to them.[4] Tobias's review of the role of interest in student learning also favors this view.[5]

Carol Dweck's work on the relationship between students' incremental versus entity views of themselves as learners could be seen as supporting the argument that students' performance-based beliefs about understanding contribute to their more performance-based understandings. If students regard their work and classroom activities as helping them build performance-based understandings, they would be more likely to focus on developing such performances, not on simply acquiring knowledge with the attitude that "you either get it or you don't." A large body of research on students' perceptions of the learning enterprise also points to the influence of students' conceptions of their goals for learning and their practices as learners.[6] These educators articulate a difference between students who apply a deep versus surface approach to learning. Students applying deep approaches enact strategies that include making personal connections to the subject matter and approaches that include applying their knowledge flexibly beyond predetermined tasks by rote. In contrast, students who are focused on surface learning enact strategies that favor recollection and application to predetermined tasks. The difference is in the desired goal: to comprehend the subject matter for the personal gain of being able to use the knowledge flexibly and creatively where it may prove useful versus being able to provide a specific outcome predetermined by others. Research on the effect of students' applying a mastery versus a performance approach to their learning is also relevant. Dweck and others have found that these variations in student approaches to their learning generate important differences in the outcomes of learning.[7]

In reviewing our findings and comparing them with the results presented in Chapter Eight, we note that in the classrooms where the TfU elements were more explicitly integrated into the teacher's practice, students were more likely to notice and appreciate the usefulness of the TfU elements and tended to develop higher levels of understandings (see Chapter Eight). For example, in the history and physics classes we studied the teachers often had open conversations with their students about what it means to understand and about how the curriculum and pedagogy were organized around building this type of understanding. Although our speculations about causal connections warrant more exploration, in light of the literature and these compelling correlational findings we strongly recommend that other teachers interested in integrating Teaching for Understanding talk explicitly with students about understanding and how to develop it. Teachers should hold class conversations that not only honor and draw out the variety of beliefs students bring to the classrooms but that also explicitly present the tenets and underlying philosophies of Teaching for Understanding to the students.

Admittedly, the data correlating students' conceptions of the TfU framework elements in their classrooms and their conceptions of understanding with our assessments of their subject matter understanding do not establish any causal relationship among these three outcomes. Nevertheless, these data clearly raise two questions and two possible answers to those questions.

First, might the correlation across classrooms suggest that students understand more when the framework elements are more fully and explicitly part of the teacher's practice? In the classrooms where the researchers observed more explicit and complete integration of Teaching for Understanding, students more readily recognized and appreciated the TfU elements. Students in these classrooms also scored higher in the measures of their subject matter understanding than students in the classrooms where TfU was less fully and explicitly enacted. The hypothesis is that greater student understanding was the result of these practices being more explicitly and fully in play in the classroom.

Second, might the correlation between students' views of understanding and their level of understanding indicate that a performance-based conception of understanding facilitates better understanding of both subject matter and the process of learning itself? These correlations exist across classrooms, suggesting the possible causal effect of students' conceptions on the development of their understandings apart from the specific practice of their teacher.

We believe that our findings suggest that explicit enactment of Teaching for Understanding may support the development of students' understanding of subject matter. Further, we argue that discussing students' ideas about understanding and learning along with the performance-based view underlying the TfU framework may help students achieve active, creative, autonomous understanding.

We end the chapter with one student's responses to some of our interview questions:

Was this class taught any differently?

It was really different from last year and [from the rest of the school]. It was always different because they wanted you to understand why you were doing things and not just knowing, like they taught for textbooks and all that.

What's the difference between understanding and just knowing?

When you know, you know what happened on such and such a date, like what happened in Bunker Hill. But not *why* it happened.

So you say this class had been taught differently?

I didn't like my last year's class. It was kind of like . . . we learned things but looked at things from the outside, but we never went inside. But if it's real, we kind of go in the inside . . . inside the things that happened and [inside] countries and histories, and think like that.

What do you mean by really going inside?

It's understanding, I think. Because [for example] when I did my report on Nigeria last year . . . I said things like what kind of nature was there and what happened, but I didn't say . . . It was just giving an overview, but I wasn't elaborating or explaining . . .

Any other thing that you think you do differently [in this class]?

We go deeper into things and you relate things and see the big idea and all the things around it when we make connections. In another class, Ms. Hetland begins to shake because . . . we are making connections to a lot of other things. And that is part of understanding: making these connections!

Appendix

Table 9.8. Ranking Comparisons.

Name	Class	Understanding	Conception of Generative Topics	Conception of Understanding Goals	Conception of Understanding Performances	Conception of Ongoing Assessment	Conception of Understanding
1	History	29.5	32	34	33	32.5	30
2	History	28	20	27	20	6.5	16.5
3	History	10	7.5	4	20	6.5	4.5
4	History	25	7.5	27	20	20.5	16.5
5	History	32	20	34	33	32.5	30
6	History	7	2	4	5	6.5	4.5
7	History	34.5	32	34	20	20.5	30
8	History	34.5	20	27	20	20.5	30
9	Physics	13.5	20	14.5	20	20.5	4.5
10	Physics	13.5	20	14.5	33	20.5	16.5
11	Physics	18	32	27	20	32.5	30
12	Physics	25	32	27	5	32.5	30
13	Physics	13.5	20	14.5	20	20.5	16.5
14	Physics	25	30	14.5	20	20.5	30
15	Physics	25	30	14.5	20	32.5	30
16	Physics	25	20	27	20	20.5	16.5
17	Physics	32	20	14.5	33	32.5	30

Table 9.8. Ranking Comparisons (continued).

Name	Class	Understanding	Conception of Generative Topics	Conception of Understanding Goals	Conception of Understanding Performances	Conception of Ongoing Assessment	Conception of Understanding
18	Physics	35	20	14.5	20	20.5	16.5
19	English	18	20	14.5	20	20.5	16.5
20	English	3.5	20	27	5	6.5	16.5
21	English	29.5	7.5	27	20	20.5	16.5
22	English	21	7.5	27	5	20.5	16.5
23	English	10	7.5	4	5	20.5	4.5
24	English	3.5	2	4	5	6.5	4.5
25	English	16	2	27	20	20.5	16.5
26	English	3.5	20	14.5	5	6.5	4.5
27	English	21	32	27	20	20.5	30
28	Math	7	7.5	4	5	1	4.5
29	Math	10	20	4	20	20.5	16.5
30	Math	1	20	4	20	6.5	16.5
31	Math	13.5	7.5	14.5	20	6.5	16.5
32	Math	3.5	7.5	14.5	5	20.5	16.5
33	Math	21	20	14.5	33	20.5	30
34	Math	7	20	14.5	20	6.5	4.5
35	Math	18	20	14.5	20	6.5	16.5

Note: 1 = lowest ranking, 35 = highest ranking. Tie ranks given the average.

Promoting Teaching for Understanding

Part Four

Promoting Teaching for Understanding

Chapter Ten

How Can We Prepare New Teachers?

Vito Perrone

There is much about our Teaching for Understanding (TfU) formulation that appears natural for classroom teachers. Few would say, for example, that student understanding is not their purpose. Moreover, the central ideas in our formulation—generative topics, understanding goals, performances of understanding, and ongoing assessment—do not seem particularly complex as ways to think about the teaching-learning exchange. Making TfU commonplace, the usual rather than the occasional practice, nonetheless represents a significant challenge.

In our ongoing work we have put considerable energy into assisting practicing teachers to gain personal control of the TfU framework and develop aspects of their teaching practice around it. We have also introduced the framework into the Harvard Teacher Education Programs, believing that it would be particularly helpful for those who are preparing to teach to have both theoretical and practical experience with the framework as part of their preservice education.

Teaching for Understanding receives major attention in the yearlong core course entitled Teaching and Curriculum. Because the basic ideas, essentially those relating to the comprehension and design levels[1] (having an understanding of the basic ideas and being able to use the formulation for the development of curriculum and some introductory teaching), are developed primarily in the first semester, I describe in this account how the TfU framework is introduced and used at that time, though some of the discussion covers aspects of work related to enactment and integration (putting the ideas into practice and making them central to most aspects of the teaching and learning exchange) in the second semester.[2] I provide a good deal of detail about our process, as the intent in this chapter is to suggest a rich array of possibilities for others who wish to incorporate Teaching for Understanding into their teacher education programs.

The framework itself is directly introduced midway through the course. Much of the language, however, is brought forth earlier. Common questions addressed in early class sessions and throughout most of the year in relation to all aspects of the teaching and learning exchange are: What are the purposes? Why is that topic important to teach? Is it central to the field? Will it relate well to student interests and intentions? Is it related to other fields and easily made a part of interdisciplinary studies? If you were teaching X, what would you want students to understand? What would cause you to say they understand? What would they be able to do? Further, in relation to our ongoing discussions and activities, we pose such questions as: Do you recognize that much of what you are asked to do each day in this class are performances? Can you make a metaphor or model of one or more of the ideas under discussion? Are there things you know about in relation to the topic under discussion but do not understand? Is there a difference between "knowing about something" and "understanding something?" In the classroom account we just read, is the teacher teaching for understanding? How is the teacher staying close to students' learning? And we have only touched the surface. The point is that when the Teaching for Understanding framework is formally introduced through readings and classroom exercises, much of the language is clear operationally. Moreover, the importance of TfU has become manifest by this time.

To help readers gain insight into the work of the core course and the attention provided to Teaching for Understanding, this chapter first describes those elements that particularly serve as background to the formal introduction of the TfU framework as well as the curriculum development work associated with it.[3] This is followed by an account of our direct focus on the framework and curriculum design. The chapter closes with aspects of our evaluation of the curriculum units prepared by the preservice students and discussions related to the application phase—the actual teaching of the units.

Moving Toward the Teaching for Understanding Framework

Unlike our workshops with in-service teachers, in which we are compelled to move quickly to the language of the framework, there is time in the Harvard Teacher Education Program to assume a more natural pacing, letting the teaching and curriculum course itself model much of what our Teaching for Understanding formulation is about, coming to the formal language and curriculum design at a point after the students have already gained some active experience with the ideas.

The syllabus, which students receive one week before the course begins, states:

> One way to think about this course—a way you might also think about the courses you teach—is to ask: What do we most want to be able to say about the students who complete the course? We want to be able to say that you
>
> - Understand the importance of your own biographies
> - Possess good reflective skills
> - Appreciate the importance of collective thought
> - Understand teaching as both moral and intellectual
> - Are good observers of teaching-learning practice
> - Are effective journal writers
> - See the importance of teaching for understanding
> - Are reasonably skilled curriculum makers
> - Are good problem posers regarding teaching, learning, and curriculum
> - Are reasonably confident about working with young people in the schools
> - Have begun to develop a repertoire of teaching approaches

- See students as having the potential to be powerful learners
- Have a personal philosophy of teaching to work from
- Can describe good teaching
- Have workable understandings of the importance of multiculturalism

For the initial meeting of the course we ask students to "write your largest hopes for the course—what you most want to be able to say about yourself as you leave," making clear the importance of starting with these kinds of large purposes. We also note that when we get to the curriculum project around our Teaching for Understanding framework, purposes will be outlined as "understanding goals." Students are made aware as well that the large purposes set forth in the syllabus guide everything in the course, that we can map each of the readings back to one or more of the purposes, and that every activity we pursue, every paper students are asked to write, every focused journal entry they are to present can also be mapped back directly to the statement of purposes—just as we expect that all they do with their curriculum projects can be mapped back to their understanding goals for the unit.

We end our first meeting with the list just enumerated and a list generated by the students. Several of the hopes described by recent students are outlined here:

- Get beyond my own experience with schools—an openness to other possibilities.
- Become more articulate about teaching and learning—the importance of my subject matter and its relationship to the students and their lives.
- Learn how to use interdisciplinary approaches to teaching.
- Learn how to sustain my energy as a teacher, to be an ongoing learner, to become a student of teaching.
- Learn how to help students assume greater responsibility for their own learning and enjoy being learners.
- Develop an understanding of the teacher as coach.
- Develop a habit of reflection on teaching practice.

- Learn more about what is universal in teaching and what is more specific to the discipline.[4]

Beyond the obvious understanding that all coursework needs to begin with overarching purposes that are revisited at various times, the reciprocity of teaching—that it must take into account teacher and student purposes—is yet another of the lessons of this activity. After our integrated list the obvious question is, What will cause us to say we have met the various purposes? We ask, for example, "What might convince those of us in the course that you are articulate about the importance of your subject matter field and its relationship to your students? What would demonstrate that you are a good observer of teaching-learning practice?" This is an introduction to the matter of performances as well as what it means to establish criteria for making judgments about the degree to which the various purposes are met.[5]

Identifying Intellectual Passions

The first paper, due in the second week of the course, is a focused autobiography—an "intellectual passion paper." We ask the students to think about their deepest intellectual passion, "something you understand well, think about a lot, feel you have under control. It might be history, the growth of American labor, or the civil rights movement; it might be Shakespeare or books or animals; it could be inquiry, travel, new people, a good story, mathematical possibilities, or the stars." We ask, as yet another way to make the point, "What would people who know you well say is a unique interest—an important part of your identity? What would stand out? (He's always carrying a book; if you want to know how to tell a good story, ask Virginia.) If you have time on your hands, how are you likely to use it?"

After identifying their passions, students ask themselves: "Where did the passion come from? What was the first instance? How has this passion or deep interest been sustained over time? What were those sustaining experiences like—what characterized them?"

Students read their papers (from six to eight pages in length) in small groups. These tend to be powerful statements that help everyone know others better. Moreover, this activity influences sub-sequent interactions—they become more focused, cause us to refer to particular literature in our conversations with particular students, help us connect topics under study to the diversity of interests expressed, and the like. The larger purpose, though, is to make manifest the enormous range of interests among students in the class and to acknowledge that a similar range is likely to exist in their middle- and secondary-school classrooms. Another important point is that any topic under study—and here we introduce the language of generative topics—will be served well by pulling in the diversity of natural interests among students, causing us as teachers to think about all the possible entries to a topic that might enable every student to make a special contribution. If the foregoing are well attended to, we note, everyone's understanding of what is being studied should enlarge greatly. We come back to the foregoing understanding directly as we introduce topic mapping to the students (discussed later).

As the students read their intellectual passion papers, we ask the listeners to be attentive to the conditions surrounding the on-going development of the various passions. Although students rarely report receiving their nurturance in the schools, most agree they could have. As a collective, we note the circumstances that surrounded the various passions, asking how we might draw on these experiences in our own teaching. As it has turned out, many of the students' passions have been sustained by trips, which provoked the question, "How can we use the environments beyond schools to help sustain the interests of our various students or encourage interests that hadn't previously been developed?" Others were related to particular literature, leading to the question, "How do we assure that students have access to the large store of literature in our culture?" Some came from television, prompting the question, "How can we help our students take more from television?"

Overall, these various passions tended to grow from personal engagement, supportive environments, opportunities for personal exploration, and important personal relationships as well as through diverse resources—powerful questions, opportunities to take risks, real texts, involvement in the world, ties to real people and places, dialogue, social commitments, curiosity, and being taken seriously, among others. These features match many of the conditions that surround Teaching for Understanding and these relevant connections are noted—especially in relation to generative topics and understanding performances.

Clarifying Educational Purposes

The second paper, related to purposes, is introduced soon after the first paper and its implications are discussed thoroughly. We ask students to consider a course they will be teaching—either with another teacher during the fall semester or fully on their own in the second semester—ninth-grade composition, American literature, world history, American history, America in the twentieth century, algebra, geometry, discrete math, biology, chemistry, physics for poets, introductory Spanish, and the like. We ask them to make as persuasive a case as possible for students studying such a subject matter: "What is important about it? What would you say to students who say, 'Why are we doing this?'" The next question we pose is, "What do you most want students to leave such a course understanding and being able to do?" This is followed by, "Given such a view, what possible topics within the course are most likely to get you to where you want to be at the end? Why is this so?" Furthermore, "How would you know if students reached the understandings you set forth?"

There is a three-week period between this introduction and the second paper's completion. Students are asked for the first week to be prepared to present some of their ideas about why this is important to study. We generally ask at the outset of this session if two students are willing to stand before the class as a whole and present their response to the "Why algebra?" question. Most are willing, so we choose from different fields, asking about each: "How convincing was the statement? What made it particularly convincing or not convincing? Was it clear or not? How would the students you are working with respond? What questions would they pose? Are there sufficient examples? Do they relate to students' general experience?" These understanding performances, and we describe them as such, are discussed as initial stages on the way to the final product—a means of clarifying expectations and getting evaluative feedback while work is in progress that we are careful to describe as efforts related to ongoing assessment. We then go to small groups, where everyone has a chance to present some of his or her ideas, some work in progress, to be more universally involved in performances and ongoing assessment. In relation to this activity we also ask the students to take closer note of how often students in their school sites present their work, their understandings of what is being studied.

We then engage in a discussion about topics and the continual need for selection by asking for volunteers to discuss some of the topics they have been thinking about in relation to their subject areas and why. We begin here to consider criteria for good topics. These criteria emerged recently in this inductive process: important to understanding the field, related to the present, needed to get to a next level, naturally of interest to students, recurrent in the field, and can be engaged by students at many different levels of complexity. We noted at the time that these criteria brought forward by the students are closely related to the criteria established within our Teaching for Understanding framework, which we discuss more formally later in the semester.

The week before this second paper is due, we engage in a criteria-setting activity, asking, "What should cause the readers of the second paper to say that it is a wonderful paper (or if 'wonderful' doesn't work, an excellent paper, an A paper, or a paper that meets the expected standards)?" Students understand by this time that it is important for students to know up-front what is expected—that such an understanding is related to ongoing assessment. This activity has typically brought forward some of the following criteria for the paper:

- It addresses the basic questions in the assignment.
- The audience is clear.
- It contains more than one argument and is convincing.
- There are examples and they work in support of the argument.
- What is expected of students is realistic.
- Possible performances for students are outlined.

Mapping Generative Connections

The next set of activities, consciously constructed as scaffolds into the Teaching for Understanding framework, includes miniteaching and topic mapping. Working in pairs, students are asked to be responsible for one of the course readings—that is, to be the teachers within a group of eight others. They are instructed to "find what you consider the most 'generative' idea within the reading and use it as a basis for what you do." We discuss within this context what would make an idea or question generative, linking it back to our previous discussion of generative topics. Students' recent ideas were, among others, that a properly generative topic goes to the heart of the reading; other ideas revolve around it; it makes connections to other ideas and to diverse experience; it makes the reading larger in importance; and it helps make the reading a beginning point and not an end.

We suggest that they begin with their generative question but also include a performance activity—that they ask their colleagues to do something that will show an understanding of some important aspect of the question, the reading, or an extension of the reading. Again, the purpose of the activity is to get another window into the complexities surrounding a pedagogy of understanding—the need for consciousness about the point of entry, essentially the topic and purposes; the need for involving students in the learning through performances; and the importance of ongoing assessment.

Topic mapping, the next phase of our collective work, goes beyond the TfU framework, but we find it useful as a tool for curriculum planning. We engage in this activity prior to beginning what we call the *big curriculum project* developed around the framework—our formal entry into the framework. We typically ask class members to think about a topic they believe to be generative to teach in science, math, or humanities. We generally discuss why the topic is generative, making use of some of their ideas growing out of the second paper. We then put the topic at the center point on a board and ask students to think about aspects of the topic that could be studied, aspects that we call possible *entry points*. We suggest that the most generative topics will have fuller maps—larger numbers of entry points.[6] In addition we try to make clear that in their own classes they might wish to focus on only a few areas, not the whole, especially if they can spend only a defined time (for example, two weeks) on it. A sample topic map is illustrated in Figure 10.1.[7]

Figure 10.1. Sample Topic Map.

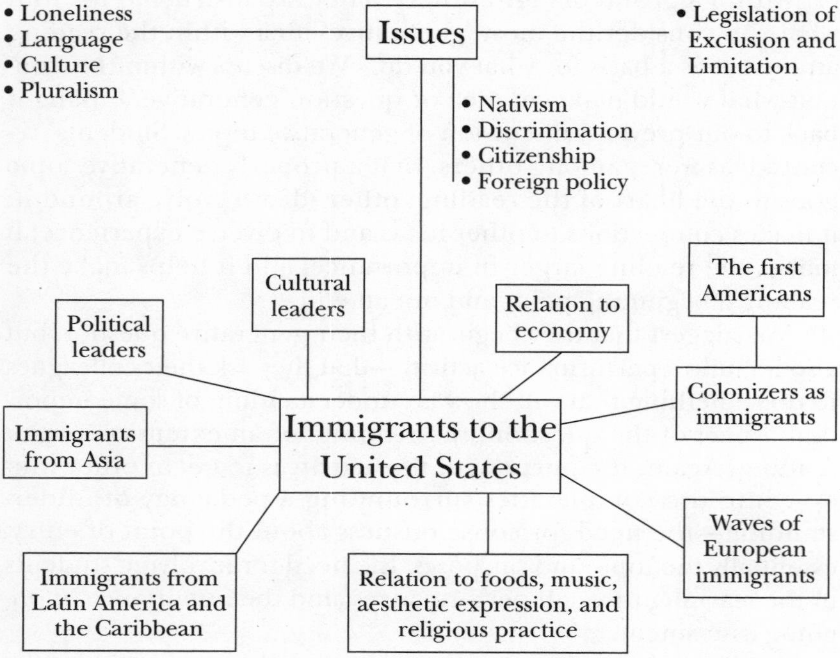

For the subsequent class period we ask the students to map the topic around which they expect to build a fifteen-day curriculum unit.[8] They bring copies for six others with whom they will meet. At this session students describe their maps, how they thought about them, and whether they believe some areas within them have more potential than others. Collectively, students add to each other's maps, providing additional possible entry points, other ways to conceptualize the topic, and the like. In relation to this activity, we invoke more fully the language of generative topics.

The foregoing exercise tends to change much of the mind-set about what is to be taught. Rather than remaining narrow subject matters, topics assume a larger and more dynamic character filled with multiple possibilities. Connections—ideas for relationships to other topics, ideas, and disciplines—emerge as important and are made visible. The thought that students might more deeply pursue different aspects of the topic that are more closely connected to their particular interests and intellectual inclinations seems realistic and exciting. Moreover, these preservice teachers can actually imagine themselves learning about things they do not really know much about. They understand that playing out in practice the implications of the foregoing changes the way the classroom functions: students carry considerably more responsibility than these preservice teachers have ever personally experienced as students or seen in the classrooms they are currently working in.

Considering Practical Realities

Drawing on these discussions of the students' personal experiences as learners and on classroom observations, we acknowledge that moving from covering to uncovering models of curriculum, from passive to active performance forms of learning, from textbooks to primary sources, from a single interpretation to multiple interpretations, and the like demands teaching-learning practices that do not well match existing norms. In relation to this discussion we make use of a focused journal entry on teacher planning. Here is an outline of the actual task:

> Engage in a conversation with your mentor teacher on how he or she does instructional planning about what to teach, what to focus on, what materials to use, what activities to pursue, what homework assignments are to be made, and how much writing to assign. Does he or she make out daily or weekly plans? What do you make of your mentor's process? Would it work for you? Why or why not? What questions are you left with after this conversation? How does your mentor's process appear similar to what you are being presented with in the course Teaching and Curriculum? How is it different? Are there constraints that make it difficult for your mentor to do all he or she would like to do?

In relation to reports resulting from the focused journal entry, we present some of what teachers have shared with us in our research around the implementation of the Teaching for Understanding framework, including some of the constraints they have identified:

- My students don't know how to read primary documents. I can't afford the time it would take to teach them how to do it successfully.

- My students aren't used to writing in math class. It would be disruptive.

- My students expect me to be an authority. It would be very difficult to move so much responsibility for the content to them.

- I am expected to *cover* [a particular subject matter]. If I followed the Teaching for Understanding format, I would only be able to cover part of it. I don't think I can do this.

- I have tried using performances before—students actually doing something. They take a lot of time and the quality is mixed.

- The students are comfortable having a textbook, knowing precisely what they are to do. The Teaching for Understanding process keeps things too uncertain. There are too many interpretations, too many diverse activities, not enough closure.

- This would be easier if my class met for a longer time each day. Forty-two minutes doesn't leave much time to do interpretive work, organize complex projects, engage in active learning.

- Where will I get all the materials needed for Teaching for Understanding?

- How can I be the only teacher doing this?

- I have 140 students each day to deal with. Teaching for Understanding calls upon me to organize many new materials, keep track of a wider range of activities, get students more involved in writing and presenting. I can't read carefully what students are beginning to produce . . .

- I have been a successful teacher doing what I have been doing. I haven't used large numbers of primary documents before. I don't really know how to use cooperative groups very well. Inquiry makes me feel less competent. I don't want to risk failure.

We acknowledge these constraints but also suggest that it is possible to go beyond them.

Formally Introducing the Teaching for Understanding Framework Through the Design of Curriculum Units

At this point, seven weeks into the first semester coursework, we introduce the TfU framework more formally, understanding that much has been done to prepare for it.[9] In relation to this introduction we ask the students to read several articles that relate to teaching for understanding.[10]

We begin by asking everyone to think about understanding, essentially what it means in practice. The students are asked to think about something within their teaching areas that they understand and over which they have control. We then ask, "What causes you to say you understand it and not just know about it?" They are asked to jot some notes to assist them in discussing this understanding. Various individuals (from among volunteers) discuss what they understand and why they say they understand. Among the recent examples were the Constitutional Convention, folktales, poetry, the writing of an essay, and density. After going through their topics along with demonstrations of their understandings, we invited class members to enter the discussion rooted in the following kind of question, "Thinking of [for example] folktales, what would you expect of a person who says he or she understands it that didn't come up in the demonstration?" In this particular case a student said, "I would expect the person to be able to tell folktales from several cultures." We asked the demonstrator if he could do that, and he proceeded to tell a wonderful Caribbean folktale involving a turtle who wanted to fly like the birds. His telling was lively and full. In each of the cases the class acknowledged that the person who volunteered understood the subject under discussion or was well on the way to understanding. We then reviewed understanding as defined in Perkins and Blythe's article[11] in relation to what we accepted in the foregoing examples to be understanding. There was a good match.

This leads us into a discussion about whether it is too much to expect that our teaching should be aimed at such understanding. Though acknowledging that it might be difficult to achieve and demands a high level of consciousness in teaching, with such ends being fully in view, few students conclude that it is impossible or not the direction that should be sought all of the time.

Introducing the Teaching for Understanding Elements

We then begin to introduce the four basic concepts in the framework one at a time, usually with some explanatory exercises alongside. We use such language as: "Deciding what to teach is a critical first step. We suggest in our Teaching for Understanding framework that we should begin with generative topics (filled out to mean ideas, questions, dilemmas, concepts, genres, and the like)."

We then discuss the criteria for generative topics: that they are central to the field, accessible at many levels (in this regard having few limits), and make good connections to other fields of inquiry. Given our previous discussions, these criteria appear clear. Earlier discussions about the importance of making connections to students' interests and the passions of teachers are also reintroduced.

The students are then asked to think about their particular areas of study: "Assuming you can teach only eight topics in the full year (each lasting four to five weeks), what are three that come to mind as really critical, certain to be among the eight? Think also about how those three match the criteria for generative topics." We then hear examples from various subject fields, a process that makes the criteria language even more familiar.

We move on from generative topics to understanding goals, suggesting that one way to think about them is to respond to the following question in relation to the various generative topics: "What do you most want your students to understand—to take away with them?"[12] With this, we ask them to write two understanding goals in relation to one of the three topics that they formulated earlier. We then hear and critique examples from various fields of study. The purpose is again to help everyone gain more comfort with the language and the formulation itself.

We enter the third concept in our framework by asking the students to think about some teaching-learning activities that have a strong relationship to the understanding goals they had previously developed—the idea of mapping activities back to the goals. This brings us directly to understanding performances, examples of what students will do (within the teaching-learning activities) to either demonstrate understanding or demonstrate that they are moving toward or developing understanding.[13] We then ask the students to develop one understanding performance to occur within one of the teaching-learning activities they have described. Seeing understanding performances as an integral part of an instructional activity and not as an add-on is initially difficult. Even as the relevant point is made about embeddedness, however, this conception generally needs ongoing work over subsequent weeks.

While trying to make clear that ongoing assessment, the fourth concept in the framework, implies that assessment in relation to understanding occurs daily through self-reflection, peer response to work, and criteria setting and that the various understanding performances are related to the ongoing assessment, we also ask the students to develop some kind of culminating activity that represents an exhibition of their understanding of what is outlined in the understanding goals. We stress that such a culminating performance works best if it brings together earlier work—that is, if it produces a cumulative quality. Although ongoing assessment is a difficult conception around which to establish initial clarity, students gain more control of the formulation as they actually work on their curriculum designs.

Designing the Curriculum Project with Teaching for Understanding

With some general guidelines about the curriculum project already in place, we ask that students come to class the following week having written up the following (with copies for six others):

1. A topic (with brief notes about why it is generative)
2. Two understanding goals
3. Three teaching-learning activities—essentially ideas that will carry them through three days of instruction where each day has one understanding performance and an example of ongoing assessment
4. Thoughts about a final culminating activity (part of an assessment plan) that will pull everything together—that is, that will be a demonstration of understanding[14]

These initial units are critiqued within the small groups and dilemmas are brought forward for more general discussion. Students rework these initial units in light of the small-group conversations, and we formally critique this version as another example of ongoing assessment. Students are then asked to add three more days of instruction with another round of ongoing assessment.

The instructions for the curriculum project are reaffirmed in the following written form.

The Curriculum Project

Set forth the generative topic you will address over a fifteen-day period that you are likely to teach in the second semester.

1. Describe what you think is important about the topic and its place within the larger framework of the course or field of inquiry. Use the criteria for generative topics.
2. Map the topic.
3. Develop two or three understanding goals for the topic.
4. Organize fifteen days of instruction.

   What will you ask students to do? To read? (Make a note of how this activity moves forward and is related to your understanding goals.)

   Define what you see as an understanding performance at least every other day—a performance that indicates students are moving toward understanding what you want them to understand.

   Over the fifteen days, try to vary your approach as much as possible.
5. Describe your assessment plan for the unit. How will you make use of the understanding performances along the way? (Self-assessment? Peer review?) Describe your ongoing assessment plans. How will the unit culminate?
6. Write a bibliography of resources and a sampler of resources.

It should be clear that much of what has been done leads up to this curriculum project. In addition students have tried out many of the ideas in the framework during the semester in their schools. For example, many who were asked to do active teaching once or twice a week used variations of the TfU model as a guide for their daily lessons.

As the curriculum project is in progress, we provide students additional materials to assist them, not only a large number of examples of understanding goals and understanding performances related to various topics in the basic subject fields but examples of full Teaching for Understanding curriculum units prepared by the previous class of teacher education students. These exemplars prove to be extremely valuable and match our discussion about the importance of exemplars in helping students understand what they are being asked to do.

We also take time for students to share dilemmas along the way and to get additional assistance. A couple of weeks before the project is due we return to the matter of criteria. We essentially ask, "What should readers take note of and be particularly attentive to?" Criteria for generative topics were developed in a recent class with the understanding that students could use them to judge the students' own projects. They require that every such topic do the following:

- Aim at student understanding (be faithful to the TfU framework).

- Be clearly important

- Feature day-to-day activities that can be connected to the understanding goals.

- Be likely to sustain students' interest.

- Encourage students to reflect on their learning (that is, have on ongoing assessment plan that is clear).

- Be flexible.

- Be thoughtful.

- Have daily activities and plans that are filled out in enough detail to enable a reader to follow them and understand how they will progress.

Note that many of the criteria we developed together are extensions of elements within the TfU framework itself.

Evaluating the Curriculum Units

The work described thus far relates to the introduction of the TfU framework through the comprehension and design levels. Those of us who worked directly with the students concluded that they had, by the completion of the first semester, come to incorporate the language of the framework into their teaching and learning discourse and to understand how to frame curriculum plans around the four elements—generative topics, understanding goals, understanding performances, and ongoing assessment.

We knew from our ongoing assessment—which we labeled explicitly as such in our discussions with students—that they were having an easier time selecting generative topics and developing understanding performances than framing understanding goals and integrating into their units the concept of ongoing assessment. In regard to understanding goals they had a tendency to write what we saw as overly broad statements and also to put forward too many for a fifteen-day unit. Moreover, though they understood the importance of ongoing assessment, they did not easily identify all the informal activities as assessment, especially those in which students provide each other feedback on activities calling for self-reflection.[15] They also were concerned about the time required to do this well in their classrooms. These observations caused us to provide some additional direct instruction as well as more examples.

Our initial assessment of the completed curriculum projects—which we emphasized to be units in progress—was that they were, for the most part, good beginning examples of Teaching for Understanding units. Most had all the elements of the framework, with generally appropriate explanations of how they matched the related criteria, and they had reasonable coherence from day to day. We also judged them to be workable in the kinds of classrooms where the students were teaching.[16] The students, in course evaluations, rated work on the curriculum project highly (4.45 on a 5-point scale).

At various times we have subjected samples of completed units to a close review of the four elements of the TfU framework. Because we were concerned about how the units would actually work in practice, our expectations were greater than the framework might suggest. We noted from these examinations that students generally made good connections to the concept of understanding performances and that this element seemed to match best their teaching and learning dispositions. Although understanding goals and ongoing assessments have been the most difficult framework elements (the latter more than the former), the more experience we have in working with the conceptions, the more examples we can draw on from the now several hundred completed curriculum projects and the easier these elements have become to incorporate successfully.

By field, math and world languages have brought the greatest challenges. Usually it has taken language students quite a long time to move away from the skills-and-grammar view of teaching that made the formulation of a generative topic seem difficult to conceptualize. At the same time, however, performance—the actual use of language—was more natural. Math students similarly have tended to be consumed by a view of the subject matter as linear and skills oriented. Although they could typically outline why various topics are important to the field of inquiry, they have had a difficult time connecting the topics to students' ongoing experiences or questions.

The Enactment Phase: Teaching the Units

The curriculum units—works in progress—were designed to be taught in the second semester. Most students were able to teach their Teaching for Understanding units. The results were presented in class as case studies, based on the following instructions:

> You will by this point have taught the unit you prepared in T-120 (or something like it). The expectation is that you will have noted in your journal on a regular basis how the unit proceeded. The focused journal entry, in the form of a case study, should include the following elements:
>
> - An overview of the unit and its purposes
>
> - A brief outline of the kinds of activities that were used to carry out the instruction
>
> - An account of how it went—what worked well, what didn't work well, what you would change in teaching the unit again
>
> - A description of how you think about the Teaching for Understanding formulation at this point
>
> - One or two questions that emerged for you that you would like your colleagues to reflect on and discuss with you

Over the past few semesters there have been many successes. In fact, in the majority of cases the units worked exceptionally well.

In most of these successful cases the student teachers reported enthusiasm among their students. Engagement was high. Also, they suggested that they were personally more focused when teaching the extended units than when attending to other instructional activities, most of which were short-term. The following statement is fairly typical: "I was more conscious about purposes—the goals were clear to me and to the students. I was, as a result, more focused in my questions, more of a coach, clearer about why students were doing so much, more engaged intellectually, more confident that students were really learning." As was the case in most of these successful units, however, the planned fifteen-day length tended to extend toward twenty or twenty-five days because of heightened student interest and the longer time that was needed for the many performance activities; many mentors suggested that this was too long, especially "with all that needs to be covered."[17]

In cases where the units have worked less well than expected, the most salient reflections related to what our students described as their students' "lack of experience with the various performance tasks." This often caused the student teachers to believe that their expectations "might have been too high" or that "the unit just wasn't realistic in relation to what students could do." They may have been correct in terms of the experience of the students. By and large, however, they seemed to understand that most of those issues could be dealt with if one began the year with activities that led in the direction of performance and higher expectations.

Although the student teachers developed additional—mostly shorter—units with the framework in mind, they made clear that they did not have the time to do the careful planning that a comprehensive Teaching for Understanding unit would take. However, they tended to make ongoing use of performances and peer response work and developed criteria with students for the assessment of various projects even though they did not develop all of their teaching around the framework. They also noted throughout the second semester many of the constraints we have found—coverage concerns, assessment as score keeping, limited expectations of student performance in their school settings, and time. They understood how important it is for a school as a whole to think about teaching and learning in understanding terms.[18]

Our task throughout these various evaluations has been to continue stressing that teachers do not go easily from the "usual practice" in schools to a pedagogy of understanding and that teachers are generally right when they say, "My students don't know how to read primary sources successfully," "They haven't had much experience doing performance activities," "They aren't very good at group activities," "They expect me to provide the important context," "It is difficult to sustain a project over five weeks," and the like. Part of the movement toward a pedagogy of understanding, we stress, is time to do the necessary scaffolding, keeping in view that students can be taught to be better question posers, interpreters, readers of primary sources, and observers, can learn to work more productively in groups, and can gain more confidence in role playing, speaking, and taking personal responsibility for a point of view. There is a natural transition that needs to be worked through.

We suggest during these reflective-evaluation sessions that teachers need to accept the fact that some of the work will be bumpy for awhile. The first project may work less well than anticipated. The group presentations may initially be flat—mostly filled with factual information. The early sets of interpretive papers might not be very well supported by data. The first sets of scientific observations may miss too much. It is important to understand that the second time or the fourth time will likely bring an improvement.

In practice, ongoing assessment is possibly the most difficult element for our students at this stage of their teaching. They manage the performances day by day and even engage in many informal and ongoing assessment activities, but pulling everything together in some large way at the end seems different. Much of this is related, it seems, to school expectations that every unit close with something that stands apart from the ongoing work. Nonetheless, the students get better over time. By the end of the semester, they tend to pose more interesting questions and ask their students to engage in more interpretation. In this, their struggles parallel our experience with experienced teachers.

Finally, for this account and in relation to evaluation, we ask students at the end of the year (in May) to reflect on their teaching, to consider their overall learning.[19] The papers as a whole are thoughtful accounts that reflect deep concerns about students and their learning and an understanding of what it takes to support a pedagogy of understanding. They demonstrate in these discussions much of what we have defined as the integration level of teacher development around the Teaching for Understanding framework. Following are segments from some representative final papers that feature this integrative language. They are organized around the four elements of the framework.

Generative Topics

I have come to see how important topic selection really is. I think I would understand math more fully if my teachers had given more thought to what they taught.

. . . [A] teacher at his/her best will make links among the various disciplines. For example, graphs and functions would be used to explain population shifts in historical migrations, ecological studies would be incorporated into the teaching of the "discovery" of the "New World," Taxi Cab (coordinate) geometry would be used to generate group building activities, Thoreau's writing from Walden Pond would be utilized in biology classrooms, and so on. The connections really are limitless, and good teaching does not construct artificial barriers between subjects but rather seeks to tear them down.

Understanding Goals

Part of the fascination, for me, is trying to figure out, first, what one would like the students to understand and to take away, and then how to approach the subject so that there's some prospect that they will take away that understanding. . . .

I am more precise now about what I want students to understand. As I have become more focused my teaching has gotten better and students are clearer about what we are doing.

Understanding Performances

In our Judeo-Christian heritage unit I had the kids become Old Testament prophets transported to the modern world. Another time we considered Oscar Schindler (we had all seen the movie) in the context of the early Jewish rabbi Hillel's famous injunction: "If I am not for myself, who will be? If I am not for others what am I? If not now, when?" At first, however, I thought that these connections would have to be considered secondary to the main task of assimilating the central ideas and history of Judaism and Christianity because the unit test was "supposed" to be counted more heavily than the other assignments. Actually the more creative and connective assignments were of a higher quality than the test!

Over the course of my student teaching stint, then, I am pleasantly surprised how little I lecture. I wonder, "Is what I have to say on a topic critical to their understanding? Will it move us forward?" This is quite a change from my first-year approach to teaching, where I felt obligated to demonstrate my competence by lecturing about three days a week. What pressure! Now I am much more interested in insuring that the onus is more on the students to take responsibility for their learning, I will not spoon it to them regularly. At times this has been difficult for them, because they have been conditioned to absorb and react rather than create and generate.

As we began *Romeo and Juliet* I asked the freshmen to paraphrase the Prologue. It was very clear from their responses that they understood very little, and that therefore I needed to rethink the way I would teach the play.

Ongoing Assessment

As teachers we are asked to reflect and think about our teaching and learning in the classroom because it is such an effective way to improve our practice. I've discovered this past term that it's very effective to ask my students to do the same to help improve their learning.

To assess a unit we did on African American Emancipation and the concept of freedom, we had the students do research and assemble and organize their discoveries into brochures. We began by soliciting them for aspects of brochures that made them really spiffy or not so hot. They gave us an incredible list of criteria from which to work. . . .

I like the idea of having multiple elements in the completion of an assignment. Having multiple elements goes along with another idea of the assessment groups that I like, and that is having opportunities to rework material. And both of these ideas go along with my own sense that I need to do a better job of linking up the pieces of a project, so that students have a better sense of the overall structure.

That the teacher education students could leave understanding the circumstances, remain committed to seeing clearly the efficacy of a more intensive Teaching for Understanding formulation, and maintain this commitment to it despite the constraints they encounter in schools speaks to their predisposition as learners and to what they incorporated into their thought through the course of their teacher education program. We believe our preservice students make a good beginning at absorbing our Teaching for Understanding framework and its theoretical and practice base. Given a reasonable level of encouragement and support, they will make teaching for understanding a central element of their work, philosophically and practically.[20]

Chapter Eleven

How Can Teaching for Understanding Be Extended in Schools?

Martha Stone Wiske
Lois Hetland
Eric Buchovecky

No innovation will generate widespread improvement in public education if it thrives only in the hands of teachers who are unusually able and supported. Much of the collaborative research on the Teaching for Understanding (TfU) framework took place in such environments by necessity; to formulate and analyze a demanding pedagogy, skillful and reflective teachers had to work closely with research partners. As these pioneer teachers talked with colleagues and publicity about the TfU project began to spread, other people in schools requested help in working with the framework.

Although the research project lacked resources to support and study these efforts systematically, its members arranged various means to encourage the use of TfU in schools. Consequently, educators in sites around the United States and in several other countries have begun to use the TfU framework as a structure for organizing their efforts to improve curriculum and pedagogy. Despite the lack of rigorous research on these endeavors, informal documentation demonstrated both the potential and the challenges of TfU in schools.

The purpose of this chapter is to show others who wish to embark on similar journeys several ways of extending TfU in the schools. Two vignettes illustrate how the TfU framework was introduced and supported in different public school settings. These examples reveal alternative ways of dealing successfully with challenges that often hamper the spread of TfU in schools. The first portrays one teacher's initiative in developing support for the TfU approach with a growing cluster of teachers in her high school. In the second vignette, TfU was one part of a complex, districtwide, multiyear project that provided both systemic support and potential distractions. Alternative starting points and support strategies, as well as crosscutting themes in these cases, indicate lessons for those who wish to integrate the TfU framework into public school practice. They suggest that both "bottom-up" teacher initiative and "top-down" leadership and support from administrators are necessary to promote widespread enactment of Teaching for Understanding.

Cambridge Rindge and Latin School

Joan Soble worked intensively for a year integrating the TfU framework into her English classes at Cambridge Rindge and Latin School[1] (CRLS) in collaboration with TfU researchers (see Chapter Four). She concluded that the TfU approach markedly improved her capacity to engage reluctant students in understanding challenging curriculum. That spring Joan and a colleague, who had worked with TfU during the early years of its development, offered a minicourse on Teaching for Understanding to other teachers.

Their five-week minicourse was one of several courses CRLS teachers could select to fulfill professional development requirements. As the assistant principal said, "Minicourses benefit both the teachers who showcase their successes and the other faculty who gain professional development credits through working with colleagues." In weekly sessions after school Joan and her colleague guided their fellow teachers to reflect on their goals, design students' understanding performances, and develop ongoing assessments for a course each teacher would teach the following fall. By the end of the minicourse several teachers were interested in continuing to work with the TfU framework.

Building Support for TfU

Joan knew from experience that learning to plan and teach with the framework is a gradual process. She was certain her colleagues needed sustained opportunities to talk and think about revising their practice with TfU. The problem was creating a structure to give them enough time to work together. After studying the complex maze of existing structures and planned initiatives at CRLS, Joan pieced together a proposal for both joint meetings and individual consultation with teachers committed to TfU.

Joan approached her housemaster at the Pilot School, one of several distinctive schools within CRLS, each with its own focus and affiliated faculty and students. The Pilot School is renowned as a democratic community where students are encouraged to share responsibility with teachers for all aspects of school life. Joan knew that Pilot teachers would be involved in several initiatives that she thought might support TfU. A new schedule would lengthen class periods and give clusters of teachers a shared planning period. Joan proposed that teachers interested in TfU be assigned a common planning period, when she would offer a yearlong minicourse on TfU. The Pilot housemaster agreed because TfU seemed compatible with her own priorities.

Through another initiative, a team of four Pilot teachers were participating in a three-year project with the Harvard Graduate School of Education to enhance teachers' scholarship in the humanities. These teachers were committed to developing interdisciplinary units to engage students in disciplined inquiry in the humanities. They all agreed to enroll in Joan's TfU minicourse. Each year one member of the team spent a partial sabbatical studying and supporting colleagues. The coming year would be Joan's turn, which reduced her teaching to one course per term. She proposed to use part of her sabbatical to guide and support colleagues interested in TfU.

Beginning the Minicourse

Joan described her planned minicourse to her colleagues at a Pilot School faculty meeting in September. She distributed an article about the TfU project to provide a more detailed picture of the project's purposes and invited interested teachers to participate.

At this point Joan recognized that several issues were important. First, teachers had to volunteer (rather than being coerced) to work with TfU. In order to make an informed choice teachers had to understand what they might gain from TfU but also develop a realistic picture of its challenges. Second, TfU had to sound similar enough to other priorities in the school to be perceived as a means to these ends rather than "one more thing." Third, the specialized meanings of TfU concepts had to be preserved so that "teaching for understanding" continued to mean this particular framework of elements. Joan had heard both the Pilot housemaster and the CRLS assistant principal endorse teaching for understanding in vague terms. Although Joan valued their support, she knew that the TfU framework was at risk for being dissolved into general rhetoric in a way that would seriously dilute its potential to make a significant difference. "I feel that I have to protect the words from being co-opted," Joan said.

Although her minicourse was open to any interested teacher in the Pilot School, Joan particularly encouraged colleagues who she thought were prepared to invest the considerable time and effort she knew TfU required. A total of seven teachers registered for her minicourse: two mathematics teachers, two history teachers, a first-year Spanish teacher, and two English teachers. Joan met with Harvard TfU project researcher Martha Stone Wiske to talk through her plans for the minicourse. Stone Wiske also attended the meetings with teachers, sometimes offered supplementary examples, and assisted Joan in consulting with teachers individually or in small groups. Joan took responsibility for planning and leading all the group meetings and consulting privately with each teacher.

Developing Teachers' Understanding of TfU

Joan began by inviting teachers to think and write about something they taught well, emphasizing what they wanted students to learn, what students did to develop this understanding, and how the teacher and students knew whether students had indeed learned successfully. Joan analyzed these reflections with the language of

TfU. At the group's meeting she identified elements of the framework in the teachers' lessons.[2] Joan also shared examples of lesson plans and materials that she had designed and taught with the TfU framework. Teachers said these models of TfU-based curriculum were most helpful in making the ideas of the framework accessible.

After this brief introduction to TfU concepts Joan urged teachers to start designing a curriculum unit they planned to teach before the Christmas vacation. "The vocabulary of the TfU framework elements and criteria can be very confusing when you first hear [it]. You need to start right away to use the ideas to think about your practice. They begin to make sense as you use them to analyze your own practice," Joan noted.[3]

The TfU teachers had a common sixty-five-minute planning period every eight days in their new rotating schedule. Joan's agendas for these meetings usually combined time for the whole group to discuss issues they were confronting in their TfU work with opportunities for individual consultation. Teachers presented their TfU plans and the problems they encountered; working in pairs or small groups they shared strategies, offered suggestions, and asked questions to advance their understanding of TfU. Between meetings teachers worked on their plans, consulted individually with Joan, and wrote reflections about the process of working with TfU.

Brent Lassow's experience illustrates how Joan helped teachers relate TfU to their individual situations. A first-year teacher of Spanish, Brent began using TfU to design a unit he planned to coteach with a veteran colleague. They planned to combine their beginning Spanish classes and have small groups of students write skits depicting the resolution of some conflict or problem typical of situations the students face in real life. It would culminate with students' performing their skits for their classmates.

At TfU meetings Brent clarified what he hoped students would come to understand from this unit. Initially, Brent listed goals of using correct Spanish and learning to collaborate. Through consultations with Joan and Stone Wiske, he clarified his central understanding goal: students will understand how to express themselves clearly in Spanish in everyday situations. With this goal in mind Brent reviewed his plans for assessing students. He had intended to follow his experienced colleague's policy of basing grades on the length of the skit. The TfU framework's emphasis on ongoing assessment with criteria related to understanding goals caused Brent to develop more specific criteria with his students: appropriate content, accurate grammar and vocabulary, pronunciation, collaboration skills, and use of conversational Spanish both in the skit and in spontaneous responses to audience questions.

Brent formulated these criteria into a series of questions that students used to assess their skits while they developed them in class. He consulted with student groups as they worked, informally assessing their progress in relation to the criteria. Brent had worried that his students might resent not being graded by the same straightforward length criterion used in the other class. But his students valued the clear published criteria. "Students right away went to work evaluating their own group's dialogues and checking to see if it was a challenging piece for them to be proud of," Brent wrote in his journal.

In the final performances students presented compelling skits on topics such as negotiating with parents about curfews and confronting students who bring weapons to school. Members of the audience became so embroiled in the issues that they eagerly stumbled past language barriers that usually prevented them from conversing in Spanish. Students clearly used Spanish to communicate authentically, but Brent discovered that grading the performances was difficult. A simple length criterion would have been easier to assess.

In her journal Joan noted:

> Brent and I discussed how the TfU framework gives us and kids a way to talk about what they're achieving and understanding, but not a way to match those understandings with particular point values. We talked about the need to juggle both absolute standards and a sense of each kid's personal best when assigning grades to a heterogeneous group of students. The more we talked, the more complicated the issue of grading became. Yet Brent was absolutely certain that he did want to deal with quality not just quantity in his assessments of his students' work. And he wanted his students to be thinking about quality as hard as he did.

All the teachers in the TfU study group encountered unique challenges in trying to incorporate the four elements of the framework into their own specific curriculum, classes, teaching styles, and collegial contexts. Joan's individual consultations and the group meetings helped them gradually understand how to use the framework elements and criteria to refine their plans.

Publicizing TfU Performances

As teachers enacted TfU in their classrooms and their students achieved impressive performances of understanding, Joan looked for ways to publicize these accomplishments. She encouraged her colleagues to showcase their work with TfU in the displays their classes prepared for the annual CRLS Arts Open House.

Joan and history teacher Betsy Grady focused on a unit they developed through their collaboration on both TfU and the humanities enrichment project. They had codesigned the unit with TfU to foster students' understanding of relating the interpretive methods of both English and history. Joan's English class studied T. S. Eliot's *The Love Song of J. Alfred Prufrock* as symbolic poetry. Betsy taught the class about the poem's "historical moment" during World War I.

As a culminating performance of understanding, pairs of students analyzed the poem's literary and historical allusions. They displayed their analyses in mixed-media posters, including the annotated pages of the poem and each student's written essay. Students presented the posters and other performances, including a rap song about *Prufrock,* at the Arts Open House.

In preparation for the open house, the class members talked about their "understanding goals" for visitors to their booth. They wanted their audience to understand not only how the students had interpreted this poem, but also how to develop their own interpretations of symbolist poetry. Students developed questions for the visitors to engage them in performing their understanding of these goals.

After the publicity from the Arts Open House, parents became more aware of TfU, and the English Department expressed more interest in Teaching for Understanding. The CRLS assistant principal advised Joan to submit a proposal for funds to prepare a videotape about TfU. Joan seized this opportunity as another way to involve her colleagues in developing and demonstrating their understanding of TfU. They videotaped interviews with themselves, their students, and their housemaster about the impact of TfU.

The group of seven TfU teachers participated in selecting and sequencing clips for the final tape. They began by listing their understanding goals for viewers of the tape.

On the tape teachers and students described their work and delineated how TfU had changed the way they taught and learned: "TfU helps teachers think about what students should learn." "It provides a language and a structure for the setting and fulfillment of high standards for all students." "I used it most in my 'standard' classes, with students of whom not much is asked. TfU structures a way for students to enter anywhere and move to understanding. It was heartening to see them working well. And students could see the quality of their work."

In the tape the Pilot housemaster remarked, "Our discussions in staff meetings are on a different level. The TfU work has helped teachers learn from each other about how to teach and what students are capable of doing. Standing back to define goals causes teachers to be learners and involves us all in a community of learning."

Sustaining Support

By the end of the year Joan and her colleagues acknowledged that TfU was often more difficult than their usual practice, but they had no doubt about its benefits. They hoped to continue the process of examining and refining their practice during the coming year. The CRLS assistant principal was eager to find ways of supporting the teachers and of extending TfU to additional faculty. She stated, "TfU is not simply a classroom innovation. It represents a deep shift in paradigm from the usual deficit mode to an emphasis on developing every student's understanding." She understood the demands of this approach well enough to realize that teachers could not accomplish it without significant time and assistance. She invited Joan to make a presentation to all CRLS housemasters and curriculum leaders about TfU with hopes that more of them would decide to support teachers in this approach. Although the assistant principal wanted TfU to become a standard approach schoolwide, she assumed that mandating this policy would assuredly undermine TfU.

Meanwhile, Joan reexamined the school for structures to support the spread of TfU. Once her sabbatical ended, she would have no time to consult individually with colleagues. The CRLS principal offered to pay her a stipend to meet after school with interested colleagues. Joan declined, knowing that she would not be comfortable receiving pay while her colleagues volunteered their time. The Pilot housemaster and the head of the Language Arts Department offered to release Joan from one course per term if she could find another faculty member with time to teach the course. This path through the maze proved fruitful; Joan identified a teacher from another house who had already expressed interest in TfU and was eager to teach Joan's course. This arrangement freed Joan during the school day for individual consultations with CRLS teachers who wanted to work with TfU.

Conclusions

At CRLS a single savvy teacher initiated the construction of supports necessary to integrate TfU into her school. Among the ingredients for success were these: the teacher had sustained opportunities to learn how to integrate TfU into her class through a year of intensive consultation with a TfU specialist; she was familiar with the politics and culture of her school and knew how to negotiate arrangements and rewards; and she built upon a well-deserved reputation for following through on ambitious plans in winning support from administrators at the department, house, and school levels, who gave her leeway to develop an important educational change. She rewarded their faith by planning and conducting an effective project.

Joan applied the TfU framework to the design of the project by making TfU generative for teachers, establishing clear goals, outlining sequences of understanding performances, and creating opportunities for teachers to assess their unit plans and enactments through rounds of assessment from themselves, from Joan, and from their peers. She orchestrated two public culminating performances—at the open house and in the videotape—that helped the teachers recognize how far they and their students had progressed. They also demonstrated the benefits of TfU to other potential participants and supporters.

Norfolk

Teaching for Understanding entered Norfolk, Virginia as part of a comprehensive systemwide school reform effort called the ATLAS (Authentic Teaching, Learning and Assessment [for All Students]) Communities.[4] The ATLAS design called for a broad range of innovations in pedagogy, school governance, and community involvement; Teaching for Understanding provided a unifying framework that helped focus and integrate these multiple reform initiatives. This case illustrates both the benefits and challenges of attempting systemic school change. It is a study in balancing flexibility with focus and rigor in the steady work of educational improvement.

Getting Started: The Need to Focus on Just One Thing

The ATLAS Communities design reflected the ideas of its developers: Howard Gardner of Project Zero at Harvard University, Theodore Sizer of the Coalition of Essential Schools at Brown University, James Comer of the School Development Program at Yale University, and Janet Whitla of the Education Development Center in Newton, Massachusetts. The project aimed to synthesize elements of their various initiatives in a pathway of schools (one elementary, one middle, and one secondary school) to "break the mold" of traditional K–12 schooling. In the fall of 1993 the four partner organizations of ATLAS presented different aspects of their work to the Norfolk site team, which included school principals, a site-based project coordinator, and school-based developers (usually teachers who had been released from teaching duties to support ATLAS activities with teachers, administrators, and parents).

After reviewing the menu of initiatives introduced by the ATLAS organizations, the Norfolk site team decided to focus on using the Teaching for Understanding framework from Project Zero. The Norfolk site coordinator, Mike DeAngelo, recalled that the team chose TfU for several reasons:

1. TfU was flexible enough to use across grades K–12 and in all disciplines.
2. It provided a common language for teachers, administrators, parents, and students to talk about curriculum, teaching, and learning across the pathway of schools.

3. It offered a comprehensive vision of teaching, learning, and assessment that was compatible with the ATLAS design.
4. The TfU framework could be used to design professional development.
5. TfU did not require expensive resources, such as textbooks or curricular materials, and thereby freed ATLAS funds for other assessed needs.

Tina Blythe, who had worked at Harvard on the Teaching for Understanding project since its inception, provided technical assistance to the Norfolk schools during the first year. Tina gave Mike more information about the TfU approach and listened to his thoughts about the best ways to introduce the framework to the Norfolk schools. Mike's perspective as the on-site coordinator in Norfolk was essential in figuring out how to connect the TfU concepts, vocabulary, and activities both to the other components of the ATLAS design and to the particular personalities and school contexts in Norfolk.

Mike and Tina knew that they must tailor the change process differently for each of the three pathway schools in response to their individual school communities. Mike worked with the school-based developers to identify key priorities and teachers who might be interested in working with one another and with the ATLAS personnel on Teaching for Understanding. At the elementary school, assessment was an important issue, so Mike organized a group of about fifteen teachers to think about how assessment could promote understanding. The middle school designated a cadre of lead teachers and cluster leaders to learn about the TfU framework. At the high school, Tina presented the TfU framework to teachers in the ninth-grade clusters along with approximately eighteen other teachers including some lead teachers. Tina believed that forcing TfU on resistant teachers would be fruitless at best and preferred to work only with volunteer teachers.

Supporting Teachers' Work with TfU

After Tina's initial presentations, some fifteen to twenty-five teachers from each pathway school volunteered to explore the Teaching for Understanding framework. Tina provided an initial half-day workshop in each school to orient the teacher groups to TfU.

Subsequently, TfU teachers received support in regular small-group meetings with a TfU coach. Initially, Tina was the only person with sufficient expertise to act as the coach. During her first few visits Mike and site developers observed her coaching of teachers in small groups. After several visits Mike felt confident enough in his understanding of the TfU framework to begin facilitating and coaching small groups of teachers himself.

Teachers at each school typically met with Tina or Mike for about an hour two times a month. To avoid creating extra work for teachers, all meetings took place during the regular school day. Where possible, small groups were arranged so that teachers could meet during their common planning period. Where this was not possible, the site team arranged for substitutes to cover classes while the teachers met. In addition to Tina and Mike, the on-site ATLAS personnel consulted with individual teachers at the teachers' request.

During their individual and team meetings with Tina and Mike the teachers planned curriculum, shared experiences and examples of student work, and discussed the process of working with the TfU framework. Mike noted that the framework elements acted as "powerful provocations" for helping teachers rethink curriculum design and their practice: "Having been steeped in a traditional curriculum loaded with objectives [teachers found] the TfU framework forced them to consider what was most important for students to understand and then develop experiences and activities (performances of understanding) that would help students both build and demonstrate their understanding of these important ideas."

Mutual Adaptation

As the Norfolk teachers worked with the TfU ideas, Mike began to understand the framework better and saw how it related to other ATLAS projects and to Norfolk priorities. Mike wished to keep the TfU framework as the priority initiative in Norfolk but recognized that he would need to modify it to incorporate some other key ideas. For example, the concept of essential questions was central to the principles of the Coalition of Essential Schools and compatible with the TfU elements of generative topics and understanding goals. The coalition's emphasis on student exhibitions could easily be related to TfU's ongoing assessments and understanding performances. Meanwhile, Mike and Tina noticed some common shortcomings in teachers' early understanding of TfU. For instance, several teachers were focusing on setting explicit standards for student performances but were neglecting to design cycles of ongoing assessment into students' work. With these issues in mind, Mike "translated" the TfU framework into what was called the ATLAS Curriculum Planning Framework. In addition to the TfU elements, it includes essential questions and student exhibitions. It also expands ongoing assessment into two elements: ongoing assessment strategies and performance standards and rubrics.

Tina and Mike also realized that learning to relate elements of TfU to other aspects of the ATLAS design and integrate these concepts into their practice was a gradual process for teachers. Some ideas associated with the ATLAS design, which initially appeared compatible with TfU, were absorbing attention and time without significantly improving learning. For instance, teachers were attracted to the idea of portfolio assessments and interdisciplinary curriculum projects. When teachers first tried to enact these strategies, however, they did not always advance students' understanding. Mike and Tina consulted with teachers to revise their designs to focus more directly on understanding. They emphasized that curriculum projects should address explicit understanding goals and focus on engaging students in understanding performances. Similarly, portfolios had to be structured as ongoing assessment of understanding performances to support students in developing and demonstrating their understanding.

The melding of multiple, potentially interfering initiatives into one clear, focused approach required vigilance by the facilitators on two fronts. On one front they modified the TfU framework slightly to accommodate compatible ideas from other projects. On the other front they protected TfU terms, concepts, and activities from drifting into superfluous or counterproductive window dressing. Competing distractions were either eliminated, discouraged, or integrated with the central purposes, language, and activities of TfU.[5]

Mike also extended and reinforced TfU by using it as a general framework for designing professional development and school change. Thus staff developers identified their understanding goals, designed professional development activities to engage teachers in performances of understanding, and used ongoing assessment to monitor their own and teachers' progress. This approach not only gave teachers an opportunity to be learners in a TfU setting but also gave staff developers first-hand experience with the framework. Through this experience all the participants understood the framework better and became more sensitive to the resources and supports that its implementation required.[6]

Mike's efforts to make TfU the central planning framework extended to the administrative and organizational components of the ATLAS schools in Norfolk. The ATLAS project had created school planning and management teams at each school, including representatives of the building administration, faculty, and parents. Mike urged these committees to adopt the TfU framework as a guide for setting and pursuing their own agendas. Gradually, TfU language and ideas pervaded the ATLAS Community. As Mike says, "The use of TfU has become an expectation in the school, and people find it valuable."

Changing School Structures and Norms

As Norfolk teachers shifted from planning curriculum to applying TfU principles in the classroom, they confronted incompatible school policies, norms, and structures. One of the first constraints was time. Teachers who engaged their students in understanding performances quickly recognized the need for longer class periods. This posed a particular problem at the high school, which ran on a fixed schedule of forty-five-minute classes. Teachers raised this problem with their site-based ATLAS management team during the first year. In response a task force consulted other schools about alternative schedules and proposed options to the entire faculty. Subsequently, the high school initiated a block schedule in which classes met for ninety-minute sessions on alternate days.

In addition to longer blocks of contact time with students, teachers needed time within their regular schedule to meet with one another to share and reflect on their experiences with TfU. Finding common planning periods for all groups, especially as more teachers began to use TfU, was not feasible. Providing substitutes to free teachers to meet was not ideal as it took teachers away from students and disrupted school routines.

After reviewing various options, the site-based management team instituted monthly late arrival days for the following year. On these days teachers reported at the normal starting time to meet with colleagues, but students arrived one and a half hours later. Thus teachers engaged in professional dialogue early in the day, while their minds were fresh, without seriously disrupting the school day. This program was so successful in the ATLAS schools during the second year that the district administration began to implement it in other schools in the district.

TfU's emphasis on developing understanding over time forced teachers to consider understanding goals for whole units, not just instructional objectives for single lessons. Teachers soon realized that students did not have enough time to develop understanding of everything in the current curricula and that not all of those topics were equally important. As teachers considered ways to pare down and focus their program, however, they worried about being held accountable for teaching the mandated district curricula. Mike noted: "Teachers received conflicting messages from district curriculum coordinators and school-based administration. So while the [TfU] framework provided a way to think about the curriculum, teachers did not have the authority to make important decisions in their classrooms."

Teachers took this issue to the site-based management team, which arranged meetings with the principals, superintendent, and district curriculum coordinators. As a result of these negotiations, teachers in the ATLAS schools were granted greater authority in making curricular decisions. The district curriculum coordinators took a more interactive role in working with teachers in the ATLAS schools to identify the most essential parts of the curriculum for students to understand. While granting this autonomy, the district also established new forms of accountability. Students are required to perform "benchmark exhibitions" at fifth, eighth, and eleventh grade. Students must either write a position paper on a subject of their choice concerning a social issue or prepare a report about a science research study they conducted. Then they must defend their research before a panel of judges drawn from the school faculty and the community. Some elementary schools require students to produce a product every nine weeks, in connection with the curriculum cycles, that demonstrates their understanding of the subject they have been studying. In one school these products are displayed outside the parent resource room.

Enacting TfU in the classroom also challenged the teacher evaluation process. As teachers moved away from a series of independent lessons toward curriculum units with understanding performances that spanned multiple class periods, the existing check-sheet-based teacher observation protocol did not provide a sufficient assessment of a teacher's work. Evaluative observations needed to be framed within the larger context of the generative topic, essential questions, and understanding goals. At the instigation of the site-based management team the teacher evaluation process was modified. The evaluator met with the teacher before and after the classroom observation to understand the teacher's curriculum design in TfU terms. Teacher evaluators also interviewed students to hear them explain the essential questions and understanding goals and how their work related to them. The teacher evaluation process became more collaborative, as administrators assumed the role of "critical friend" more than judgmental evaluator. Teachers were generally pleased with these changes and felt that their evaluations more accurately reflected their work and engendered improvement.

Conclusions

The Norfolk case illustrates the advantages of a well-managed systemic change process focused on the implementation of Teaching for Understanding. The project was introduced and supported by administrators, but teachers were permitted to volunteer rather than being required to work with TfU. A strong on-site "champion" simultaneously protected the TfU framework from dilution and adapted it to encompass local priorities. As participating Norfolk teachers who used the TfU framework confronted obstacles in the existing structures and organization of their schools, this champion worked with site-based teams to negotiate appropriate adjustments. Because TfU was part of a systemwide initiative backed by all components of the school community, these teams were able to persuade administrators and faculty to make the systemic changes necessary to support work with TfU.

In Norfolk, TfU served as a general framework for guiding not only classroom practice but also professional development programs and broader school change efforts. As more teachers, administrators, and parents understood the framework elements, TfU provided a shared language with which the school community conversed about its educational program.

Two Levels of Support for TfU in Schools

Before one derives further conclusions from these vignettes, it is wise to recall that they are not based on rigorous research. They summarize TfU work in two sites where supports for TfU have been unusually well organized and sustained. We do not offer them as typical stories but rather as cases that suggest feasible ways of overcoming problems that frequently hamper the spread of TfU in schools. We constructed the vignettes to incorporate themes[7] that teachers often mention in reflecting on the process and effects of TfU. As such, they serve to illustrate our hunches about what it will take to make this promising framework workable in a larger number of school settings.

Teaching for Understanding is a demanding, comprehensive framework for guiding educational practice. It is not an isolated curriculum innovation but a more far-reaching and fundamental change in pedagogical approach. As teachers attempt to use the TfU approach, they reconsider existing curriculum, assessment, educational activities, and cultural norms in the classroom. Ultimately, these changes within the classroom usually challenge the prevailing culture and structure of the school community surrounding the classroom.

Because the enactment of TfU stimulates both deep and broad changes in educational practice, it requires support on two levels. One level addresses the substance of classroom practice and focuses on supporting the teacher as the primary locus of change. The other level deals with the systemic context that shapes what teachers and students do and focuses on school organizational structures, cultural norms, and policies.[8] The vignettes illuminate the dimensions of both classroom practice and systemic context factors that may support or impede the integration of Teaching for Understanding in schools. They reveal that TfU appears to proceed most effectively when on-site personnel have sufficient understanding and power to generate, coordinate, and sustain support at both levels over at least two years.

Classroom Practice Support for TfU

At the classroom practice level teachers need opportunities to experience cycles of learning, enacting, assessing, and revising their practice in relation to the Teaching for Understanding framework. As characterized in Chapters Four and Five, the process of learning to teach for understanding may be conceived as an example of developing and demonstrating understanding. Therefore, the TfU framework itself provides a structure for supporting teachers in understanding TfU at the level of classroom practice. These vignettes illustrate features of effective support at this level, which have been apparent in many other cases too.

Models of practice that exemplify TfU. Joan's strategy of explicating the elements of TfU from an analysis of teachers' own best practices worked well. Like other experienced TfU teachers, Joan also found it useful to introduce TfU ideas by showing teachers materials she had designed and used with her own students, such as unit plans named with the elements of the framework, lesson materials and assessment materials, and samples of student work. Some teachers have benefited from reading written cases or watching and discussing videotapes of classroom practice that exemplifies TfU. Abstract principles become accessible through exemplars that instantiate the elements and criteria of the TfU framework.[9]

Dialogue with fellow teachers about their experiences with TfU. Such conversations with colleagues may address strategies, challenges, problems and solutions, and feelings aroused by both the difficulties and the satisfactions of this kind of classroom practice. Our experience suggests that teachers can benefit from dialogue with other teachers who may or may not teach the same subject, work with similar students, or work in the same school or district. These shared interests appear not to be so important as an atmosphere where experimentation is endorsed, reciprocity in exchanging suggestions and requests for help is expected, and reflective analysis is encouraged.

Individual coaching from a TfU specialist. Although teachers benefit from collegial exchange, they also need focused, individualized help in articulating their own goals, designing plans, assessing their performances, and sustaining energy for the very hard work of improving teaching practice. Teachers need flexible, tailored support that allows them to talk about the TfU framework in relation to their own strengths, interests, and concerns and those of their students. A consultant who understands TfU, understands the subject matter of the teacher's practice, and is familiar with the teacher's context is likely to be able to serve as an effective coach. In this relationship, as in all others where understanding is the goal, an atmosphere of mutual respect, trust, and honesty encourages the risk-taking and courage that learning requires. Our experience suggests that tailored consultation is valuable every week or two during a teacher's early efforts to design and enact curriculum with the TfU framework.

Fairly intensive support over time. These vignettes suggest an aspect of support that is more often noted because of its absence. Learning to teach for understanding seems to require successive revisions of teachers' ideas and practice, fueled by cycles of learning, performing, and assessing. Our experience suggests that teachers must enact these cycles within a reasonable time frame (for example, over a period of one to three months after initial introduction to TfU ideas), several times (perhaps two or three times within a year), and across a sustained period (at least a year or preferably two) in order to develop better understanding of TfU.

If after their initial exposure to TfU ideas teachers do not have a ready opportunity to apply the ideas in practice and receive feedback on these performances, their momentum is likely to dissipate. Initial efforts to use TfU may be fairly clumsy so teachers need coaching to develop performances that generate successful learning in the classroom. Teachers often perceive the power of TfU only after they look back over one or more curriculum units in which they tried to incorporate elements of the framework. In hindsight teachers can often define their goals more clearly, identify features of performances that were particularly powerful for students, and discern the depth and resilience of their students' understandings. These kinds of evidence of change in teachers and learners eventually begin to generate the self-sustaining incentives that support TfU. But these results do not become apparent until teachers have received relatively intensive and sustained support.

Because teachers' lives are busy and TfU is demanding, this approach is easily overwhelmed by competing demands. The seeds of TfU need to be planted, fertilized, and protected until TfU takes root in a teacher's own practice—until it becomes an internalized framework through which the teacher automatically and independently analyzes and judges his or her practice.

Systemic Supports for TfU

Isolated teachers who are unusually able and courageous may be able to integrate Teaching for Understanding into their classroom practice. Their work will rarely thrive or spread to other teachers, however, unless it is supported by more systemic factors in school departments, buildings, and districts. Both vignettes in this chapter reveal that extending TfU to clusters of teachers depends upon adjustments in school structures, incentives, and cultures.

Structures

Important structural factors include the allocation of time for TfU within the regular school work week. Teaching for Understanding is more easily accomplished when teachers have longer time blocks for class meetings than the typical forty- or fifty-minute periods. Teachers also need time within the regular school week to meet with colleagues and consultants to plan, discuss, and review curriculum materials and classroom experiences. Revising class schedules is a complex administrative undertaking, and time is always a precious commodity. The required adjustments depend on administrative approval and often require the development of consensus by a range of stakeholders within the school.

Another structural element that affects the integration of TfU is the definition of staff roles and relationships. At CRLS, Joan negotiated release from some of her teaching responsibilities so that she had time available during the school day to consult with colleagues about their TfU efforts. In Norfolk, Mike's role was defined to include on-site professional development consultation with teachers. In other schools where the administration did not create or assign this role to anybody, the teachers suffered from insufficient support.

One of the most important structural supports is curriculum and assessment policies that are consistent with TfU or that at least do not directly oppose this approach. In Norfolk the existing curriculum guidelines required teachers to cover more material in their courses than they could manage when they tried to enact TfU. The TfU initiative threatened to founder until administrators explicitly exempted teachers from meeting these coverage requirements.

Finally, Teaching for Understanding appears to be reinforced when it becomes the prevailing structure for designing many educational initiatives within a school system. In Norfolk and at CRLS the TfU framework served as a model for professional development as well as classroom practice. In Norfolk, Mike encouraged staff developers and school leaders to use TfU explicitly so that teachers experienced the model as learners. He believed that as administrators employed the TfU Framework to design, enact, and assess their own educational programs they might also become more sensitive to its demands and rewards. Using the Teaching for Understanding framework so that it is reflected at multiple levels seems promising as a way of extending and deepening understanding of TfU within a community of educators.

Incentives

Teachers are encouraged by incentives or rewards that directly endorse their efforts to enact TfU. A few pioneers may be drawn to TfU if it happens to appeal to one of their professional passions. Unless they are positively rewarded, however, most teachers are not likely to commit the sustained effort that understanding TfU requires. Busy teachers with many competing responsibilities have tended to devote more attention to TfU when they were required to complete specific TfU activities in order to earn professional development points or in-service credits. Other forms of reward that appear to be supportive include release time during the school day to complete the reflection and planning that learning TfU requires.

In Norfolk, teachers negotiated teacher evaluation criteria and procedures that rewarded rather than punished teachers for concentrating on developing students' long-term understanding. Teacher evaluation procedures that incorporated TfU elements as criteria for assessing practice would presumably constitute a powerful incentive, so long as they were backed by a process of support that also exemplified the TfU framework.

Our experience suggests that teachers who integrate the TfU framework into their practice eventually find that TfU generates its own rewards in the form of student understanding and more explicit and coherent professional practice. Until teachers reach this level of intrinsic motivation, however, external rewards or accountability requirements appear to be an important incentive.

School Culture

To the extent that TfU shifts the educational paradigm in a school, its support depends on the development of compatible cultural norms and values, as well as more concrete structures and incentives. TfU is most likely to succeed in schools and school systems where informed endorsement of its principles is broad and deep.

In Norfolk and at CRLS, teachers working with TfU were supported by administrators in their department, their building, and the central office who understood the demands and valued the goals of Teaching for Understanding. In the Pilot School at CRLS a long-standing commitment to democratic values and to students as responsible for their own learning created a culture conducive to TfU. In Norfolk a widespread commitment to developing students' understanding fueled a willingness to reconsider many policies that undermined this goal.

Endorsement of teachers as risk-takers and learners, of students as active participants in generating and assessing their own learning, of schools as sites of inquiry where time is provided to wonder deeply and converse honestly—all of these norms and values are consistent with Teaching for Understanding. In schools where teachers are expected to deliver a standardized curriculum, where students are rewarded for recalling and reproducing what they have been told, or where time is divided into small segments structured by rigid requirements, TfU is not likely to flourish. Such a culture does not allow or encourage the creative invention that understanding requires.

Themes in Extending TfU

These vignettes can (and should) be interpreted as cautionary tales about the demands of TfU, but they also contain optimistic implications about the power of TfU. The framework has the potential not only to structure individual teachers' classroom work but also to provide a generic guide for focused educational improvement efforts. The following themes, which are illustrated by these two vignettes, have recurred in other schools where TfU has been the focus of an extended school change process.

TfU encompasses other school improvement initiatives and accommodates many approaches.

The TfU framework is comprehensive and coherent. It provides a structure for clarifying and aligning curriculum, pedagogy, and assessment. It directs the development of practice that connects students' interests to the heart of particular subject matters. It is applicable across multiple grade levels and subject matters. And it is flexible enough to guide teachers with a range of styles, concerns, and priorities. Rather than prescribing specific curriculum content or pedagogical methods, the TfU framework offers a structure through which teachers can focus on understanding while addressing additional priorities. Finally, the TfU framework draws attention to ways of identifying and building on learners' (including teachers') strengths and interests rather than filling their empty cavities or fixing their deficits. These characteristics allow the framework to be a generative topic for schoolpeople concerned about a range of problems and interested in a range of solutions. Educators may begin from multiple starting points and use TfU to focus inquiry into their central concerns, namely what to teach and how to ensure that all students learn.

TfU explicitly focuses on learners and understanding.

Despite its breadth and flexibility, TfU centers attention clearly on rigorous understanding goals. As the framework orients educators to their core purposes, it helps them distinguish and address these fundamental ends instead of being mired by secondary concerns or distractions. Originally, the TfU framework was developed to guide teachers' efforts to improve student understanding of subject matter. Subsequently, it also served to guide improvement of teachers' understanding of curriculum and pedagogy. Teachers' understanding of TfU, in the performance sense, is enhanced if the school around them is a learning community. These vignettes suggest that TfU can also serve to guide the members of a school system in defining and pursuing their focus as learners about learning. Whatever the scope of the educational task, the TfU framework can be used to clarify and bend work toward explicit understanding goals.

TfU is learned through performances that yield visible results.

By emphasizing performances of understanding, the TfU framework guides the refinement of visible products and performances. Teachers and students involved in TfU produce evidence of their understanding, often in forms that attract the attention of their colleagues. Both the performers and the audience learn from public performances of understanding. Such evidence of powerful teaching and learning can help build commitment to TfU in schools where "walking the walk" is more important than "talking the talk." Teachers, administrators, and parents who are wary of one more educational fad believe the proof is in the pudding. Visible results attract their attention.

TfU provides a common language for defining good work and holds teachers and students accountable.

TfU promotes the collaborative definition and application of explicit criteria for assessing teaching and learning through cycles of developing, critiquing, and improving performances of understanding. Teachers say the language and the elements of the TfU framework provide a structure for dialogues about what to teach and how to teach. Through cycles of ongoing assessment, TfU encourages teachers and learners to build on their strengths, gradually improving performances in relation to explicit criteria and standards for excellence. Through the application of shared criteria to public performances, TfU draws learners into collaborative inquiry, thereby overcoming the norms of privacy that often isolate both students and teachers from helpful dialogue with peers. The TfU structure helps both students and teachers clearly conceptualize their classroom agendas and their own progress. In this way it helps them articulate and justify their work to others such as parents, administrators, and colleagues. Because schools are notoriously fraught with competing, often tacit agendas, well-defined means of defining and tracking progress can help to consolidate support from potentially competing stakeholders.

It is no accident these major themes in the way TfU guides school improvement recapitulate the elements of the framework itself. The process of improving schools is fundamentally an educational endeavor. The learners in this process are all the members of the school community. TfU helps them focus, assess, and refine their performances toward the stated goal of teaching for understanding. A reason to emphasize this analogy is to encourage supporters of TfU to practice what they preach. This is a good motto for several reasons. First, people can often learn from models. Exemplifying a pedagogical approach is an effective way of teaching about the approach. Second, the salesperson who uses his or her own product musters credibility for the product, especially if it works. Third, school leaders who attempt to apply the TfU framework in their own educational endeavors gain an intimate understanding of the framework and what is required to understand it thoroughly. From this experience they can discern situations in which TfU might be appropriately extended. Furthermore, they become deeply familiar with the challenges that TfU presents and sensitive to the kinds of support that its enactors require.

Conclusion

When educators first learn about TfU, many think, "I already do this." That is beneficial if it makes the framework seem accessible and endorsing of existing good practices. Yet those who have used the framework to reconsider and reshape their practice perceive that it has changed their approach profoundly. Many claim that TfU supports a paradigm shift from the usual deficit model of schooling in which teachers attempt to fix what is wrong with learners. TfU shifts the focus from teachers and transmission of information to learners and helping them construct understanding.

Such a paradigm shift requires integrated, coordinated, and sustained support for change on two levels. On the level of classroom practice, teachers need support for using the TfU framework to rethink goals and redesign curriculum and assessment. To make

Teaching for Understanding the accustomed approach in multiple classrooms requires a second level of support focused on school organizational structures, policies, incentives, and cultural norms that are conducive to TfU. These systemic supports complement forms of assistance focused on teacher development.

Finally, TfU thrives in a culture that endorses continual inquiry guided by ongoing assessment of teachers' and students' performances. TfU is not a solution so much as a structure for stimulating and framing dialogues about what should be learned and how to teach. It supports and thrives in schools that are communities of learners.

Melding Progressive and Traditional Perspectives

Howard Gardner

The forty-fifth yearbook of the National Society for the Study of Education (NSSE), published in 1946, was devoted to "the measurement of understanding."[1] Over three dozen distinguished contributors stressed the need to go beyond the recall of facts or the use of skills in precisely the situation in which those facts and skills were initially learned. Instead, they called for attention to a "higher type" of educational outcomes or mental processes. As two authors put it:

> When a geometry student sees the usefulness of the Pythagorean theorem for laying off the corners of a tennis court, we may be sure that he has some understanding of that theorem. When a fifth grade pupil by means of his maps discovers for himself a probable connection between the physical features of a region and the manner of life of its inhabitants, we may be sure that he too has some understanding, in this case of the geographic principles involved. And when a primary-grade pupil translates the statement $5 + 2 = 7$ into a concrete representation, by setting up one group of five objects and another of two objects and then combining them into a new group of seven, we can be sure once again that he also has some understanding, this time of the abstract relationship in the statement.[2]

These brief quotations confirm that the issues treated in the present book are not new ones. Indeed, as Philip Jackson has argued, the contrasting traditions of "mimetic" and "transformational" education have been with us since classical times.[3] There have always been individuals who have stressed traditional means and goals: a fixed curriculum, specific concepts and facts to be learned, canonical books to be read, exercises to be done. And just as predictably, there have been individuals who have challenged this orthodoxy. Called transformationalists, reformers, or more recently, progressives, these latter individuals have focused on the diverse forms of knowledge, the several uses to which knowledge can be put, and the important role of the individual and the context in determining what to teach, how to construe it, what questions to raise, and how to make use of what has been learned. (For a parallel contemporary effort, see Cohen, McLaughlin, and Talbert.[4])

Both at the time of the NSSE yearbook and at this writing a half-century later, individuals who challenge the skills-and-content mentality have been seen as progressives. Indeed, there is little question that the NSSE writers had been influenced by the recent publication of the fabled Eight-Year Study—a detailed investigation that documented the efficacy of progressive education at the secondary level.[5] Yet the authors of the yearbook would have felt little impulse to get on the soapbox unless they thought that most American classrooms—no matter how they characterized themselves—rarely called for or assessed rich forms of learning and understanding.

We believe that our own perspective goes beyond these earlier discussions—including the NSSE yearbook—in a number of respects. First of all, our view of understanding grows out of a theoretical framework, one grounded in the cognitive discoveries of the last half-century. Concern with the way knowledge can be represented mentally and the ways those representations are performed publicly allows one to be far more specific in determining what learners have mastered (or failed to master) and how such mastery can be demonstrated. Second, we have sought to examine in an integrated fashion the various components of the understanding process: how goals, performances, and assessments can work together, and how teachers, students, and curriculum planners can complement one another in a pedagogy that places understanding up front.

Finally, and most important, we believe that our approach can alleviate the tension between traditional and progressive perspectives, making possible an education that melds the strengths of each.

As we see it, our own educational goals are ambitious but in no sense unorthodox or revolutionary. We seek students who are literate, who have mastered the disciplines, who can—and want to—use their minds well. We assume that the most traditional of current school commentators—Allan Bloom, Chester Finn, E. D. Hirsch, Diane Ravitch—would be sympathetic with these ends.

Yet we eschew any a priori commitment to traditional ways of teaching or assessment, in part because they have already been shown inadequate for many students in many circumstances. We are uncomfortable with commitments to coverage because we are convinced that efforts to cover too much inevitably slight understanding. We are uncomfortable with most short-answer standardized tests because we do not believe understandings can typically be probed through that instrumentation. We are uncomfortable with coverage that is "flat" because we believe students are motivated to learn if they encounter ideas that are generative and central to the discipline being studied. And we reject the "transmission model" of pedagogy; we believe that students who are deeply involved in the learning process and actively constructing knowledge are most likely to master material and—more important—most likely to want to continue to learn on their own in the future.

Indeed, as we examine current debates in education we are struck by the extent to which so many of them occur at a level that does not influence the crucial encounters among teachers, students, and curricular materials. Certainly it matters whether or not there are charter schools, whether or not there are voucher systems, and whether or not there are national standards, and if there are, who determines them and how specifically targeted they are. But at the end of the day education is well served only if students understand important disciplinary materials and develop the ability—and the inclination—to continue to learn outside formal school settings.

In this book we have sought to describe our TfU framework in some detail and to illustrate how it has been used and adapted in a number of settings. At the least our work constitutes an *existence proof:* that is, a concerted collaborative effort among teachers and researchers can yield an educational program that is rooted in sound theoretical analysis, pursues ambitious goals of understanding, seeks student work that embodies fledgling understandings, provides feedback that coaches and directs student efforts, and ultimately elicits performances that exhibit increasingly sophisticated forms of understanding.

Such a thumbnail sketch, however, can be misleading. It glosses over the fact that the framework itself emerged slowly, after years and multiple cycles of positing, piloting, revising, and perfecting. There is no need for new groups of educators to rehearse this sometimes agonizing process in its entirety, but it is also the case that the deceptively simple framework cannot be assimilated in one sitting.

Other obstacles must also be acknowledged. Students are accustomed to classes where demands are less and where assessment is swift if impersonal: they often resist an approach that is far more labor intensive and that requires considerably more student input both into the work and its evaluation. Truth to tell, many teachers feel precisely the same way. Parents may be perplexed by a sudden switch in criteria of excellence, particularly one remote from their own experience. In the absence of a milieu that extends beyond a single classroom—indeed, one that ideally pervades the entire school or community—a steady focus on understanding may isolate both students and teachers.

It is no wonder then that leaders of major reform efforts are not content, as we have been, to work with individual teachers in congenial settings. Many seek to work at the level of the school, the district, and networks of schools around the country.[6] But each of these efforts itself encounters problems. It is much easier to start a new public school or create a charter school than to alter the course of an already established school.[7] Networks of schools may cut across geographic barriers, but they have difficulty working within established districts that have their own biases, priorities, and funding mechanisms. Often it is more feasible to achieve reform within individual departments,[8] but in such circumstances students may get caught in a cross fire when neighboring teachers and departments differ in their student expectations and evaluations.

Thus we would be disingenuous if we were to suggest that it is easy to launch full-blown *education for understanding*. Major changes in American education are difficult to achieve; this assertion has proved particularly true with respect to reforms that go beyond structural changes and invade the heart of classroom practice.[9] One of our recurring nightmares has been that we would revisit one of our research sites a few years hence only to overhear one teacher muttering to another, "Oh, Teaching for Understanding— we used to do that." If our work has the impact that we wish for it, such impact is most likely to accumulate gradually in diverse settings where someone's attention has been caught by our vision and where that person has succeeded in mobilizing the energies of others in his or her surroundings. More rapid change seems possible only in those jurisdictions that are both homogeneous and authoritarian—two adjectives that certainly have not characterized American public education to this point.

Still, we are emboldened to conclude our study on an upbeat note. We believe it possible to teach for understanding and that the rewards of such efforts are sufficiently palpable to motivate all parties—teachers, administrators, families, and students—to persist in the endeavor we have charted here. As successful experiences accumulate, curious educators will be able to visit relevant sites and benefit from the experiences there; no doubt, on the basis of our contacts with others and our own continuing experiments, we and our colleagues will further hone our own coaching and mentoring skills. Indeed, several of us have used portions of the framework in our own teaching and have seen firsthand how our own skills have been enhanced.

Furthermore, both the times and the circumstances may be on our side. Though the calls for "back to basics" and the "three R's" will never die—and there are reasons why they should not—citizens the world over will eventually become convinced that neither basics nor skills are worthwhile unless they can be mobilized in significant performances of understanding. We believe that future citizens will reach this conclusion for three reasons.

First, nearly all tasks that can be carried out by computational or algorithmic systems will be thus realized. Second and relatedly, cutting-edge work will be at a greater premium than ever before, and it cannot be carried out in the absence of significant understandings. Finally and most significantly, although both physical and economic well-being are surely important, human beings are fundamentally organisms that strive to master their environment—their physical surroundings, their social surroundings, the symbols created by others, and their own thoughts and feelings. They want to achieve such mastery both for their own feelings of competence and because they can marshal such competencies in the service of other persons and issues that they value.

Such mastery can never occur if education is restricted to the accumulation of facts, concepts, and skills; it can only come about if individuals have the opportunity to use these acquisitions in ways and in situations where they are appropriate. In our terms, individuals require the opportunity to perform their understandings—and those charged with individuals' well-being equally require the opportunity to observe these understandings, provide feedback and critique when needed, and provide applause when merited. Transcending stale and unproductive controversies, education for understanding puts the focus of education where it should be: on people's ever-increasing grasp of the world.

Notes

Introduction

1. Blythe, T. *The Teaching for Understanding Guide.* San Francisco: Jossey-Bass, 1997.

Chapter One

1. See Murnane, R., and Levy, F. *Teaching the New Basic Skills: Principles for Educating Children to Thrive in a Changing Economy.* New York: Free Press, 1996.
2. Whitehead, A. N. *The Aims of Education and Other Essays.* Old Tappan, N.J.: Macmillan, 1929.
3. In 1900 only 8 percent of those of secondary school age were attending a post-eighth-grade school. Not until after World War II did the percentage of Americans completing high school become great enough to justify labeling the accomplishment universal.
4. Cremin, L. A. *The Transformation of the School: Progressivism in American Education, 1876–1957.* New York: Vintage Books, 1961, p. 21.
5. Cremin, *The Transformation of the School,* p. 130.
6. Dewey, J. *The Child and the Curriculum* and *The School and Society.* Chicago: University of Chicago Press, 1969.
7. Mayhew, K. C., and Edwards, A. C. *The Dewey School: The Laboratory School of the University of Chicago, 1896–1903.* Rockaway Beach, N.Y.: Lieber-Atherton, 1966.
8. Quoted in Handlin, O. *John Dewey's Challenge to Education: Historical Perspectives on the Cultural Context.* New York: HarperCollins, 1959, p. 42.
9. Cremin, *The Transformation of the School.*
10. Dewey, J. *Experience and Education.* New York: Macmillan, 1959.
11. Cremin, *The Transformation of the School;* and Graham, P. A. *Progressive Education from Arcady to Academe: A History of the Progressive Education Association, 1919–1955.* New York: Teachers College Press, 1967.

12. Kilpatrick, W. H. *Project Method.* New York: Teachers College Press, 1918.

13. Cremin, *The Transformation of the School,* p. 130.

14. Bruner, J. S. *The Process of Education.* Cambridge, Mass.: Harvard University Press, 1960; and Bruner, J. S. *Toward a Theory of Instruction.* Cambridge, Mass.: Belknap Press, 1966.

15. Bruner, J. S. *Man: A Course of Study.* Occasional paper, Social Studies Curriculum Program, no. 3. Cambridge, Mass.: Educational Services, 1965.

16. *Science: A Process Approach* was a project of the American Association for the Advancement of Science.

17. For further discussion of *The New Social Studies* project, see Fenton, E. *Teaching the New Social Studies in Secondary Schools: An Inductive Approach.* Austin, Tex.: Holt, Rinehart and Winston, 1966.

18. Educational Development Center. *Guide to the Elementary Science Study.* Newton, Mass.: Educational Development Center, 1966, pp. 1–2.

19. Educational Development Center, *Guide to the Elementary Science Study,* p. 2.

20. Schaffarzick, J., and Sykes, G. (eds.). *Value Conflicts and Curriculum Issues: Lessons from Research and Experience.* Berkeley, Calif.: McCutchan, 1979.

21. For an excellent discussion of the political debates surrounding *Man: A Course of Study,* see Dow, P. B. *Schoolhouse Politics: Lessons from the Sputnik Era.* Cambridge, Mass.: Harvard University Press, 1991.

22. See the chapter "Science Education: From Sputnik to the Toyota." In V. Perrone, *Working Papers: Reflections on Teachers, Schools, and Communities.* New York: Teachers College Press, 1989.

23. Whether this continues depends in part on how the discussions about standards play out. As various states develop frameworks to help schools develop curriculum, they appear to be adding more and more specific content. Moreover, given the related interest in state and national testing, we may yet see greater curriculum specificity. These are not good signs; they are likely to work against a focus on teaching for understanding in the schools.

24. We must acknowledge, however, that putting these standards and frameworks into practice is not an easy task. The barriers remain large; the typical school organization often leaves little time for teachers to plan, the history of textbook dominance is long and pervasive, learning is tied heavily to tests of information and not performance. Moreover, the belief in schooling as it has been, a nostalgia for all that schooling has represented, is still large. For a further elaboration of the barriers to change, see Cuban, L. *How Teachers Taught: Constancy*

and Change in American Classrooms, 1890–1980. New York: Teachers' College Press, 1993; and Cuban, L., and Tyack, D. *Tinkering Toward Utopia: A Century of Public School Reform.* Cambridge, Mass.: Harvard University Press, 1995.

25. National Research Council, National Committee on Science Education Standards and Assessment. *National Science Education Standards: An Enhanced Sampler.* Washington, D.C.: National Research Council, 1993, p. 1.

26. As noted later, this formulation matches well our definition of a *generative topic.*

27. National Research Council, National Committee on Science Education Standards and Assessment, *National Science Education Standards,* p. 53.

28. National Research Council, National Committee on Science Education Standards and Assessment, *National Science Education Standards,* pp. 55–58.

29. National Council of Teachers of Mathematics. *Curriculum and Evaluation Standards for School Mathematics.* Reston, Va.: National Council of Teachers of Mathematics, 1989, p. 125.

30. Mathematical Sciences Board of the National Research Council, National Academy of Sciences. *On the Shoulders of Giants.* Washington, D.C.: National Academy of Sciences, p. 8.

31. National Council of Teachers of English. *Criteria for Planning and Evaluating English Language Curriculum.* Urbana, Ill.: National Council of Teachers of English, 1991, p. 36.

32. National Council of Teachers of English, *Criteria for Planning and Evaluating English Language Curriculum,* p. 38.

33. National Council of Teachers of English. *Standards for the English Language Arts.* Urbana, Ill.: National Council of Teachers of English, 1996.

34. National Commission on Social Studies in the Schools Curriculum Task Force. *Charting a Course: Social Studies for the 21st Century.* Washington, D.C.: National Commission on Social Studies in the Schools, 1989, p. 27.

35. National Commission on Social Studies in the Schools Curriculum Task Force, *Charting a Course,* p. 23.

36. The important point to note is that the suggested content is limited to "big ideas," what we call in our Teaching for Understanding framework *generative topics.*

37. Bradley Commission on History in Schools. *Building a History Curriculum: Guidelines for Teaching History in Schools.* Washington, D.C.: Educational Excellence Network, 1988, p. 6.

38. Bradley Commission on History in Schools, *Building a History Curriculum,* pp. 6–7.

39. Thomas Holt, quoted in National Commission on Social Studies in the Schools Curriculum Task Force, *Charting a Course*, pp. 48–49. Holt has also written for the College Board Series on Academic Disciplines an instructive booklet called *Thinking Historically* (New York: College Entrance Examination Board, 1990) that outlines what it means to teach history for understanding. This work stresses the narrative of history and active involvement of students in creating a narrative. He uses the reconstruction period after the Civil War as an example.

40. National Center for History in the Schools. *National Standards for History*. Los Angeles: National Center for History in the Schools, 1996. The standards for U.S. history and world history have come under considerable criticism for not stressing sufficiently the long-standing themes of U.S. and Western European nationalism in world history. Efforts at greater inclusion of these themes have not received universal praise, but the focus on understanding has not been challenged.

41. "What they have learned" is essentially "what they remember" for the particular testing period. Insufficiently considered, however, is how much is forgotten or put out of mind soon after the test.

42. For discussion of the descriptive review, see Carini, P. F. *The Art of Seeing and the Visibility of the Person*. Grand Forks: University of North Dakota, 1979; and Carini, P. F. *The School Lives of Seven Children: A Five Year Study*. Grand Forks: North Dakota Study Group on Evaluation, University of North Dakota, 1982.

Chapter Two

1. Mayer, R. E. "Models for Understanding." *Review of Educational Research*, 1989, *59*, 43–64.

2. Gentner, D., and Stevens, A. L. (eds.). *Mental Models*. Hillsdale, N.J.: Erlbaum, 1983.

3. Gentner, D., and Gentner, D. R. "Flowing Waters or Teeming Crowds: Mental Models of Electricity." In D. Gentner and A. Stevens (eds.), *Mental Models*. Hillsdale, N.J.: Erlbaum, 1983.

4. Johnson-Laird, P. N., and Byrne, R.M.J. *Deduction*. Hillsdale, N.J.: Erlbaum, 1991.

5. Entwistle, N. J., and Marton, F. "Knowledge Objects: Understandings Constituted Through Intensive Academic Study." *British Journal of Educational Psychology*, 1994, *64*, 161–178.

6. Schank, R. *Explanation Patterns: Understanding Mechanically and Creatively*. Hillsdale, N.J.: Erlbaum, 1986.

7. Ohlsson, S. "Abstract Schemas." *Educational Psychologist*, 1993, *28*(1), 51–66.

8. Collins, A., and Ferguson, W. "Epistemic Forms and Epistemic Games: Structures and Strategies to Guide Inquiry." *Educational Psychologist,* 1993, *28*(1), 25–42.

9. Perkins, D. N. "Epistemic Games." In S. Ohlsson (ed.), *Learning and Instruction,* forthcoming; Perkins, D. N. "The Hidden Order of Open-Ended Thinking." In J. Edwards (ed.), *Thinking: International Interdisciplinary Perspectives.* Victoria, Australia: Hawker Brownlow, 1994.

10. Case, R. *The Mind's Staircase: Exploring the Conceptual Underpinnings of Children's Thought and Knowledge.* Hillsdale, N.J.: Erlbaum, 1992.

11. Johnson-Laird and Byrne, *Deduction.*

12. Winograd, T., and Flores, F. *Understanding Computers and Cognition: A New Foundation for Design.* Norwood, N.J.: Ablex, 1986.

13. McClelland, J. L., and Rumelhardt, D. E. (eds.). *Parallel Distributed Processing: Explorations in the Micro-Structure of Cognition.* Vols. I and II. Cambridge, Mass.: MIT Press, 1986.

14. Cain, K., and Dweck, C. S. "The Development of Children's Conception of Intelligence: A Theoretical Framework." In R. Sternberg (ed.), *Advances in the Psychology of Human Intelligence.* Vol. 5. Hillsdale, N.J.: Erlbaum, 1989; Dweck, C. S., and Bempechat, J. "Children's Theories of Intelligence: Consequences for Learning." In S. G. Paris, G. M. Olson, and H. W. Stevenson (eds.), *Learning and Motivation in the Classroom.* Hillsdale, N.J.: Erlbaum, 1980; Dweck, C. S., and Licht, B. G. "Learned Helplessness and Intellectual Achievement." In J. Garbar and M. Seligman (eds.), *Human Helplessness.* Orlando: Academic Press, 1980.

15. Collins, A., Brown, J. S., and Newman, S. F. "Cognitive Apprenticeship: Teaching the Craft of Reading, Writing, and Mathematics." In L. B. Resnick (ed.), *Knowing, Learning, and Instruction: Essays in Honor of Robert Glaser.* Hillsdale, N.J.: Erlbaum, 1989.

16. Brown, A. L., and Campione, J. C. "Communities of Learning and Thinking, or a Context by Any Other Name." In D. Kuhn (ed.), *Developmental Perspectives on Teaching and Learning Thinking Skills. Contributions to Human Development,* 1990, *21* (special issue), 108–126; and Brown, A. L., and Palincsar, A. S. "Guided, Cooperative Learning and Individual Knowledge Acquisition." In L. B. Resnick (ed.), *Knowing, Learning, and Instruction: Essays in Honor of Robert Glaser.* Hillsdale, N.J.: Erlbaum, 1989.

17. Tishman, S., Perkins, D. N., and Jay, E. *The Thinking Classroom.* Needham Heights, Mass.: Allyn & Bacon, 1995.

18. Gardner, H. *The Unschooled Mind: How Children Think and How Schools Should Teach.* New York: Basic Books, 1991.

Chapter Three

1. Dewey, J. *The Child and the Curriculum* and *The School and Society.* Chicago: University of Chicago Press, 1969.
2. For more on the importance of relating curriculum to core concepts in the disciplines, see Schwab, J. J. "The Structures of the Disciplines: Meanings and Significances." In G. W. Ford and L. Pugno (eds.), *The Structure of Knowledge and the Curriculum.* Skokie, Ill.: Rand McNally, 1964; and Shulman, L. S. "Those Who Understand: Knowledge Growth in Teaching." *Educational Researcher,* 1986, *15*(2), 4–14.
3. On multiple intelligences and the value of approaching learning through more routes than merely the usual text and mathematical forms that are prevalent in schools, see Gardner, H. *Frames of Mind: The Theory of Multiple Intelligences.* New York: Basic Books, 1993.
4. For teachers' efforts to manage multiple agendas, see McDonald, J. P. *Teaching: Making Sense of an Uncertain Craft.* New York: Teachers College Press, 1992; and Lampert, M. "How Do Teachers Manage to Teach? Perspectives on Problems in Practice." *Harvard Educational Review,* 1985, *55*(2), 178–194.
5. For research on factors that shape schoolteachers' conceptions of subject matters, see Ball, D. L. "The Mathematical Understandings that Prospective Teachers Bring to Teacher Education." *Elementary School Journal,* 1990, *90*(4), 449–466; and Stodolsky, S. S. *The Subject Matters: Classroom Activity in Math and Social Studies.* Chicago: University of Chicago Press, 1988.
6. For approaches to teacher development that focus on developing teachers' conceptions of subject matter, see Borko, H., and Putnam, R. T. "Expanding a Teacher's Knowledge Base: A Cognitive Psychological Perspective on Professional Development." In T. R. Guskey and M. Huberman (eds.), *Professional Development in Education: New Paradigms and Practices.* New York: Teachers College Press, 1995; and Grossman, P. "Of Regularities and Reform: Navigating the Subject-Specific Territory of High Schools." In M. W. McLaughlin and I. Oberman (eds.), *Teacher Learning: New Policies, New Practices.* New York: Teachers College Press, 1996.
7. Stanislavski, C. *An Actor Prepares.* (E. R. Hapgood, trans.) New York: Theatre Art Books, 1948.
8. It is worth noting that this understanding framework emerged from attempts to become more systematic in assessing the quality and nature of students' understanding in TfU classrooms. Once again, efforts to assess learning pushed educators to become more articulate about their understanding goals. Teachers and researchers worked

together in analyzing students' work and characterizing it in relation to research on conceptions of knowledge and cognition.

9. For a fuller discussion of understanding as performance, see Chapter Two in this book and Perkins, D. *Smart Schools: From Training Memories to Educating Minds.* New York: Free Press, 1992.

10. Bruner, J. S. *Beyond the Information Given: Studies in the Psychology of Knowing.* New York: Norton, 1973.

11. Gardner, *Frames of Mind.*

12. Hawkins, D. *The Informed Vision: Essays on Learning and Human Nature.* New York: Agathon Press, 1974.

13. Parts of this section are adapted from a memo prepared by Howard Gardner. The TfU project built upon ideas developed by Gardner, David Perkins, and their colleagues at Project Zero about assessments of learning through analysis of portfolios of students' products and performances. See the chapter "Assessment in Context: The Alternative to Standardized Testing," in H. Gardner, *Multiple Intelligences: The Theory in Practice.* New York: Basic Books, 1993.

14. See Chapter One for a history of assessment practices. For more on current thinking about performance assessments, see Sizer, T. R. *Horace's Compromise: The Dilemma of the American High School.* Boston: Houghton Mifflin, 1984; and Baron, J. B., and Wolf, D. P. (eds.). *Performance-Based Student Assessment: Challenges and Possibilities: Ninety-fifth Yearbook of the National Society for the Study of Education, Part I.* Chicago: University of Chicago Press, 1996.

15. Schwartz, J. L., and Viator, K. (eds.). *The Prices of Secrecy: The Social, Intellectual, and Psychological Costs of Current Assessment Practices.* Report to the Ford Foundation. Cambridge, Mass.: Educational Technology Center, Harvard Graduate School of Education, Sept. 1990.

16. On negotiating intellectual authority and changing classroom roles, see Wiske, M. S., and Houde, R. "From Recitation to Construction: Teachers Change with New Technologies." In J. L. Schwartz, M. Yerushalmy, and B. Wilson (eds.), *The Geometric Supposer: What Is It a Case of?* Hillsdale, N.J.: Erlbaum, 1993; and Wiske, M. S. "How Teaching for Understanding Changes the Rules in the Classroom." *Educational Leadership,* 1994, *51*(5), 19–21.

17. On curriculum as a process of negotiating meanings, see Grundy, S. *Curriculum: Product or Praxis.* Bristol, Pa.: Falmer Press, 1987. On professional development as a process of working with and by teachers rather than on them, see Fullan, M., and Hargreaves, A. *What's Worth Fighting for in Your School.* New York: Teachers College Press, 1996; Guskey, T. R., and Huberman, M. (eds.). *Professional Development in Education: New Paradigms and Practices.* New York: Teachers College

Press, 1995; and Cochran-Smith, M., and Lytle, S. L. *Inside/Outside: Teacher Research and Knowledge.* New York: Teachers College Press, 1993.

18. See Chapter Eleven on the role of the TfU framework in structuring organizational learning at the level of a department or school.

19. For more on the need for classroom pedagogy, teacher development, and school change to proceed in complementary ways see Elmore, R. F., and McLaughlin, M. W. *Steady Work: Policy, Practice and the Reform of American Education.* Santa Monica, Calif.: Rand, 1988; Wasley, P. "Stirring the Chalkdust: Changing Practices in Essential Schools." *Teachers College Record,* 1991, *93*(1), 28–48; and Nelson, B. S., and Hammerman, J. K. "Reconceptualizing Teaching: Moving Toward the Creation of Intellectual Communities of Students, Teachers, and Teacher Educators." In M. W. McLaughlin and I. Oberman (eds.), *Teacher Learning: New Policies, New Practices.* New York: Teachers College Press, 1996.

Chapter Four

1. This classification of kinds of understanding TfU bears some resemblance to the taxonomy of educational objectives described in Bloom, B. *Taxonomy of Educational Objectives.* White Plains, N.Y.: Longman, 1956. Some of the same terms appear both in our set and in his six classes of educational objectives: knowledge, comprehension, application, analysis, synthesis, and evaluation. Bloom distinguishes a classification system from the more rigorous taxonomy that is conceived as a hierarchical order such that "the objectives in one class are likely to make use of and be built on the behaviors found in the preceding classes in this list" (p. 18). In our project we did not presume that such a clear and hierarchical relationship exists. For example, we thought some teachers might be able to design or enact good performances of understanding without being able to explain how these activities exemplify the criteria of understanding performances according to the Teaching for Understanding framework. We assumed, however, that performances of one kind would probably enhance performances of the others. Thus the levels of understanding TfU indicated a range of mutually reinforcing performances to support as we tried to help teachers learn how to teach for understanding.

2. As Joan reflected on her year of work with the Teaching for Understanding framework, she felt the need to "protect the vocabulary" of the framework. She realized that for her, the phrase "teaching for understanding" meant a particular complex set of ideas and activities.

When other people used the phrase in a general or casual way, she knew that her meanings were not shared. Her concern can be viewed as related to the role of "shared vision" in learning organizations as discussed by Peter M. Senge in *The Fifth Discipline: The Art and Practice of the Learning Organization*. New York: Doubleday, 1990. Senge uses "shared vision" to mean a very specific, explicit shared purpose that gives focus and meaning to the work of people in an organization: "Vision establishes an overarching goal. . . . A shared vision also provides a rudder to keep the learning process on course when stresses develop" (p. 209).

3. National Council of Teachers of Mathematics. *Curriculum and Evaluation Standards for School Mathematics*. Reston, Va.: National Council of Teachers of Mathematics, 1989.

4. For research on the impact of conceptions of subject matter on both teachers' and students' thinking about learning, see Stodolsky, S. S. *The Subject Matters: Classroom Activity in Math and Social Studies*. Chicago: University of Chicago Press, 1988; Grossman, P. L. *The Making of a Teacher: Teacher Knowledge and Teacher Education*. New York: Teachers College Press, 1990; and Grossman, P. L. "Content as Context: The Role of School Subjects in Secondary School Teaching." *Educational Researcher*, 1995, *24*(8), 5–11, 23.

5. For more on the value of analyzing student performances, see Jamentz, K. "Assessment as a Heuristic for Professional Practice." In M. W. McLaughlin and I. Oberman (eds.), *Teacher Learning: New Policies, New Practices*. New York: Teachers College Press, 1996.

6. For a summary of research on the kinds of content knowledge teachers need to help students construct understanding, see Borko, H., and Putnam, R. T. "Expanding a Teacher's Knowledge Base: A Cognitive Psychological Perspective on Professional Development." In T. R. Guskey and M. Huberman (eds.), *Professional Development in Education: New Paradigms and Practices*. New York: Teachers College Press, 1995.

7. Shulman, L. S. "Knowledge and Teaching: Foundations of the New Reform." *Harvard Educational Review*, 1987, *57*, 1–22.

8. For further analysis of the influence of school contexts on teachers' and students' assumptions and behavior, see McLaughlin, M. W., Talbert, J. E., and Bascia, N. *The Contexts of Teaching in Secondary Schools: Teachers' Realities*. New York: Teachers College Press, 1990.

9. For analyses of school improvement as teacher development through continuing inquiry, see McDonald, J. P. *Teaching: Making Sense of an Uncertain Craft*. New York: Teachers College Press, 1992; Cochran-Smith, M., and Lytle, S. L. *Inside/Outside: Teacher Research and Knowledge*. New

York: Teachers College Press, 1993; and McLaughlin, M. W., and Oberman, I. (eds.). *Teacher Learning: New Policies, New Practices.* New York: Teachers College Press, 1996.

10. The influence of school cultures, including norms and values, on teachers' work has been examined in Sarason, S. B. *The Culture of the School and the Problem of Change.* Needham Heights, Mass.: Allyn & Bacon, 1982; Cuban, L. *How Teachers Taught: Constancy and Change in American Classroom, 1890–1980.* White Plains, N.Y.: Longman, 1984; Fullan, M. G. *The New Meaning of Educational Change.* New York: Teachers College Press, 1991; Fullan, M. G. *Change Forces: Probing the Depths of Educational Reform.* Bristol, Pa.: Falmer Press, 1993; and Oakes, J., and Quartz, K. H. *Creating New Educational Communities: Ninety-Fourth Yearbook of the National Society for the Study of Education, Part I.* Chicago: University of Chicago Press, 1995. For policy perspective on the interaction of teaching and school cultures, see Cohen, D. K., McLaughlin, M. W., and Talbert, J. E. (eds.). *Teaching for Understanding: Challenges for Policy and Practice.* San Francisco: Jossey-Bass, 1993; and Elmore, R. F., Peterson, P. L., and McCarthey, S. J. *Restructuring in the Classroom: Teaching, Learning, and School Organization.* San Francisco: Jossey-Bass, 1996.

Chapter Five

1. The emphasis on culminating projects as an important part of the TfU sequence connects the framework with other models of project-based learning, such as the "learning expeditions" advocated by Expeditionary Learning Outward Bound and the "project approach" to early childhood education put forth by Lillian Katz and Sylvia Chard. These models all assume a performance view of understanding and draw on the power of generative projects to motivate learning. TfU makes an additional contribution by situating class projects within the context of clear understanding goals and the process of ongoing assessment. Teachers engaged in project-based teaching often find the TfU framework particularly accessible. Our colleagues at Project Zero, Heidi Goodrich, Thomas Hatch, Gwynne Wiatrowski, and Chris Unger, have written more about the use of projects in *Teaching through Projects: Creating Effective Learning Environments.* Reading, Mass.: Addison-Wesley, 1995. Information on learning expeditions can be found in Mednick, A., and Cousins, E. (eds.). *Fieldwork.* Vol. II. Dubuque, Iowa: Kendall/Hunt, 1995. Lillian Katz and Sylvia Chard describe the project approach in *Engaging Children's Minds: The Project Approach.* Norwood, N.J.: Ablex, 1989.

2. The issue of transfer is an important aspect of Teaching for Understanding. Eric paid careful attention to the shepherding of transfer by engaging in a practice that David Perkins and Gavriel Salomon describe as "hugging." The practice of hugging involves situating the skills to be learned and transferred within a meaningful instructional context as opposed to trying to develop them in isolation. The issue of transfer and the practice of hugging are dealt with more extensively in Perkins, D., and Salomon, G. "The Science and Art of Transfer." In A. Costa, J. Bellanca, and R. Fogarty (eds.), *If Minds Matter: A Foreward to the Future.* Palatine, Ill.: Skylight, 1992. In addition, readers may want to see Campione, J. "Forms of Transfer in a Community of Learners: Flexible Learning and Understanding." In A. McKeough, J. Lupart, and A. Marini (eds.), *Teaching for Transfer: Fostering Generalization in Learning.* Hillsdale, N.J.: Erlbaum, 1995.

3. Lois taught this unit during both of the years she was involved in the research project. Derek chose Phillis Wheatley the first year; Renee, whose work appears in Chapter Seven, chose her the second year.

4. The power of well-framed questions to direct and focus students' learning as Lois's throughlines did can also be seen in the five "habits of mind" of the Central Park East Secondary School (see Meier, D. *The Power of Their Ideas.* Boston: Beacon Press, 1995) and the "guiding questions" used by the Coalition of Essential Schools and Expeditionary Learning (see Mednick, A., and Cousins, E. [eds.]. *Fieldwork.* Vol. II. Dubuque, Iowa: Kendall/Hunt, 1995).

5. The culture of thoughtfulness and thinking that Eric sought to establish is an important component of effective TfU practice. Though not explicitly addressed in the framework, these issues are developed further in a number of related works, including Tishman, S., Perkins, D., and Jay, E. *The Thinking Classroom: Learning and Teaching in a Culture of Thinking.* Needham Heights, Mass.: Allyn & Bacon, 1995; and Schrag, F. *Thinking in School and Society.* New York: Routledge, 1988.

6. Issues associated with control, sharing authority, and authenticity are dealt with in much of the democratic schools literature. See, for example, Meier, *The Power of Their Ideas;* Glickman, C. "Education as Democracy: The Pedagogy of School Renewal." Paper presented at the annual meeting of the American Educational Research Association, New York, Mar. 1996; and Apple, M., and Beane, J. (eds.). *Democratic Schools.* Alexandria, Va.: Association for Supervision and Curriculum Development, 1995.

Ann Brown, among others, has written extensively on the creation of classrooms as communities of learners. See, for example, Brown, A. "Communities of Learning and Thinking: Or a Context by Any Other

Name." *Contributions to Human Development,* 1990, *21,* 108–126; and Brown, A. "Social Interaction and Individual Understanding in a Community of Learners: the Influence of Piaget and Vygotsky." In A. Tryphon and J. Voneche, (eds.), *Piaget-Vygotsky: The Social Genesis of Thought.* Hove, England: Taylor & Francis, 1996. In addition two recent edited volumes bring together the work of many individuals working in this area: Oakes, J., and Quartz, K. H. (eds.). *Creating New Educational Communities: Ninety-Fourth Yearbook of the National Society for the Study of Education.* Chicago: University of Chicago Press, 1995; and McGilly, K. (ed.). *Classroom Lessons: Integrating Cognitive Theory.* Cambridge, Mass.: MIT Press, 1994.

7. The role of subject matter knowledge has been investigated by Susan Stodolsky, Deborah Ball, and Pamela Grossman, among others; see, for example, Stodolsky, S. S. *The Subject Matters: Classroom Activity in Math and Social Studies.* Chicago: University of Chicago Press, 1988. For an examination of the roles of both subject matter and pedagogical knowledge, see Grossman, P. *The Making of a Teacher: Teacher Knowledge and Teacher Education.* New York: Teachers College Press, 1990. For an in-depth look at the role of subject matter knowledge in mathematics, see Ball, D. L. *Research on Teaching Mathematics: Making Subject Matter Knowledge Part of the Equation.* East Lansing: National Center for Research on Teacher Education, Michigan State University, 1988.

8. Some of these supporting structures can be characterized as forms of distributed cognition. Gavriel Salomon, Roy Pea, and David Perkins have written about distributed intelligence; see, for example, Salomon, G. (ed.). *Distributed Cognitions.* New York: Cambridge University Press, 1993.

9. For more on the concept of appropriation, see Newman, D., Griffin, P., and Cole, M. *The Construction Zone: Working for Cognitive Change in School.* New York: Cambridge University Press, 1989; and Leont'ev, A. N. *Problems of the Development of Mind.* Moscow: Progress, 1981.

Chapter Six

1. For a rich account of the debate around curriculum, see Kliebard, H. M. *Forging the American Curriculum.* New York: Routledge, 1992; and Kliebard, H. M. *The Struggle for the American Curriculum 1893–1958.* New York: Routledge, 1995.

2. Bailyn, B. *On the Teaching and Writing of History.* Hanover, N.H.: Montgomery Endowment, Dartmouth College, 1994.

3. Stout, N. S. *Getting the Most Out of Your U.S. History Course.* Lexington, Mass.: Heath, 1994.

4. Please note that the fragments included in this chapter are not direct quotes from single students in our project. The examples were created on the basis of multiple performances that we encountered in the field, with the purpose of illustrating the four dimensions of the Understanding framework here proposed.

5. See Kuhn, T. *The Structure of Scientific Revolution*. Chicago: University of Chicago Press, 1970. For an updated analysis of the debate generated by this book, see also Kuhn, T. *What Are Scientific Revolutions?* Cambridge, Mass.: MIT Press, 1987.

6. Because of its rapid growth cycle, yeast has proven very appropriate for students' experimentation in genetics. For a detailed description of how yeast can be used in the classroom, see Manney, T. R., and Manney, M. "Yeast: A Research Organism for Teaching Genetics." *American Biology Teacher,* 1992, *54*(7), pp. 426–431.

7. A portrait of this intuitive epistemology as it plays out in the developing child can be found in Carey, S., and Smith, C. "On Understanding the Nature of Scientific Knowledge." In D. Perkins, J. L. Schwartz, M. M. West, and M. S. Wiske (eds.), *Software Goes to School.* New York: Oxford University Press, 1995.

8. For a comprehensive account of representations of scientific knowledge in school contexts, see Neil, W., and Wilkof, J. (eds.). *Science, Curriculum and Liberal Education: Selected Essays.* Chicago: University of Chicago Press, 1978.

9. About science, see Kuhn, *The Structure of Scientific Revolution*; and Kuhn, *What Are Scientific Revolutions?* About history, see Carr, E. *What Is History?* New York: Vintage Books, 1961; Le Goff, J. *History and Memory.* New York: Columbia University Press, 1992; and Ricoeur, P. *Time and Narrative.* Vols. I, II, and III. Chicago: University of Chicago Press, 1984. See also White, H. *Metahistory: The Historical Imagination in Nineteenth Century Europe.* Baltimore: Johns Hopkins University Press, 1973.

10. See Habermas, J. *Knowledge and Human Interest.* Boston: Beacon Press, 1971; and Heller, A. *Everyday Life.* London: Kegan Paul, 1984.

11. See Dewey, J. "The Logical and Psychological Aspects of Experience." In D. Vanderberg (ed.), *Theory of Knowledge and Problems of Education.* Urbana: University of Illinois Press, 1970; Phenix, P. "The Disciplines and Curriculum Content." In D. Vanderberg (ed.), *Theory of Knowledge and Problems of Education.* Urbana: University of Illinois Press, 1970; Phenix, P. *Realms of Meaning.* New York: McGraw-Hill, 1987; and Neil and Wilkof, (eds.), *Science, Curriculum and Liberal Education.*

12. For a careful analysis of students' developing historical cognition, see the pioneering work of Lee, P., Dickinson, A., and Ashby, R. "Some Aspects of Children's Understanding of Historical Explanation." Paper presented at the American Educational Research Association,

San Francisco, 1995; and Lee, P., Dickinson, A., and Ashby, R. "Children's Ideas About Testing Historical Claims and of the Status of Historical Accounts." Paper presented at the American Educational Research Association, New York, 1996. See also Carretero, M., Arsenio, M., and Pozo, J. L. "Cognitive Development, Historical Time Representation and Causal Explanations in Adolescence." In M. Carretero, M. Pope, R. J. Simous, and J. L. Pozo (eds.), *Learning and Instruction: European Research in an International Context.* New York: Pergamon Press, 1996.

13. Kohlberg, L. *Essays on Moral Development.* San Francisco: Harper San Francisco, 1981; and Perry, W. G. *Patterns of Development in Thought and Values of Students in a Liberal Arts College: A Validation of a Scheme.* Cambridge, Mass.: Bureau of Study Counsel, Harvard University, 1968.

14. For a developmental scheme from early intuitive theories to disciplinary understanding, see Gardner, H., and Boix Mansilla, V. "Teaching for Understanding in the Disciplines and Beyond." *Teachers' College Record,* 1994, *96*(2), 198–218.

15. For comprehensive accounts of intuitive theories, misconceptions, and the development of domain-specific cognition, see Bruner, J. T. *Schools for Thought.* Cambridge, Mass.: MIT Press, 1993; Gardner, H. *The Unschooled Mind: How Children Think and How Schools Should Teach.* New York: Basic Books, 1991; Hirschfeld, L., and Gelman, S. *Mapping the Mind: Domain Specificity in Cognition and Culture.* New York: Cambridge University Press, 1994; and Perkins, D., and Simmons, R. "Patterns of Misunderstanding: An Integrative Model for Science, Math and Programming." *Review of Educational Research,* 1988, *58*, 303–326. For an example of emphasis on continuities between intuitive and disciplinary understanding in science, see Arca, M., Guidoni, P., and Mazzoli, P. *Enseñar ciencia: Como empezar: Reflexiones para una educacion cientifica de base* [Teaching science: Where to start: Reflections on a basic science education]. Barcelona: Paidos, 1990.

16. Heller, *Everyday Life.*

17. Phenix, *Realms of Meaning.* See also Phenix, "The Disciplines and Curriculum Content."

18. Lee, Dickinson, and Ashby, "Children's Ideas About Testing Historical Claims and of the Status of Historical Accounts"; see also Seixas, P. "Parallel Crises: History and the Social Studies Curriculum." *Curriculum Studies,* 1993, *25*(3), 235–250.

19. Lee, P., Dickinson, A., and Ashby, R. "Researching Children's Ideas About History." Paper presented at the International Conference on Cognitive and Instructional Processes in History, Madrid, 1994.

20. Habermas, *Knowledge and Human Interest.* For an account of the difficulties in linking theory and practice, see the introduction in Habermas, J. *Theory and Practice.* Boston: Beacon Press, 1973.
21. Seixas, "Parallel Crises."
22. For a comprehensive account of the cognitive use of symbol systems,
see Gardner, H. *Frames of Mind: The Theory of Multiple Intelligences.* New
York: Basic Books, 1983. For an account of the uses of various symbol
systems as entry points to content in the classroom, see Gardner, H.
Multiple Intelligences: A Theory in Practice. New York: Basic Books, 1993.
23. Kindfield, A. "Biology Diagrams: Tools to Think With." Paper presented at the annual meeting of the American Educational Research
Association, Chicago, Apr. 1991.
24. Gardner, *The Unschooled Mind.*
25. For an account of patterns of imaginative elaborations in students'
spontaneous narratives in history, see VanSledright, B., and Brophy,
J. "Storytelling, Imagination, and Fanciful Elaboration in Children's
Historical Reconstructions." *American Educational Research Journal,*
Winter 1992, *29*(4), 837–859.
26. Hirsh, P. *Cultural Literacy.* Boston: Houghton Mifflin, 1987.

Chapter Eight

1. Six interviews from each classroom were randomly selected and
rescored in order to obtain interrater reliability ratings. Overall, the
reliability was 81 percent across all four dimensions (92 percent for
knowledge, 83 percent for method, 75 percent for purposes, and 79
percent for forms). Researchers discussed any discrepant interrater
reliability scores and agreed on a final assessment.
2. See Chapter Ten for a detailed description of the way Eric was introduced to TfU as a student teacher.
3. Grossman, P. L., and Stodolsky, S. S. "Content as Context: The Role
of School Subjects in Secondary School Teaching." *Educational Researcher,* 1995, *24*(8), 5–11, 23.

Chapter Nine

1. Dweck, C. "Motivational Processes Affecting Learning." *American Psychologist,* 1986, *41*(10), 1040–1048.
2. Entwistle, N. J., and Entwistle, A. C. "Contrasting Forms of Understanding for Degree Examinations: The Student Experience and Its
Implications." *Higher Education,* 1991, *22,* 205–227; Entwistle, A. C.,
and Entwistle, N. J. "Experiences of Understanding in Revising for

Degree Examinations." *Learning and Instruction,* 1992, *2,* 1–22; and Dweck, C., and Elliot, E. S. "Achievement Motivation." In E. M. Hetherington (ed.), *Socialization, Personality, and Social Development.* New York: Wiley, 1983.

3. Unger, C. "Students' Conceptions of Understanding and Learning for Understanding." Paper presented at the annual meeting of the American Educational Research Association, Atlanta, 1993.

4. Pintrich, P. R., Marx, R. W., and Boyle, R. A. "Beyond Cold Conceptual Change: The Role of Motivational Beliefs and Classroom Contextual Factors in the Process of Conceptual Change." *Review of Educational Research,* 1993, *63*(2), 167–200.

5. Tobias, S. "Interest, Prior Knowledge, and Learning." *Review of Educational Research,* 1994, *64*(1), 37–55.

6. Dweck, "Motivational Processes Affecting Learning"; Dweck and Elliot, "Achievement Motivation"; Entwistle and Entwistle, "Contrasting Forms of Understanding for Degree Examinations"; Entwistle and Entwistle, "Experiences of Understanding in Revising for Degree Examinations"; Marton, F., and Saljo, R. "On Qualitative Differences in Learning I: Outcome and Process." *British Journal of Educational Psychology,* 1976, *46,* 4–11; Marton, F., and Saljo, R. "Approaches to Learning." In F. Marton, D. J. Hounsell, and N. J. Entwistle (eds.), *The Experience of Learning.* Edinburgh: Scottish Academic Press, 1984; Svensson, L. "Skill in Learning." In F. Marton, D. J. Hounsell, and N. J. Entwistle (eds.), *The Experience of Learning.* Edinburgh: Scottish Academic Press, 1984.

7. Dweck and Elliot, "Achievement Motivation"; Dweck, "Motivational Processes Affecting Learning": Entwistle and Entwistle, "Contrasting Forms of Understanding for Degree Examinations"; Entwistle and Entwistle, "Experiences of Understanding in Revising for Degree Examinations"; Marton and Saljo, "On Qualitative Differences in Learning I"; Marton and Saljo, "Approaches to Learning"; Svensson, "Skill in Learning."

Chapter Ten

1. Comprehension and design are two levels of understanding the Teaching for Understanding framework. Two other levels are enactment and integration. Chapter Four provides further information about the meaning of these categories and their use in helping teachers understand and implement TfU.

2. Note that what now occurs has been evolving over several years. In 1994, for example, Teaching for Understanding was a unit within the

course; students came away with a good deal of knowledge about the Teaching for Understanding formulation, but it seemed too much like just another approach to teaching. We wanted it to be more. It has now become in a real sense the entire course.

3. Students come to this course after an intense four-week prefall program called the "summer component." Within it they read extensively about the philosophy, history, and sociology of American secondary schools. This critical context also includes work around matters of teaching and learning and related matters of multiculturalism (growing out of various case studies and discussions with practicing teachers). Also in the summer component, students begin to maintain an active teaching-learning journal (which continues to be a central part of their work over the full academic year), part of the reflective process we introduce. Reflection is a habit of mind critical to Teaching for Understanding, as it raises consciousness about practice and individual students, helps keep track of interesting questions and responses, and is a means through which to consider other entries to whatever topic is being studied. It is also a self-evaluation process that we view as an important element of Teaching for Understanding. We call attention to the foregoing aspects of journal writing at many points.

In addition students are asked in the summer component to "teach something you understand well to your section members." We ask them to think about one important thing they want their colleagues to leave with—essentially an understanding—and determine how they will know if that occurred. We suggest that they consider some kind of performance activity, which we discuss. One other aspect of this teaching miniactivity is that students provide to two of their colleagues a written statement that clearly outlines their purposes for the teaching and what they expect will occur. These two students offer a critique of the statement of purposes and the like. This begins a conversation about assessment. The point is for students to reach the fall course with some familiarity with the language of Teaching for Understanding.

4. Many of the goals listed by students reflect some of the work of the summer component, especially in relation to the work of the Coalition of Essential Schools.

5. Alongside the course, but an integral part of it, the students are in middle or secondary schools two full days per week. These are the settings they will be in for their second semester, a fourteen-week intensive internship experience. During the first semester the students move from an observational role to an active instructional role very

quickly. Weekly, they have an active focused journal assignment that grows out of their work in the schools. Many have a relationship to our work around Teaching for Understanding.

6. We share in this regard the work of teachers we know who make decisions about themes to explore during the school year through a mapping process. They ask what themes are being considered, what the connections are, and what relationships and possible directions are open. Maps that are particularly expansive in their possibilities are seen as more generative than those that are less full. Beyond this particular application, however, we use the example to make another possibly more important point: that curriculum planning is usually enhanced when engaged in more collectively. Each person's ideas get extended, new connections are developed, possibilities never considered become manifest.

7. The map displayed here was developed largely in one of our collective activities in class, though it has been reorganized for this presentation (essentially making it a bit more orderly).

8. We ask the students to select a topic they are actually expected to teach in the second semester. Most are able to do this, but if they are uncertain about the precise courses they will teach, we encourage them to select a topic within their subject field that they would like to teach.

9. Also at about this time, we share with the mentor teachers of our students that they are beginning to develop a fifteen-day curriculum project around a topic they are expected to teach in the second semester. We also outline for them the Teaching for Understanding framework that guides the work (through a couple of articles and the instructions for the curriculum project). We encourage them to ask the students how it is going and discuss various aspects of it with them. Our purpose is to help mentors encourage the students to try out their curriculum directions and not pose barriers because the process seems complex.

10. These are the articles: Perkins, D., and Blythe, T. "Putting Understanding Up Front." *Educational Leadership,* 1994, *51*(5), 4–7; Perrone, V. "Teaching for Understanding in the Classroom." *Educational Leadership,* 1994, *51*(5), 11–13; Hawkins, D. "Critical Barriers to Science Teaching." *Outlook,* Winter 1982, 3–25; and Shulman, L. "Aristotle Had It Right on Knowledge and Pedagogy." Occasional Paper, no. 4. East Lansing: Holmes Group, Michigan State University, 1988.

11. Perkins and Blythe, "Putting Understanding Up Front."

12. They have already seen in their reading examples of understanding goals formulated around several different subject matter topics.

13. We stress here the idea of moving toward understanding as a means of acknowledging that understanding often needs scaffolding—steps that lead in constructive directions.

14. We acknowledge that ongoing assessment means more than a final culminating activity. In our discussions we make clear that we should know long before any culminative activity about students' progress toward understanding what we want them to understand (the understanding goals). About this point we offer the following explanation: "Remember that assessment should mean more than informing *you* of student progress; it should also help students enlarge *their* understandings of what is being studied. For this, it can't just be an end-of-unit test. At its best, assessment should occur throughout the unit (or course). It begins when you ask students what they already understand about the topic under study. It includes the various understanding performances that are embedded in the daily instruction. It provides opportunities to reflect on their own and others' performance, and it involves students in developing criteria for assessment (we will take this step with regard to your curriculum unit)." In addition we provide examples of ongoing assessment in each of the subject areas. The example in literature is this: "As students work through a piece of literature, they write successive drafts of a paper on a particular topic, reflecting in journals about how their thoughts on the topic are changing. The teacher and a classmate read each draft, offering two or three suggestions for developing the ideas as well as for improving the style."

15. Math and language students struggled the most often, insisting, as those from other subject matters didn't, that their fields are different, have to be learned skill by skill, and are self-contained.

16. Copies of the projects were placed in the library so that students could use each other's work. This represented another example of our ongoing need to share curriculum development efforts. In this regard one of the preservice teachers prepared a stimulating four-week TfU unit about the Great Depression. She spent approximately sixty hours in the archives reading old newspapers and magazines on microfiche, essentially gathering primary materials to support her unit that would call upon students to build their own narratives. She said to us at the time, "Let's assume I could do one of these units a year. It would take me nine to ten years to get enough material for a yearlong course, assuming I built it around nine or ten generative topics." She was right—if she continued to see herself as a single teacher doing everything herself. But, as we shared with her and continue to suggest to ongoing students, in a school in which a teaching

for understanding culture exists, five teachers could produce in two weeks the primary sources for ten units—enough for an entire year's course. And this doesn't take into account the many primary-source curriculum projects existing in the United States that could be used.

17. Nonetheless, several mentors like the curriculum units so much that they plan to teach them in subsequent years.

18. Even as we continue to assist individual teachers to work with the Teaching for Understanding framework, it seems clear that there are limitations when only one or two teachers in a school are working with these directions.

19. We asked the teaching fellows to select two or three representative papers for the purpose of drawing together some of the students' reflections on their teaching experience.

20. Graduates have been reasonably successful keeping a teaching for understanding orientation intact. Those in coalition schools, of course, find a particularly supportive environment. Others find it more complex but possible, even though it is often something they engage in for particular units and not others. The idea of coverage and tests is still overwhelming in most schools. Interests in certainty and simplicity still outweigh interests in ambiguity and complexity. One of our graduates is involved in a major segment of the project's research; he is teaching one of his courses completely around the Teaching for Understanding framework and its intellectual foundation. His work here is inspiring (and reported on elsewhere in the book). But it is only one course, not the mainline college preparatory course, and it is clearly not seen by his colleagues as the most appropriate way to teach physical science.

Chapter Eleven

1. This vignette is based on notes that Stone Wiske made after observations at CRLS and meetings with Joan Soble approximately twice a month during Joan's sabbatical year. It also draws on reflective journals and portfolios that the teachers in Joan's yearlong minicourse kept to document their experiences with TfU.

2. Joan organized her minicourse as a kind of teacher research seminar in which the members reflected on their own practice and gradually came to use the language and concepts of TfU in those reflections. Vito Perrone led a similar process in his teacher education course as described in Chapter Ten. Joan's approach also resembled models of research that invite teachers to write about and talk about their practice in what Barbara Scott Nelson and James K. Hammerman call in-

tellectual communities. See Nelson, B. S., and Hammerman, J. K. "Reconceptualizing Teaching: Moving Toward the Creation of Intellectual Communities of Students, Teacher, and Teacher Educators." In M. W. McLaughlin and I. Oberman (eds.), *Teacher Learning: New Policies, New Practices.* New York: Teachers College Press, 1996.

For more about practice improvement through teacher research, see Hollingsworth, S., and Sockett, H. (eds.). *Teacher Research and Educational Reform: Ninety-Third Yearbook of the National Society for Education, Part I.* Chicago: University of Chicago Press, 1994; Altrichter, H., Posch, P., and Somekh, B. *Teachers Investigate Their Work.* London: Routledge, 1993; and Cochran-Smith, M., and Lytle, S. L. *Inside/Outside: Teacher Research and Knowledge.* New York: Teachers College Press, 1993.

3. Joan knew from her own experience that learning to teach with the Teaching for Understanding framework proceeds through an interaction of comprehension (talking about practice), design (planning curriculum), and enactment (trying TfU approaches in the classroom). See Chapter Four for further description of these categories of performances of understanding TfU.

4. The Norfolk vignette is based on research conducted by Eric Buchovecky that included review of progress reports prepared by Mike DeAngelo and interviews with others directly involved in the Norfolk project.

5. This conscious management of TfU concepts and language in relation to other initiatives and practices resembles the "mutual adaptation" identified in the Rand study of educational innovations (Berman, P., and McLaughlin, M. W. *Federal Programs Support Educational Change:* Vol. VIII. *Implementing and Sustaining Innovations.* Prepared for the Office of Education, U.S. Department of Health, Education, and Welfare. Santa Monica, Calif.: Rand, May 1978), in which both the new innovation and current practices are adjusted to accommodate one another. What is notable in this case is Mike and Tina's explicit attention to vocabulary as well as strategies to retain the focus on understanding: for example, ensuring that portfolios included performances of understanding and were subject to ongoing assessment as a process of improving understanding.

6. Note that this process of using TfU to orchestrate several levels of developing understanding mirrored the strategy that the TfU project used with teachers and that Joan used with her colleagues. For research on the benefits of engaging teachers in the same kind of learning that they are expected to enact with students, see Borko, H., and Putnam, R. T. "Expanding a Teacher's Knowledge Base: A Cognitive

Perspective on Professional Development. In T. R. Guskey and M. Huberman (eds.), *Professional Development in Education: New Paradigms and Practices*. New York: Teachers College Press, 1995.

7. Although we did not conduct formal research on the process of extending TfU in schools, we made several efforts to collect and analyze the experiences of researchers and school people who worked extensively with TfU in schools. For example, researchers from the TfU project served as consultants in a range of schools that requested assistance in integrating TfU into their practice. In several cases the researchers wrote reflective memos about their experiences or prepared progress reports for their clients. These writings constituted an additional source of information for this chapter beyond the materials concerning CRLS and Norfolk. In June 1995 the TfU project held a meeting for teachers and researchers who had worked extensively with TfU in schools. The purpose was to share views about the process and effects of integrating TfU into schools, not merely supporting individual teachers. A summary of themes from this meeting was circulated to the participants for corrections and elaboration. These insights from experienced supporters of TfU in schools informed this chapter and our continuing work.

8. Regarding the necessity of supporting change at both the classroom level and the school context level, see Cox, P. L. "Complementary Roles in Successful School Change." *Educational Leadership*, 1983, *41*(3), 10–13. For a discussion of school change as a process of interrelationships between individual and organizational learning, requiring both top-down and bottom-up strategies, see Fullan, M. *Change Forces: Probing the Depths of Educational Reform*. New York: Teachers College Press, 1993.

9. See Britt Mari Barth for a model that develops understanding of a concept through dialogue relating the word, exemplars, and attributes for the concept: Barth, B. M. "La determination et l'apprentissage des concepts." In J. Houssaye, (ed.), *La pedagogie: Une encyclopedie pour aujourd'hui*. Paris: ESF Editeur, 1993.

Conclusion

1. Henry, N. B. (ed.). *The Measurement of Understanding: The Forty-Fifth Yearbook of the National Society for the Study of Education*. Vol. 1. Chicago: University of Chicago Press, 1946.

2. Brownell, W. A., and Sims, B. M. "The Nature of Understanding." In N. B. Henry (ed.), *The Measurement of Understanding: The Forty-Fifth Yearbook of the National Society of the Study of Education*. Vol. 1. Chicago: University of Chicago Press, 1946, p.27.

3. Jackson, P. *The Practice of Teaching.* New York: Teachers College Press, 1986.

4. Cohen, D. K., McLaughlin, M. W., and Talbert, J. E. (eds.). *Teaching for Understanding: Challenges for Policy and Practice.* San Francisco: Jossey-Bass, 1993.

5. Aiken, W. *The Story of the Eight-Year Study.* New York: HarperCollins, 1942.

6. Comer, J. *School Power.* (2nd ed.) New York: Free Press, 1993; Levin, H. "New Schools for the Disadvantaged." *Teacher Education Quarterly,* 1987, *14*(4), 60–83; and Sizer, T. *Horace's School.* Boston: Houghton Mifflin, 1992.

7. Meier, D. *The Power of Their Ideas.* Boston: Beacon Press, 1995.

8. McLaughlin, M., and Talbert, J. "The Department as the Locus of School Change." Presentation to the National Academy of Education, Chicago, Oct. 25, 1996.

9. Tyack, D., and Cuban, L. *Tinkering Toward Utopia.* Cambridge, Mass.: Harvard University Press, 1995.

Index